ELEMENTS OF PLANTING DESIGN

ELEMENTS OF PLANTING DESIGN

RICHARD L. AUSTIN, ASLA

JOHN WILEY & SONS, INC.

This book is printed on acid-free paper. ♾

Published simultaneously in Canada.

Interior design and layout: Jeff Baker, BookMechanics

Library of Congress Cataloging-in-Publication Data:

Austin, Richard L.

Elements of planting design / Richard L. Austin

p. cm.

Portions of this text were originally developed as “Designing with Plants: and “Designing the Natural Landscape,” published in 1982 and 1984.

Includes bibliographical reference (p.)

ISBN 0-471-39888-8 (pbk. : alk. paper)

1. Planting design. I. Title.

SB472.45.A97 2001

715—dc21

Printed in the United States of America.

10 9 8 7 6 5 4 3 2 1

Contents

FOREWORD
Plants in the Landscape

Plants have been with us from time immemorial. Just as humankind developed step by faltering step from ancient ancestors, so have the plants we know today struggled to survive the rapidly changing environment on our earth. Many of these plants were lost along the way while others, such as the Ginkgo, have survived without much modification. Most of them, however, have adapted to change, and we see them today in a variety of forms.

When we think of the role of plants in our lives, each of us thinks of plants in relation to our own experiences. Probably the first thing that comes to mind for many of us is the plant origin of the food we eat. Perhaps for lunch we had fresh corn on the cob and a salad of lettuce and tomatoes, topped off with a slice of juicy watermelon for dessert. Even the animals we depend upon for protein depend upon plants in the form of pasture grass, hay, or grain for nourishment.

In landscape compositions, we are often unaware of the visual impact plants have upon us. In the autumn woods we note the bright colors of foliage and fruit displayed in great profusion; we listen to the sigh of the wind in the pines; we smell the smoke of a campfire. We see a distant mountaintop, white with a snowy crown. It contrasts with the blue of the autumn sky and the golden yellow of the dancing aspen leaves framing the view. One can find a sense of well being in the landscape — a peace of mind not present amid the cacophonies of noise, offensive odors, and sights of the crowded urban world.

Landscape architects can use a technical knowledge and a "feel for plants" to create opportunities for this sense of well being, and for this aesthetic experience. Landscape architects look beneath the superficial and study the characteristics of plants and what makes them appealing to the senses. The color value of plants is self-evident to many of us, yet some subtleties require a second look, a deeper perception. The red twigs of a dogwood shrub against the white of winter snow, the mottled bark of a sycamore or a true Chinese elm, and hundreds of other examples add up to many enjoyable experiences when plants are used for more than decoration. We find color variations throughout the year —the variety of colorful flowers that bloom in different seasons, the fresh light green of new leaves in the spring, the deep green hues of summer foliage, the bright contrasts of fall colors, and the delicate variations of browns on twigs and bark in winter.

Texture is another characteristic that plants exhibit in great variety. Some plants are coarse, such as the Catalpa, with its large leaves, or the tropical banana plant. Others have medium-sized leaves or leaves that are small and narrow. Deciduous trees with small twigs produce fine-textured effects when bare. In stark design contrast, the large twigs of the Kentucky coffee bean or the tree of heaven give a design composition a course impression.

Plants, as design elements, come in all sorts of shapes and sizes. Form, as a design feature, is a very important when choosing plants for a composition. Next to color, people often recognize this characteristic more readily than any other, so it may be used more frequently to focus attention or to provide variety in a planting space. Grasses and creeping ground covers give us low, spreading forms to provide our spaces with a living surface. Slightly higher are prostrate types such as Andorra creeping juniper and many of the cotoneasters. They are in turn exceeded by the round forms of Mugo pine and boxwoods, the vase shape of certain junipers, the towering pyramids of narrow-leaved evergreens and sweet gums, the irregular asymmetry of Meyers juniper and selected firethorns, and the broad crowns of many deciduous shade trees. The list goes on and on, and a designer may use numerous form varieties in a single composition.

The landscape architect is often called upon to draw attention to a particular area. This can be done by focusing the attention of the viewer, through contrast, upon a specific plant or mass of plants different from those nearby. For example, one 10-foot pyramidal green juniper among 15 low-spreading green junipers would compel the viewer's attention through shape and size alone. Change it to a silver-gray Rocky Mountain juniper and you reinforce the accent of form and size with color. Change the low plantings to low shrubs of contrasting texture and you have brought contrast and accent into play for maximum visual experience.

In similar fashion plants are selected to serve as background for objects the way a group of buildings can be viewed against a mountain slope or a piece of garden sculpture. If our goal is to focus upon a specific object in a composition, background plants must be subordinate to the object and not dominate it. If they become more attractive to a viewer than the object, the composition fails. If they blend into a monotonous sameness of color, shape, and texture effect, the composition fails again.

There are many other related factors to be considered by a landscape architect: defining usable space, reinforcing nonplant design elements, complementing architectural accents, framing aesthetic views, screening out undesirable views, controlling pedestrian circulation, or providing interesting sources for sounds, seasonal changes, or shadow patterns for aesthetic effect.

The landscape architect should understand the fact that plants have a positive psychological effect upon people. Garrett Eckbo (1969) refers to plants as "our poetic lifeline back to Mother Nature in an increasingly denatured world."[1] The garden was the site where ancient Chinese philosophers contemplated the human role in the world. To many, plants may be symbolic of happenings in other times and places. To some the drooping branches of weeping willows suggest drooping spirits. The fragrance of spring flowers can lift our spirits, and the putrid smell of Gingko fruits can offend. A farmer, coming in from the summer wheat field, appreciates the shade of cottonwoods near the house. These natural air conditioners fend off the rays of the sun and, through transpiration, add evaporative, cooling effects to a space.

The landscape architect uses plants in many ways to modify the climate of a space. Windbreaks, shelterbelts, and plantings for glare control and the control of soil moisture, drifting snow, and sinking cold air in a valley are all specific uses for which plants can be designed. We know that trees and shrubs serve as filters to screen out pollutant particles and also reduce irritating noises significantly within the crowded urban space.

During the Dust Bowl days of the 1930s, we became acutely aware of the need for plantings to combat soil erosion. The Soil Conservation Service was organized to research the problem in consultation with other agencies and individuals. Improved tillage techniques for the soil surface were developed, as were plant uses to combat wind and rain erosion. Windbreak and shelterbelt plantings of trees and shrubs, ground-cover plantings of indigenous plant materials, dust- and sand-control plantings, grassed water channels, stream-bank stabilization, and watershed protection plantings were design applications originating from this era.

Plants also serve as indicators of soil and erosion conditions. Sedges and cattails say "It is wet"; cacti and succulents say "It is dry." Ericaceous plants say "It is an acid soil," and saltgrass and atriplex say "It is salty here."

Certain plants produce symptoms that indicate the

presence of air pollutants of various kinds. Grapes and redbud leaves become deformed, curled, cupped, and streaked with yellow when some chemical weed controls appear in the air. Tomato plants quickly succumb to gases such as methane, and dwarf Yaupon holly is quite susceptible to carbon monoxide from auto exhaust.

Many plants produce chemicals of value to the human race. The old herbalists knew of some of these many years ago. Native Americans used parts of the indigo bush, *Amorpha fruiticosa*, as a dye and the crushed fruit as a means of stunning fish. We know now that the plant contains a chemical similar to rotenone.

There are poisonous plants, too. From literature we have heard of hemlock. Our ranchers know the effect of locoweed on their cattle, and many of us have had first-hand experience with the irritation of poison ivy.

If we add the fact that perhaps a majority of us live in houses that are built in large part from lumber, we begin to see that humankind is highly dependent on plants of all types and varieties. Much of the fuel we use for heat and energy may be directly or indirectly traced to plant origins. The very paper that this book is printed upon started out as wood pulp.

Last, but by no means least, plants provide a means of livelihood, completely or partially, for many people ranging from farmers to landscape architects.

Robert P. Ealy
Professor emeritus
Department of Landscape Architecture
Kansas State University
(Adapted from the essay "Plants in our Lives")

ACKNOWLEDGMENTS

Portions of this text were originally developed by the author as *Designing With Plants* and *Designing the Natural Landscape*, published in 1982 and 1984 by Van Nostrand Reinhold Company. Special thanks to those individuals and associates that have continually adopted and used these works in their studios in the teaching of planting design.

I am especially indebted to Dr. Robert P. Ealy for his many years of mentoring friendship and patient teaching of the art of planting design.

I am also grateful for the following firms and individuals for their contributions of planting plans and graphics:

David J. Ciaccio, ASLA
Ciaccio Dennell Group; land planners, landscape architects, architects
Omaha, Nebraska

Thomas R. Dunbar, FASLA
Dunbar/Jones Partnership; landscape architecture, environmental planning, urban design
Des Moines, Iowa

Brian Kinghorn
Kinghorn Horticultural Services
Omaha, Nebraska

Kim W. Todd, ASLA
Finke Gardens and Nursery
Lincoln, Nebraska

Douglas W. Wyatt; landscape architect
Prairie Village, Kansas

Elements of Planting Design

CHAPTER 1

The Ecology of Planting Design

The common thread that links the environments we design as landscape architects is plant materials. The common philosophy that guides the selection of plants for these environments is planting design ecology.

Our repertoire of trees, shrubs, ground covers, and grasses provides the extensive and complex base of ingredients we use to manipulate the spaces around us. We improve living conditions for humans, protect and balance the habitats of wildlife, and prevent the deterioration of the aesthetic environment with the proper selection and placement of plant materials. It is important, therefore, to begin a study of the elements of planting design with the processes of plants as they occur in natural spaces.

Just as planting design is an element of landscape architecture, landscape ecology — both natural and ornamental — is the principle component of planting design. Solving intricate design problems with plants requires an understanding of "how plants live, where they live, and why they live where they do" (Dice, 1952). The selection, placement, survival, and design effectiveness of each plant or plant mass in a composition depends upon the external forces that act upon them. As landscape architects, we manipulate these forces to create planted spaces that reconstruct, replenish, or enhance livable environments.

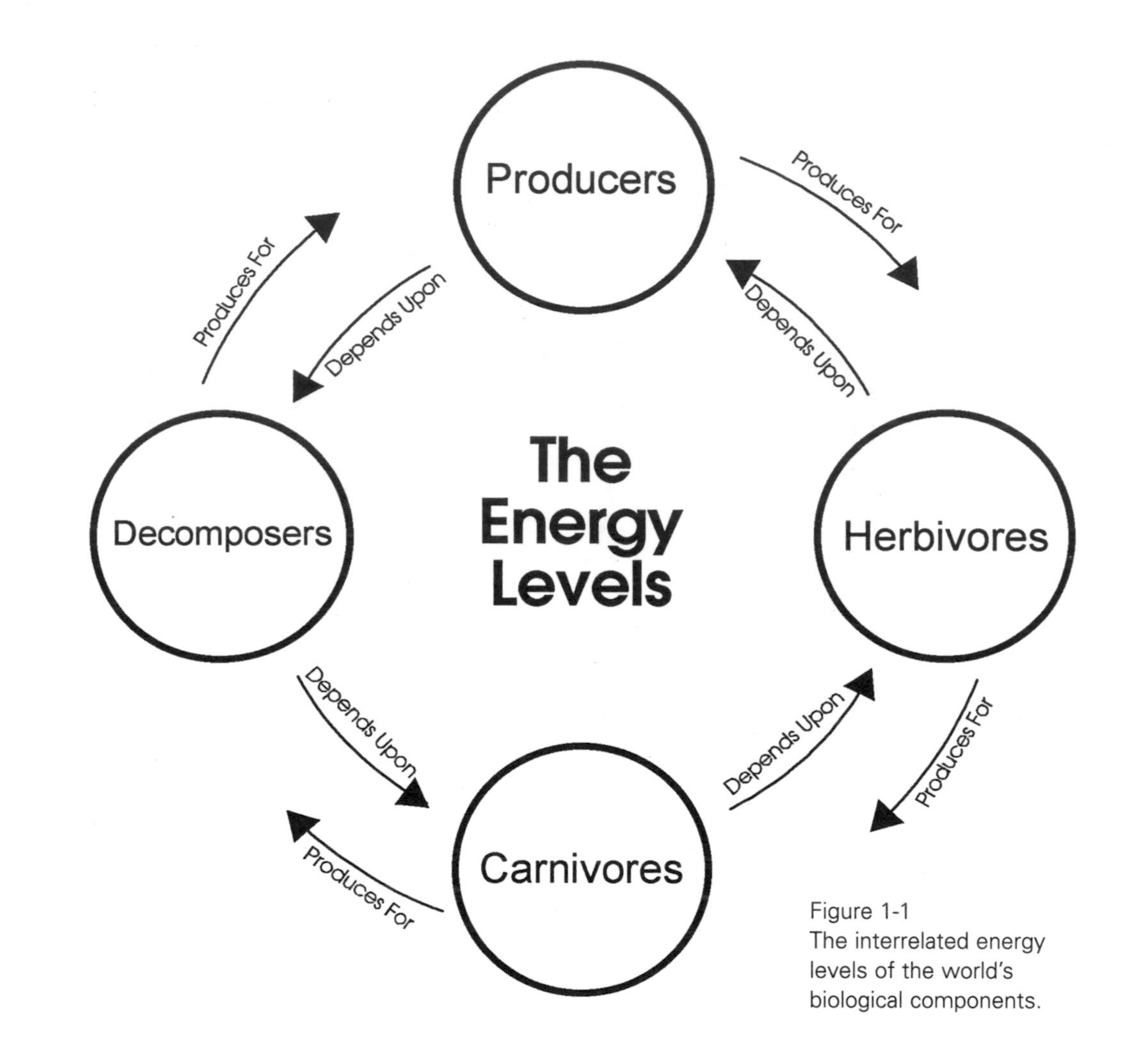

Figure 1-1
The interrelated energy levels of the world's biological components.

The Biological Components

The biological components of the physical world consist of a variety of interrelated energy levels. The first level is green vegetation, the part of the system that collects and stores energy from the sun through photosynthesis, with a corresponding release of oxygen. The rest of the plant and animal communities are dependent upon this level. Green vegetation is thus the producer level for the system. The second level, the herbivores, ranges in size from a parasitic fungus to an elephant and is dependent upon the first level for its energy and food. Levels three and four are both composed of carnivores — animals that eat herbivores. The lower form of carnivores, level three, relies exclusively on level two for energy. Level four, however, the higher form, may also get its energy from consuming members of level three. Level five is made up of bacteria, fungi, and protozoa — the decomposers — which use dead plants and animals for food and energy. This decayed matter in turn becomes an energy and food source for green vegetation, and the chain of elements and events necessary for our existence is completed (Fig. 1.1).

The Basic Communities

The community of green vegetation, known broadly as plants, is divided into four groups or subcommunities known as divisions:

1. *Thallophyta* (thallophytes) are non-chlorophyll-bearing with little or no woody structure, comprising bacteria, lichens, and fungi.
2. *Bryophyta* (mosses and liverworts) are small green plants without flowers (in the popular sense).
3. *Pteridophyta* (ferns and fern families) are green plants with vascular tissue, true roots, and a clear differentiation of leaf (frond) and stem; classes are true ferns, scouring rushes,

club mosses, the tropical genus *Psilotum*, and quillworts.

4. *Spermatophyta* (seed plants) are distinct flowering plants having an embryo that germinates and are considered to be the most highly organized. The most distinct subdivisions are the gymnosperms (plants that produce a naked seed) and the angiosperms (plants that enclose the seed in an ovary).

THE NATURAL PLANT SYSTEMS

The two basic plant ecological systems a designer must know are the *individual system* and the *population system* (Shelford, 1963).

Within the natural plant community, the individual system is one that is genetically uniform. Leaves, stems, and roots act as a total unit, and under most circumstances none of the parts can live without the others for any extended period. Some species generate vegetative parts (rhizomes or runners) that produce genetically identical plants (clones).

An individual plant in a natural environment is dependent upon and relates to the other plants around it in two ways: genetically to other members of the same species, and ecologically to other plants in the community — forming a plant population system. When a population becomes isolated and begins to inbreed with other plants within the same group, it is called a local population. It is from the local population in a specific environment that we begin to find genetic adaptation to the soil, climate, and water conditions of a site. Certain genes or gene combinations begin to restrict the area in which the plant will grow and thrive. This fundamental relationship is the key to selecting plants for a designed environment as well. An individual plant in a designed environment must depend upon and relate to the other plants in the composition. No individual plant or plant mass should be an independent element, freestanding or without ecological relationships.

The distribution of individual or populations of plants depends upon their success or failure within the particular system to which they are associated. Processes found in each living organism determine not only the continuation of the species but also its use as a design element. A plant must do more than just survive — it must complete the reproductive cycle to become fully adaptable (Shelford, 1963; Spurr, 1964). The three stages in this cycle are *germination*, *vegetative growth*, and *flowering and fruiting*.

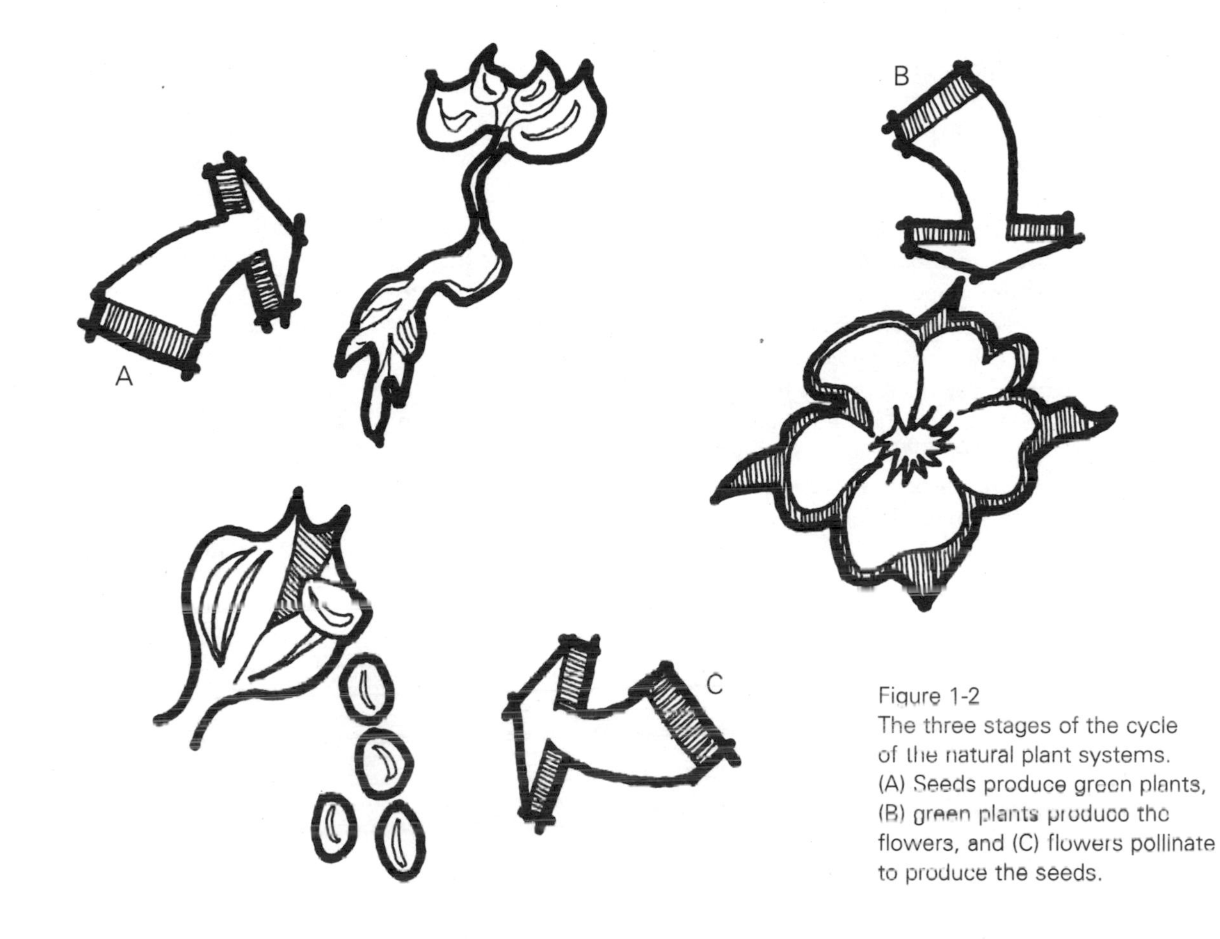

Figure 1-2
The three stages of the cycle of the natural plant systems. (A) Seeds produce green plants, (B) green plants produce the flowers, and (C) flowers pollinate to produce the seeds.

Most plants, with the exception of ferns and mosses, start from seeds. The seed is a self-contained life unit relying upon moisture as the key factor for releasing the plant embryo (Fig. 1-2).

The germination of a seed is followed by vegetative growth — represented by the development of rootlets and sprouts. The roots start downward, following water and providing the anchor system of the plant. The roots will eventually have an outer covering similar to that of bark, with root hairs forming at the ends and near the drip line of the plant to attract moisture.

The stem system in the beginning pushes the seed leaves above the surface of the ground. Eventually it provides the terminal growing points (terminal bud) that concentrate the energy direction for the pant. Side buds (lateral growth) form, and soon the structure of the plant is permanently established. Another function of the stem system is the storage of food during dormancy periods. Some plants with weak aboveground systems (such as sweet potatoes and bulbs) have developed underground stems for storage.

Aboveground development conditions the survival of most plants in the natural environment. The limbs grow and adjust as needed to expose the leaves to sunlight for the production of food. If, however, an environment becomes hostile to a plant's survival, evolutionary capabilities may emerge and allow the structure to adapt to habitat extremes such as severe loss of nutrients needed for a support structure. Good examples of this are groups of plants such as vines and creepers that have adopted a clinging or twining habit for support. Their basic structure is such that other plant features give them their form.

Once the true leaves form, the plant becomes a complete and productive organism. The leaf uses raw materials from the environment, converting and recycling ingredients into other reusable items — maintaining itself as one of the best-designed machines in nature (Fig.1-3).

The last stage in the process is flowering and fruiting. The flowers, regardless of their structural configuration, provide the link of seed fertilization by pollination. From fertilization the seeds develop, disperse, and germinate into a new plant, continuing the species (Fig. 1-4).

The existence and distribution of a plant in an ornamental setting or in a forest or open field is subject to the "approval" of the environment that surrounds it.

There are two basic levels of distribution. *Macrodistribution* is geographic: plant species occur in a general region. *Microdistribution* is ecological, with species occurring only in certain kinds of environmental situations (i.e., north-facing slopes or the edges of streams and lakes).

A few species of plants are found almost everywhere and are referred to as *cosmopolitan species*. Others are found in only one area and are called *endemic species*. Plants restricted to a given region (such as eastern North America) are *broad endemics* and include such plants as the flowering dogwood *(Cornus florida)* and ponderosa pine *(Pinus ponderosa)*. Those restricted to microenvironments in a narrow geographic area are narrow endemics and include the isolated redwoods *(Sequoia sempervirens)* of California.

The presence or absence of winter separates the distribution of plants into three groups. The first, *arctic-alpine* (harsh winter), is made up primarily of perennial herbs occurring as tundra plants. The second, *temperate*, is made up of widely distributed species genetically capable of producing individuals adapted to different climates. The third, *pantropical*, consists of species located throughout the tropics primarily in cultivated areas (Shelford, 1963).

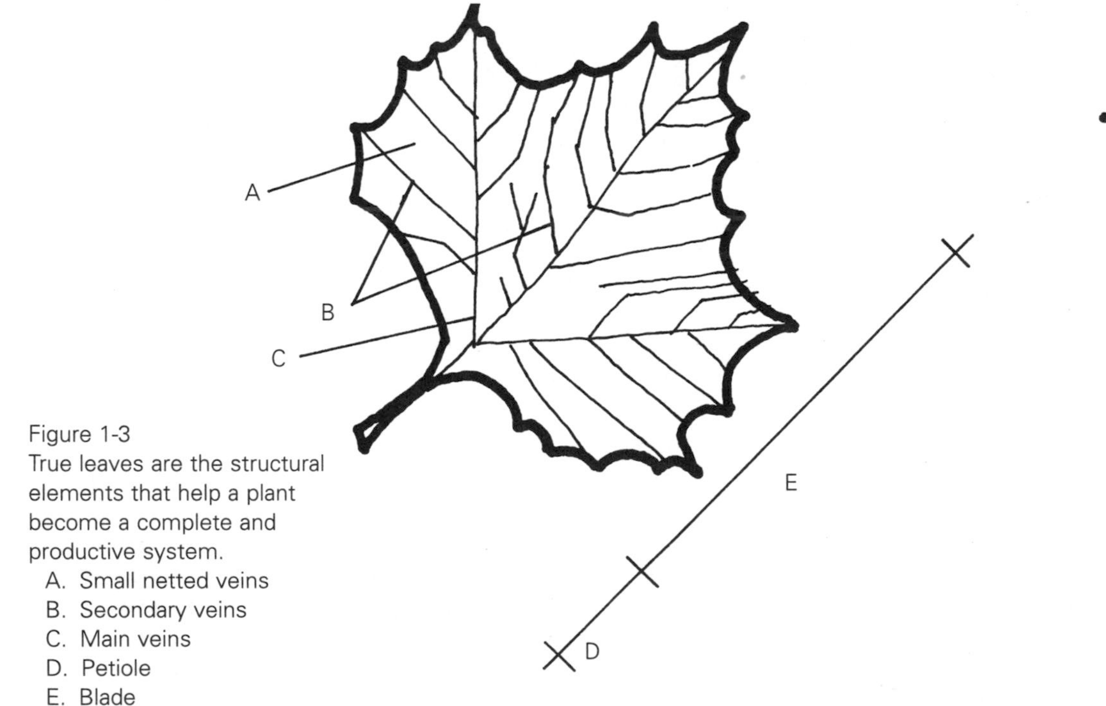

Figure 1-3
True leaves are the structural elements that help a plant become a complete and productive system.
A. Small netted veins
B. Secondary veins
C. Main veins
D. Petiole
E. Blade

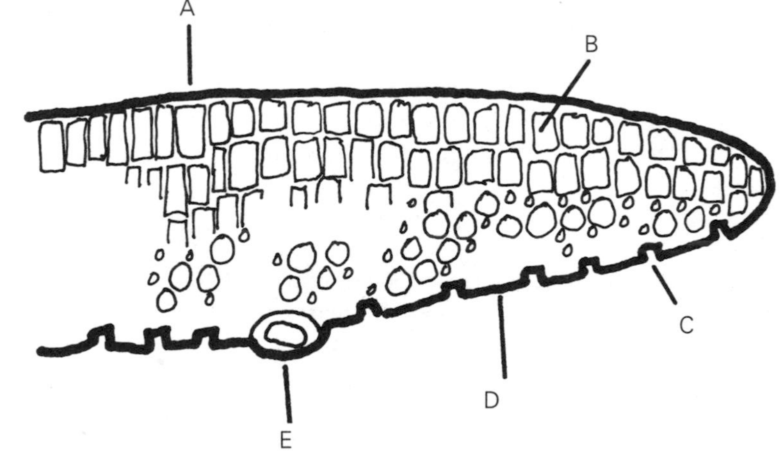

Figure 1-4
The leaf is the center of an extensive plant production system. A designed planting environment should not interrupt the needs of that system.
A. Protective layer (upper epidermis)
B. Cells for food manufacturing (parenchyma)
C. Stomata for breathing
D. Protective layer (lower epidermis)
E. Veins for conduction

The Communities of the Natural Plant Systems

The dynamic relationship between the various plant systems is governed by three principal ecological factors: climate, physiography, and soil. In order to focus attention upon the species used in a project, a careful review of these factors is important. For it is these factors, more than anything else, that will determine the geographic range and possible design functions of a plant or population of plants.

Climate

The ability of an individual plant to fulfill a specific design function is related to its hardiness and adaptability to the climate conditions that will surround it. The climate needs of broadleaf evergreens and narrow-leaf evergreens are a good example. Narrow-leaf plants will generally not survive the harsh summers of the broadleaf range without microclimate modification. Such an alteration of climate conditions may extend a plant's design effectiveness and site adaptability, but it may also increase maintenance costs.

The climate of a plant community includes temperature, precipitation, humidity, light, and wind, which act in unison from day to day and season to season.

Temperature

Temperature determines plant hardiness and growth. Each plant has a minimum and maximum temperature requirement that largely determines adaptability in a particular region or project. Adaptability is generally related to the ability of the plant to enter a dormant or resting stage during which it is able to withstand widely variable temperature extremes. Many plants, especially deciduous woody plants, protect themselves by becoming dormant until temperatures are such that growth can occur again (Fig. 1-5).

The limiting factors of temperature are:

short growing season

unfavorably high or low temperatures during growing season

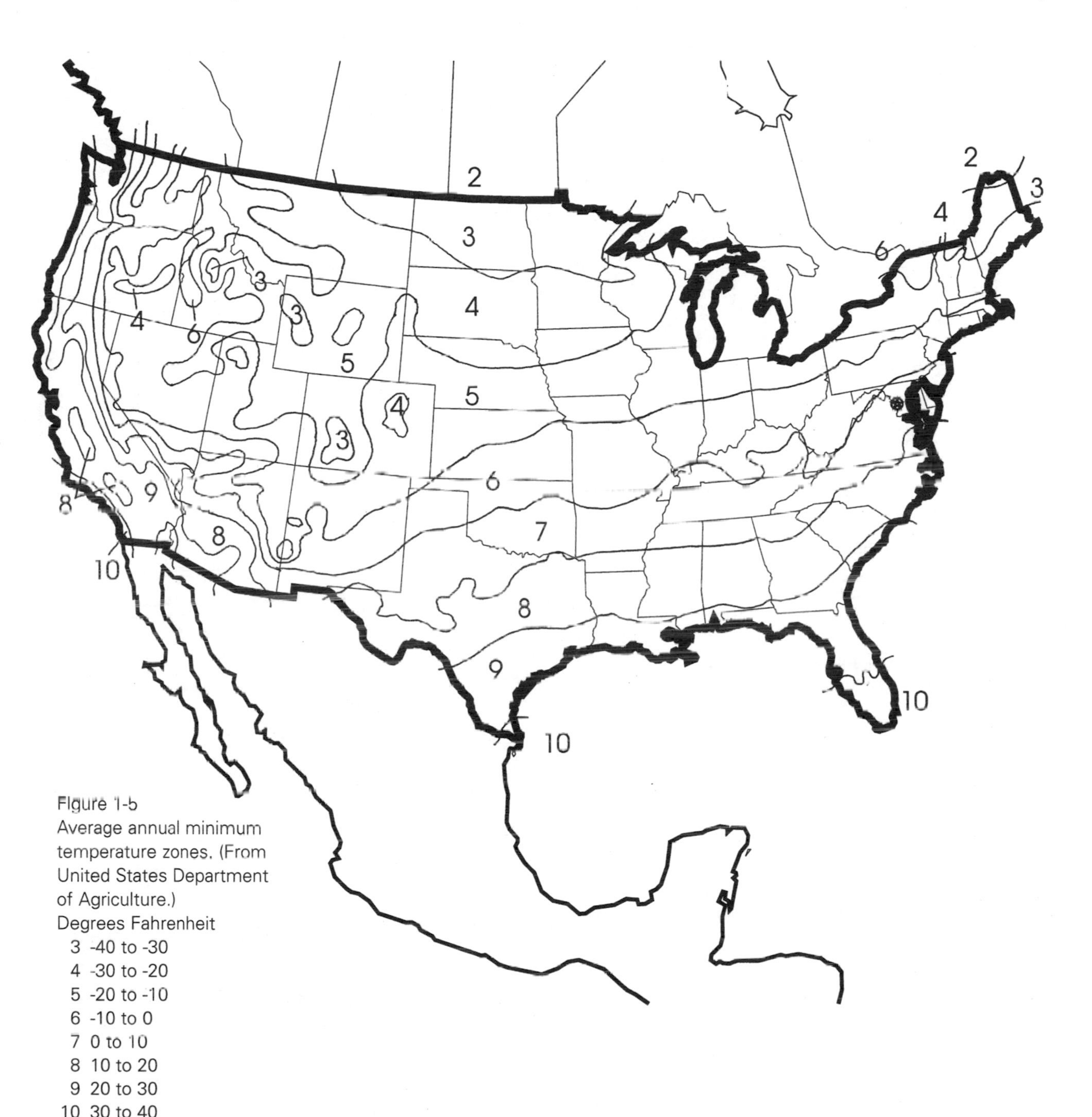

Figure 1-5
Average annual minimum temperature zones. (From United States Department of Agriculture.)
Degrees Fahrenheit
3 -40 to -30
4 -30 to -20
5 -20 to -10
6 -10 to 0
7 0 to 10
8 10 to 20
9 20 to 30
10 30 to 40

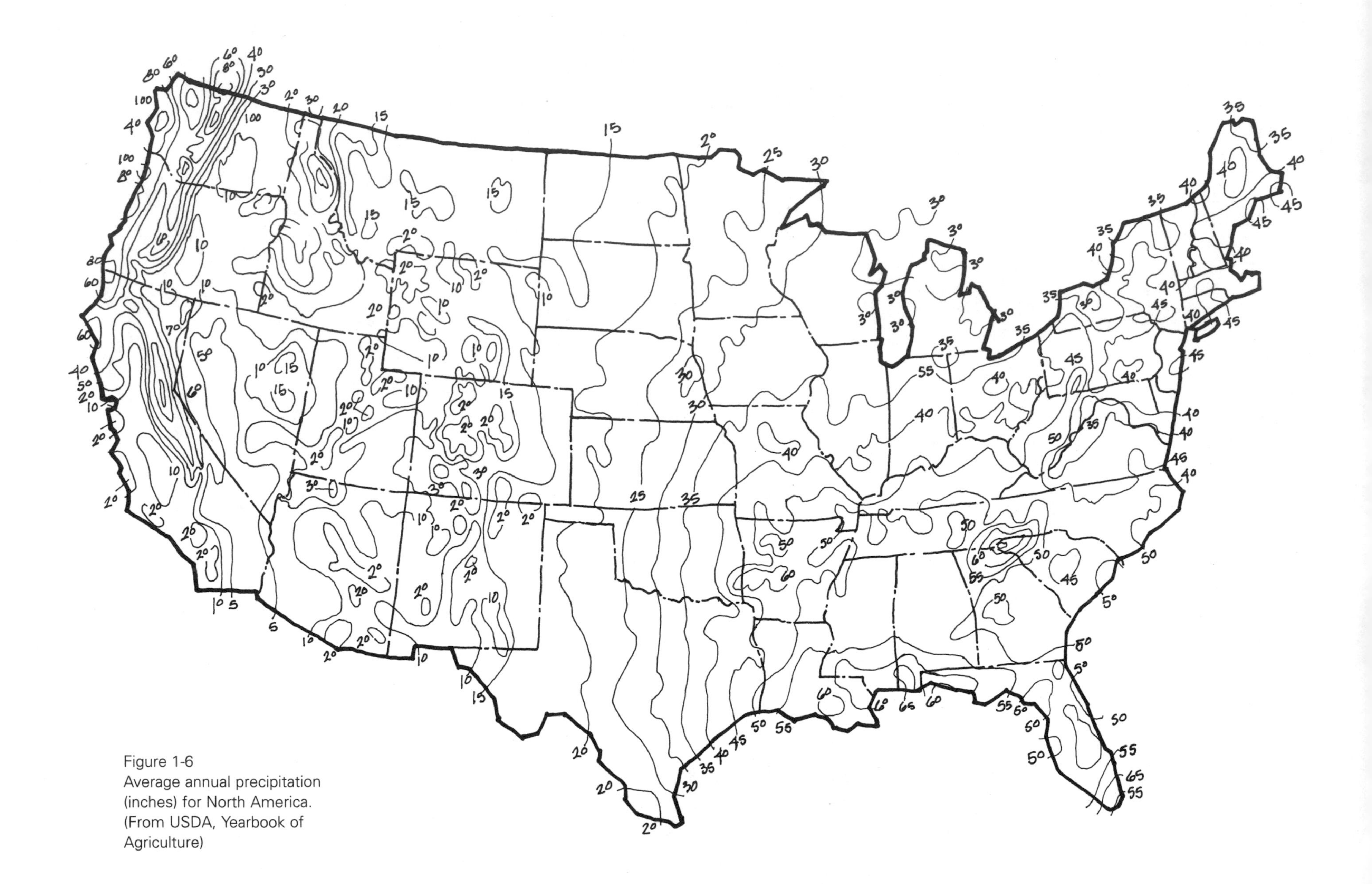

Figure 1-6
Average annual precipitation (inches) for North America. (From USDA, Yearbook of Agriculture)

harsh winter temperatures that injure or kill dormant plants

temperatures favorable to the development of pest problems.

Precipitation

Precipitation, in both natural and supplemental form, ranks next to climate in determining plant adaptability for design. It is usually gauged in inches and hundredths of inches and will largely control the distribution of vegetation. Where rainfall is heavy, a climax community could easily be a dense forest. Where it is scarce, a community may sustain only desert-like growth and will never reach its climax states.

Water may have a greater part to play in adaptability than in hardiness, but it is still important to the latter because plants under water stress may be more subject to low or high temperature injury. Plants are divided into three groups based upon their adaptability to moisture: *hydrophytes*, which are plants that will grow in water or on extremely wet sites; *mesophytes*, plants adapted to medium moisture conditions; and *xerophytes*, plants resistant to drought or extremely dry conditions. The ability of a plant to adapt to water extremes will largely determine its adaptability to a particular climate and design situation (Fig. 1-6).

Humidity

Humidity is the amount of water vapor in the air, with relative humidity corresponding to the percentage of air saturation. Air can hold more water vapor when the temperature rises; thus when air is heated, relative humidity is lowered, and vise versa. When plants cool at night and the adjacent air reaches a relative humidity of 100 percent, excess moisture falls to the ground in the form of dew or frost — depending on the temperature.

Light

Light falls to earth in the form of solar radiation and is essential to the usefulness of plants in a design, especially when color is to be a dominant element. Light is the main ingredient of photosynthesis. Light determines plant growth responses, and in many instances also relates to hardiness and adaptability. Exposure to light and temperature are interrelated, and both directly contribute to the ability of plants to adapt to local design or environmental conditions. Among the most important planting design factors to consider are the placement of plants for exposure to sun or shade (Fig. 1-7).

When dealing with light for specific plants, three aspects must be remembered:

1. *Intensity*, the plant's need for a certain level of brightness. Some plant materials cannot withstand full sunlight while others cannot tolerate shade. The landscape architect responds to this factor by filtering or increasing available light.
2. *Wavelength*, the relationship of the plant to ultraviolet (400 millimicrons) and/or infrared (760 millimicrons) light rays. The fact that a plant receives light does not necessarily mean that its light requirements are being met, as some plants need more ultraviolet (blue light) than others. The heavenly bamboo, *(Nandina domestica)* needs infrared light to produce its attractive yellows and reds and when placed in ultraviolet light remains a cool green. A designer may adjust this element to meet the needs of the materials chosen for composition.
3. *Duration*, the length of time a plant may need to be exposed to light to produce flowers, seeds, or attractive foliage. If a small flowering tree or shrub remains in full sun only a short period of time during a day, it may not receive the light it needs to achieve full aesthetic quality.

Wind

Wind plays an important role in the natural plant community by aiding in the dispersal of pollen, seeds, or insects that are vital for the continuation of basic community characteristics. The exposure of some plants to winds may directly affect their ornamental adaptability by causing the loss of stem or leaf moisture or reducing their ability to reproduce. High winds or sudden wind changes may also cause damage to some plant species or even reduce the amount of water vapor in the air. In some vegetative communities, the direction of growth and even the shape of some plants will be controlled by both seasonal and prevailing winds (Fig. 1-8).

Physiography

The basic physiography of plant communities can be determined by looking at a region's natural environment. The topography will govern the amount of light for plant growth. On level areas where the grade is fairly uniform, the transition of plants may be very broad and indefinite. On mountains and steep slopes, near saline areas, or around water, there may be a very small and well-defined plant community (Spurr, 1964).

On a micro scale, the local environmental conditions of the site must be determined by careful resource inventory. For a macro scale determination, however, the vegetative regions discussed below are presented for preplanning assistance. The United States is made up of 32 general growth regions, which stretch from the North Pacific Coast to the southern tip of Florida. These regions in turn may be divided into various forest and grassland communities (Fig. 1-9).

The North American Deciduous Forest

This forest community occupies North America from the Gulf of Mexico to the Great Lakes. It spreads from the East Coast westward to the Mississippi River and beyond and is dominated by trees with broad leaves that shed each season. Small deciduous trees and shrubs occupy its understory. The beech and sugar maple comprise the climax stand of this area.

The subdivisions of this forest are the northern and upland regions, the southern and lowland regions, and the stream-skirting forest. The natural landscape is characterized by mixed plant materials and lack of a distinctive boundary between regions.

Figure 1-7
Often in the design and development of a natural planting composition reducing the density of the overhead canopy will aid in the development of understory trees, shrubs and ground covers.

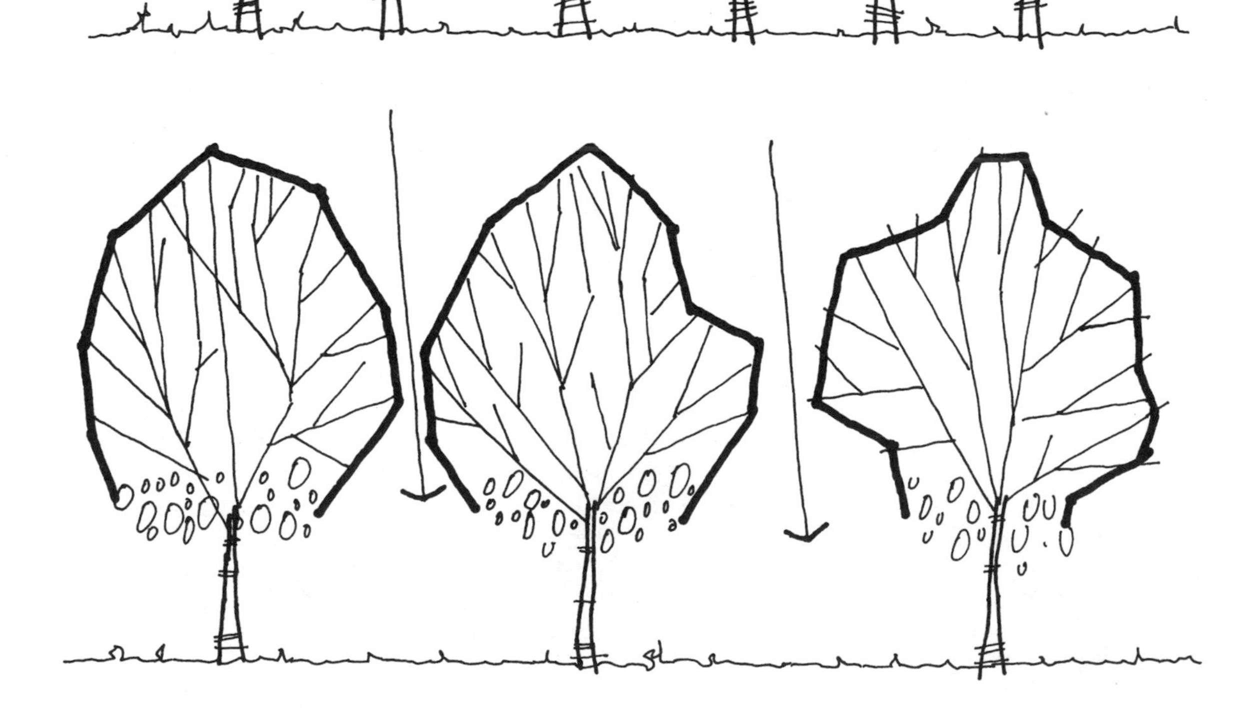

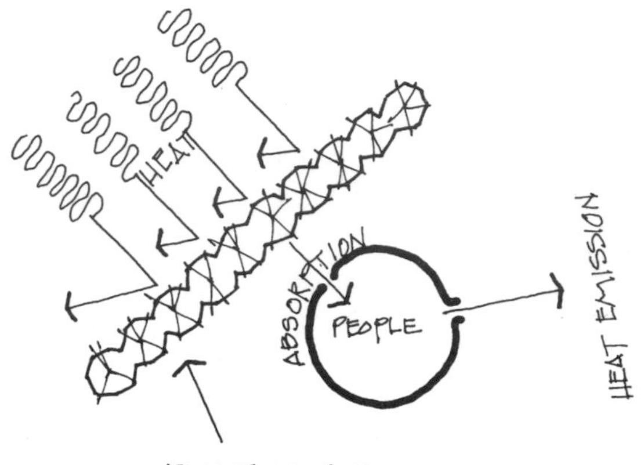

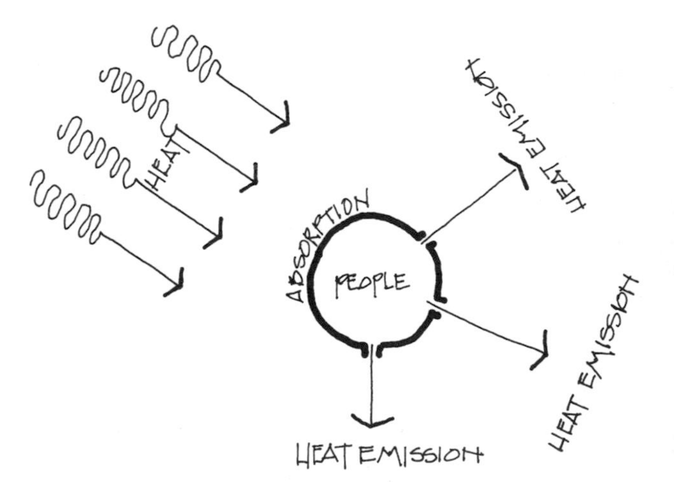

Figure 1-8
Using plants to control the effects of cold winds will help reduce heat emission, increasing the comfort of people in a planted space.

Figure 1-9
Plant growth regions of the United States.

1. North Pacific Coast
2. Willamette Valley — Puget Sound
3. Central California Valleys
4. Cascade–Sierra Nevada
5. Southern California
6. Columbia River Valley
7. Palouse-Bitterroot Valley
8. Snake River Plain — Utah Valley
9. Great Basin — Intermontane
10. Southwestern Desert
11. Southern Plateau
12. Northern Rocky Mountains
13. Central Rocky Mountains
14. Southern Rocky Mountains
15. Northern Great Plains
16. Central Great Plains
17. Southern Plains
18. Northern Black Soils
19. Central Black Soils
20. Southern Black Soils
21. Northern Prairies
22. Central Prairies
23. Western Great Lakes
24. Central Great Lakes
25. Ozark-Ohio-Tennessee River Valleys
26. Northern Great Lakes–St. Lawrence
27. Appalachian
28. Piedmont
29. Upper Coastal Plain
30. Swampy Coastal Plain
31. South-Central Florida
32. Subtropical Florida

The northern and upland region has five subregional areas, which are composed of the following vegetative types (Figs. 1-10 to 1-12):

1. *Tulip-oak.* This part of the forest is most abundant between altitudes of 500 feet (150 m) and 1,000 feet (300 m).
2. *Oak-chestnut.* This area is found from Cape Ann, Massachusetts, to the southern end of the Appalachians at elevations between 1,500 and 2,000 feet.
3. *Maple-basswood-birch.* This forest area is found primarily in the Appalachians at altitudes of 2,500 feet (760 m) to 4,200 feet (1,275 m).
4. *Maple-beech-hemlock.* These are found in southern Michigan, northern Ohio, and Indiana.
5. *Maple-basswood.* These are found in northern Illinois, southern Wisconsin, and parts of eastern Minnesota.

The annual rainfall of this forest area ranges from 28 inches (70 cm) to 40 inches (100 cm). The trees of the forest canopy are 75 feet (23 m) to 100 feet (30 m) in height and 23 inches (58 cm) to 30 inches (76 cm) in caliper. Their branching heights are 32 feet (10 m) to 40 feet (12 m), and they shade about 90 percent of the forest floor.

The canopy layer is made up of the limbs, upper trunk, and leaves of the dominant forest vegetation. The understory is composed of young and suppressed individuals of the larger species, while the main seedling trees (or larger shrubs) are the abundant pawpaw. The spicebush is the dominant material of the shrub layer, and the herb layer is characterized by common nettle and wild ginger.

The southern and lowland forests are subdivided into:

1. *Oak-hickory.* These are found primarily from New Jersey to Alabama and westward to Texas.
2. *Magnolia-maritime.* This begins in the southwest corner of Virginia, extends southward to meet the magnolia forest in South Carolina, and goes along the coast to the southeast corner of Texas.

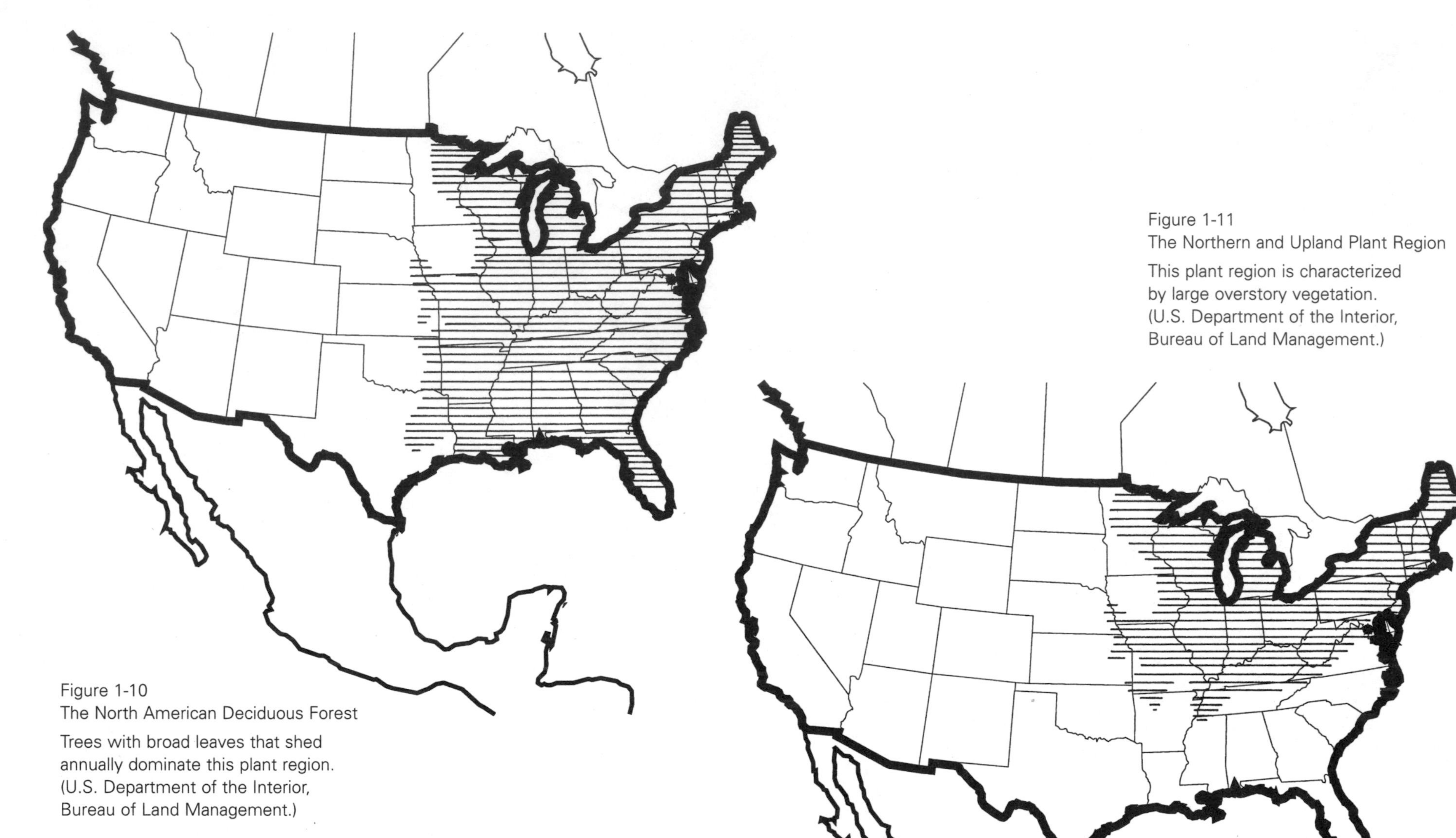

Figure 1-11
The Northern and Upland Plant Region
This plant region is characterized by large overstory vegetation. (U.S. Department of the Interior, Bureau of Land Management.)

Figure 1-10
The North American Deciduous Forest
Trees with broad leaves that shed annually dominate this plant region. (U.S. Department of the Interior, Bureau of Land Management.)

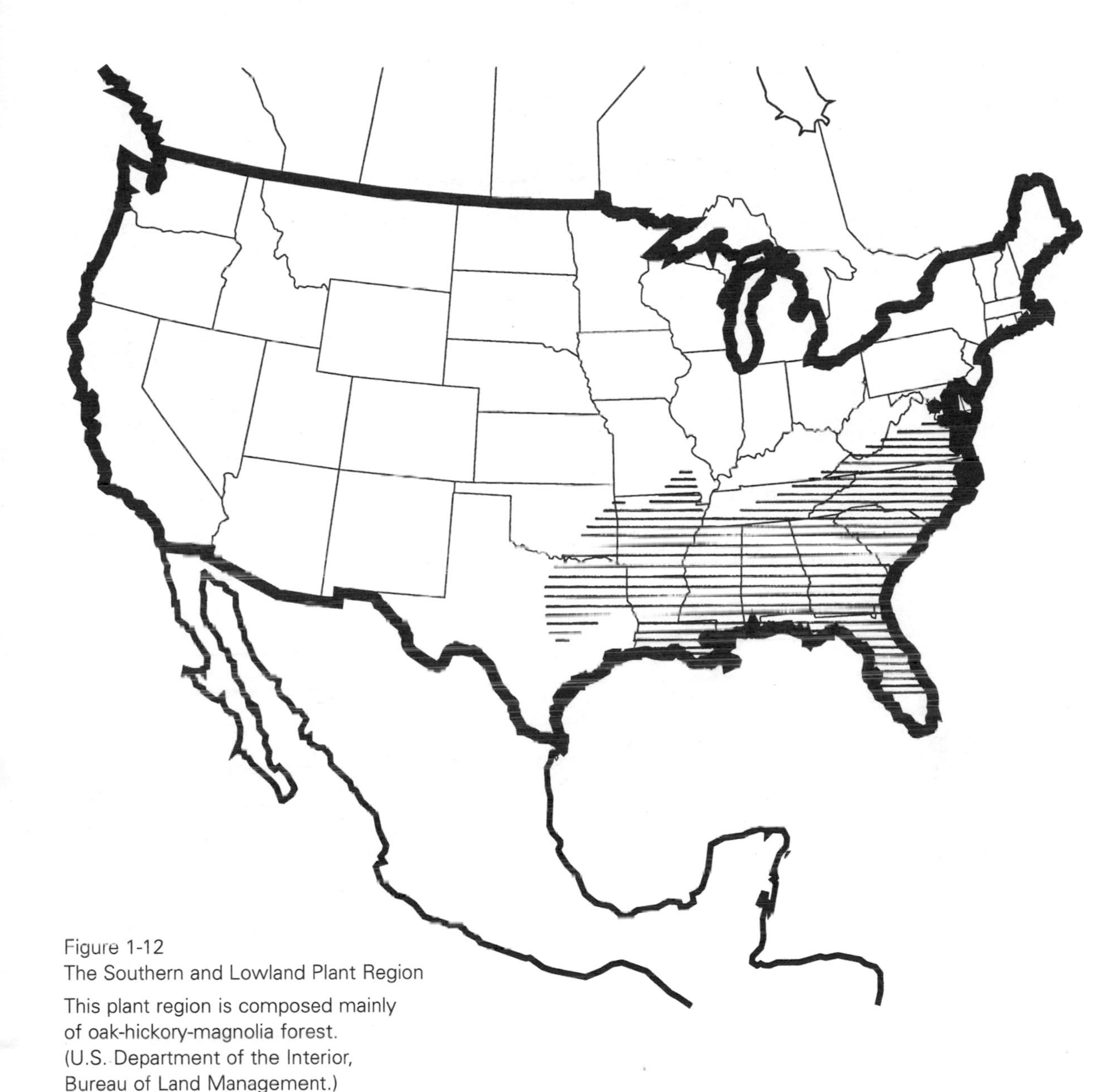

Figure 1-12
The Southern and Lowland Plant Region
This plant region is composed mainly of oak-hickory-magnolia forest. (U.S. Department of the Interior, Bureau of Land Management.)

Rainfall for this region is from 40 inches (100 cm) to 60 inches (150 cm) annually and is greatest in the spring and summer (Spurr, 1964.)

The floodplain forest is mixed with other deciduous forests and grassland areas of North America. Because of constantly changing environmental conditions brought on by shifting channels, islands, and sandbars, vegetation often stops short of the climax stage (Fig. 1-13).

Two types of landscape habitats are characteristic of this area. The first is *terrestrial*, which is dry at low water. Early spring flooding that causes the submergence of vegetation for anywhere from a week to as long as two months is typical of these forest areas. The second is *aquatic*, which is covered with water most of the year.

Small tree thickets are common, especially the sandbar willow, which helps stabilize sands along river channels. These are usually followed immediately by cottonwood seedlings, and then by sugarberry, elm, and sweetgum. Several hundred years may be necessary for an oak forest to appear in areas 40 feet (12 m) to 45 feet (14 m) above the low water level (Shelford, 1963).

The Boreal Coniferous Forest

This forest originally extended from some parts of Indiana and Ohio, to the mouth of the Mackenzie River in Canada, to the Brooks Mountain Range in Alaska. In this area, the climate ranges from cool to cold, and there is precipitation all year, with much coming in the summer. The climax evergreens may be pines, with long needles, or spruce, hemlock, and fir, with short, thick leaves (Fig. 1-14).

This forest area can be subdivided into the boreal forest east of the Rocky Mountains; the vegetation of the valley areas and lower slopes of the northern Rocky Mountains; and the forests of the Rocky Mountains and the Sierra Nevada (Shelford, 1963).

The Montane Coniferous Forest and Alpine Communities

This region is found from the upper eastern slope of the British Columbia coastal mountains, the Cascade Mountains, and the coast range of northern California.

Figure 1-13
The Floodplain Forest Region

This region is characterized by terrestrial (occasionally flooded) and aquatic (submerged or partly submerged) vegetative types. (U.S. Department of the Interior, Bureau of Land Management.)

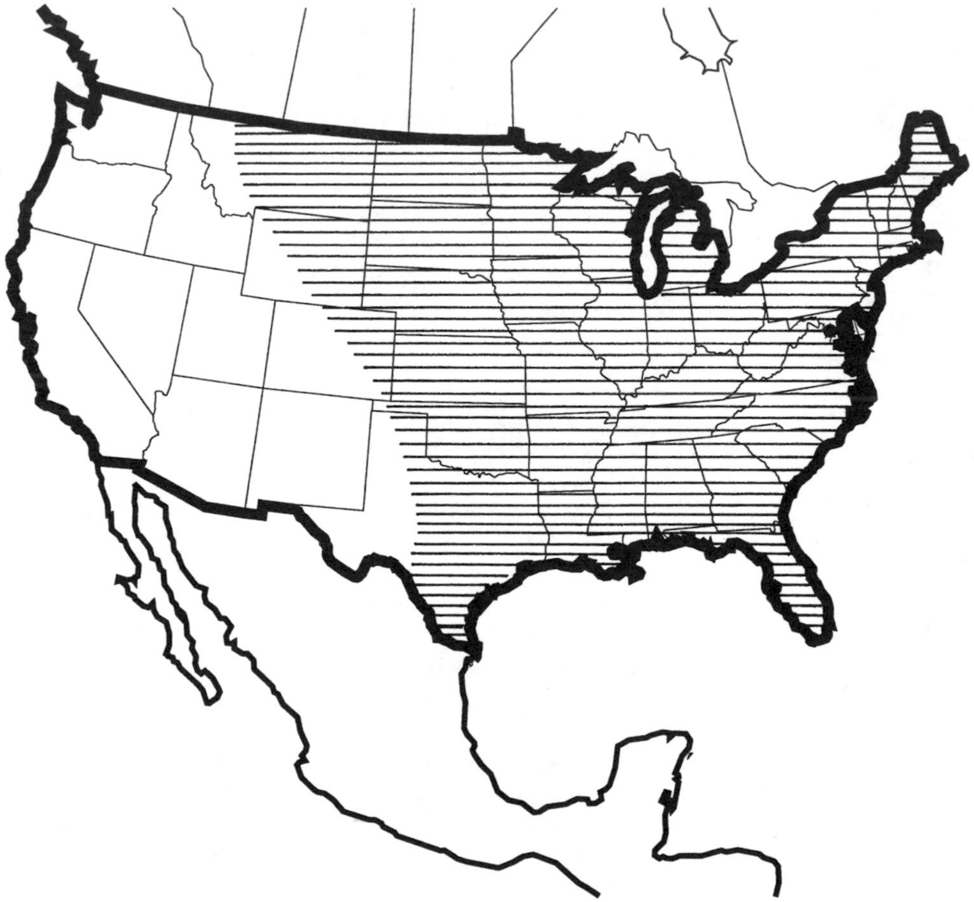

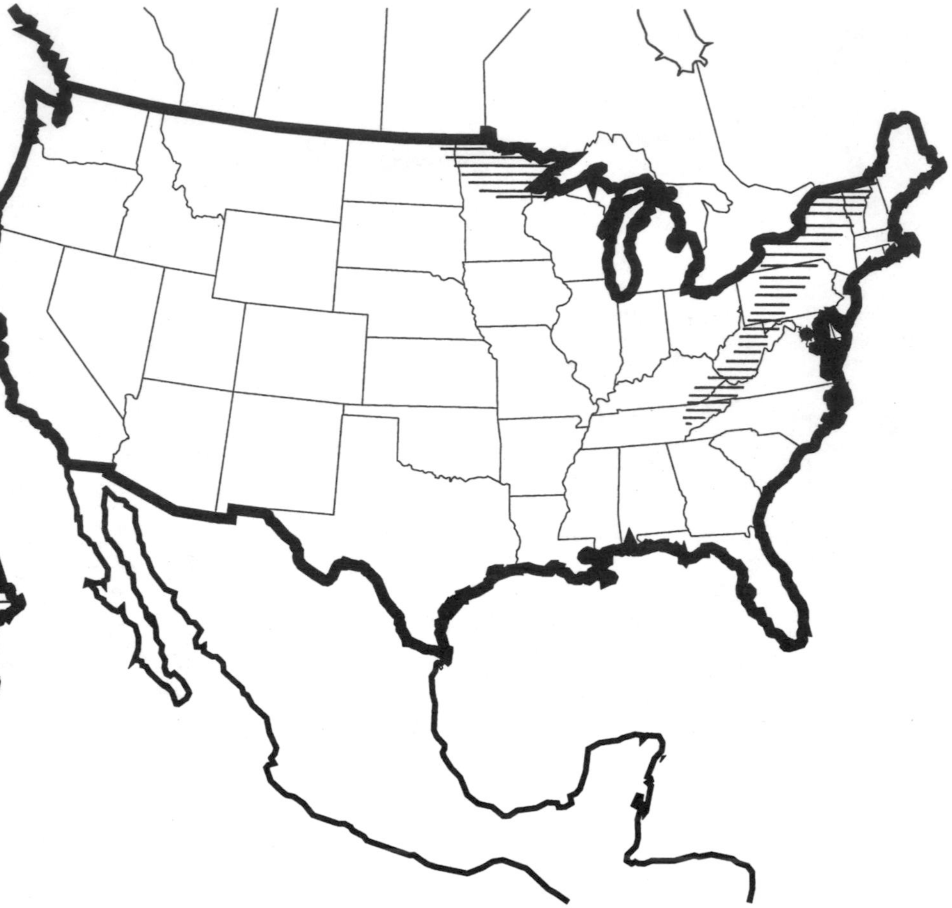

Figure 1-14
The Boreal Coniferous Forest Region

This region is divided into the boreal forest east of the Rocky Mountains in northern Minnesota and in the Appalachian region, and the vegetation of the valley areas of the northern Rocky Mountains of Canada. (U.S. Department of the Interior, Bureau of Land Management.)

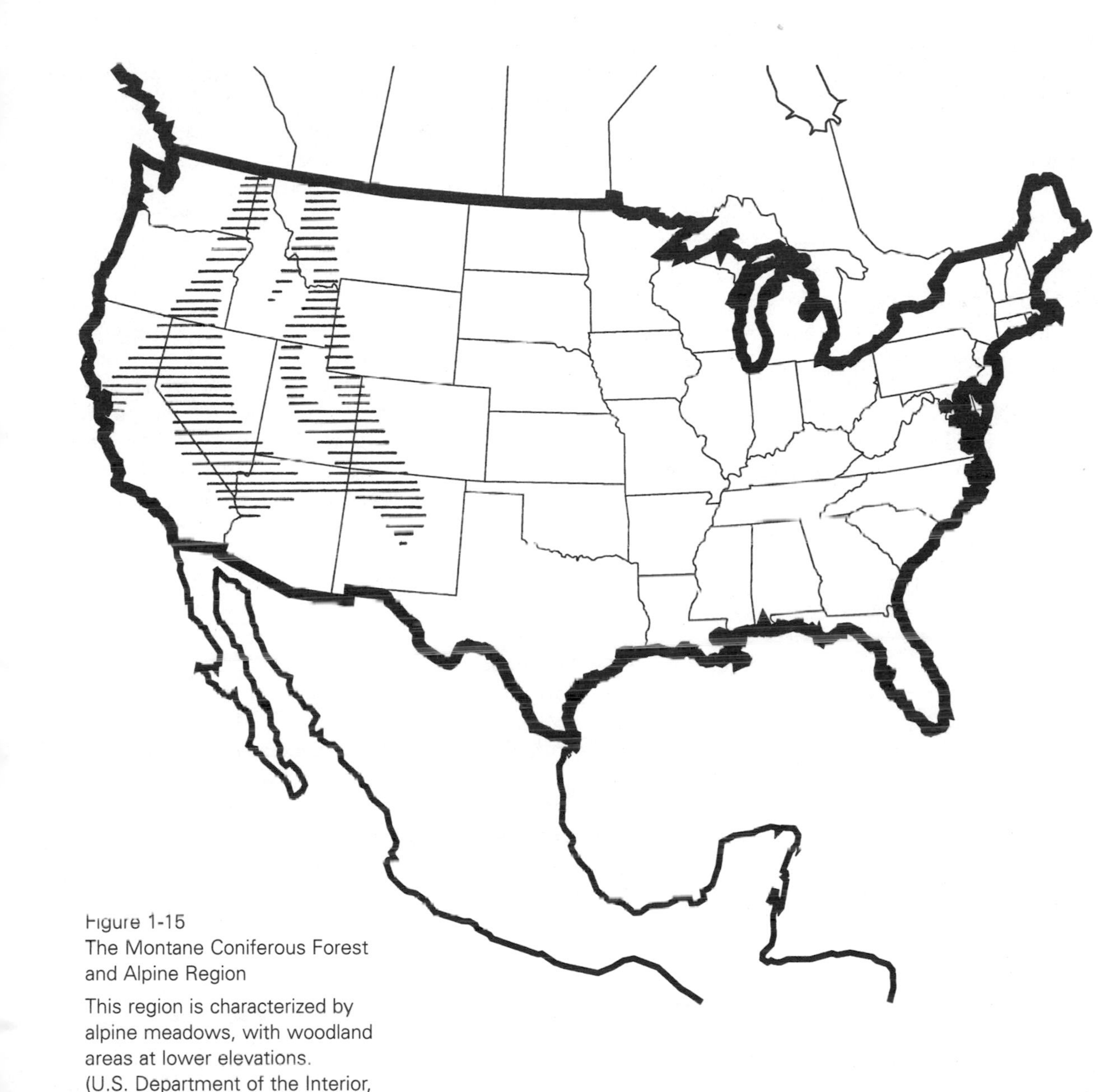

Figure 1-15
The Montane Coniferous Forest and Alpine Region
This region is characterized by alpine meadows, with woodland areas at lower elevations.
(U.S. Department of the Interior, Bureau of Land Management.)

Its eastern boundary is the boreal forest in the north and the Great Plains grassland in the south. Alpine meadows occur at higher elevations above the forest's vegetation, while various woodlands occur below at lower elevations (Fig. 1-15) (Shelford, 1963).

The Northern Pacific Coast–Rainy Western Hemlock Forest

This forest area is found adjacent to the Pacific Coast from the middle of California to southern Alaska. The mature, dominant vegetation is very tall — 125 feet (38 m) to 300 feet (90 m) — and up to 20 feet (6 m) wide. Understory trees or shrubs may find it impossible to survive unless openings are provided in the canopy (Fig. 1-16). Shrub and herb layers cannot develop properly in the mature forest and are restricted to a few species. The frost-free period will vary from 120 days to 210 days, with a mean annual temperature range from 40°F (4°C) to 56°F (13°C).

The Broad Sclerophyll–Grizzly Bear Community

This vegetation ranges from central Oregon through California and may be either forest, woodland, or chaparral. Fewer than 20 percent of the dominant species are deciduous.

Annual rainfall in the northern areas ranges from 16 inches (40 cm) to 38 inches (95 cm), whereas the southern chaparral averages 21.6 inches (54 cm) and remains dry June through September.

The sclerophyll vegetation will vary from a large oak forest with a grass ground cover, to a scattered woodland with chaparral or sagebrush undergrowth, to a bush vegetation (Fig. 1-17) (Shelford, 1963).

The Desert and Semidesert Communities

These communities occupy the Great Basin portion of western Utah and a part of Nevada. The vegetation is shrubby and dominated by sagebrush, with some contact with ponderosa pine forests.

Rainfall for most of this area will average below 10 inches. The temperature in January will average between 29°F (-17° C) and 39°F (3.90°C), with July averaging

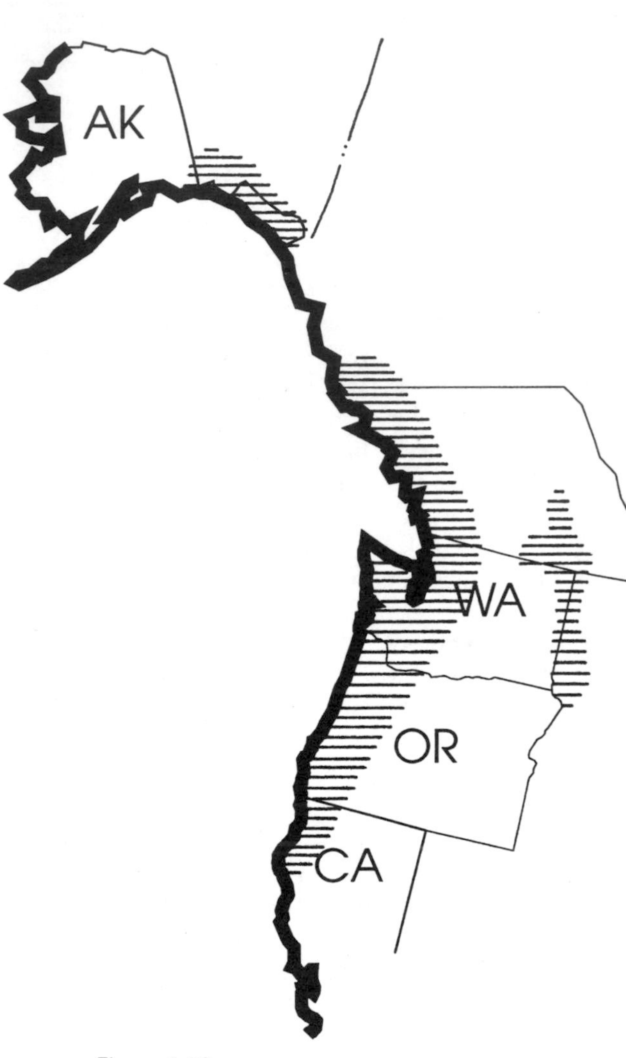

Figure 1-16
The North Pacific Coast–Rainy Western Hemlock Forest

This region has a dominant overstory reaching as high as 300 feet tall. (U.S. Department of the Interior, Bureau of Land Management.)

between 70°F (21°C) and 78°F (26°C). The major plants are deciduous shrubs and dense stands of tall sagebrush (Fig. 1-18) (Shelford, 1963).

THE WOODLAND AND BRUSHLAND COMMUNITIES

This vegetation occurs in the foothills of the Rocky Mountains from Montana and Oregon to Mexico. It is characterized by short-trunked trees, a scattered growth of shrubs and herbs, and a dense growth of shrubs thinning into grassland and desert at lower elevations. The annual rainfall is from 12 inches (30.48 cm) to 25 inches (63.5 cm), and the temperature of the seasons is quite variable.

The following specific communities may be recognized: the western juniper-buckbrush region; the pinyon-juniper region; the oak-juniper region; the oak woodland region; and the oak bushland (Fig. 1-19) (Shelford, 1963).

THE NORTHERN GRASSLANDS

This vegetative region is characterized by perennial grasses stretching from Alberta to Mexico City, and from the Pacific Coast to western Indiana. The northern part is moist and cool; the southern part is drier. There are four major grassland areas important in this natural landscape (Fig. 1-20) (Shelford, 1963).

The tall-grass prairie

This grass range once extended through what is now the Midwest agricultural region of the United States, from Manitoba to Oklahoma and eastward into Ohio and southern Michigan. It is now extensively plowed and is principally found in Kansas, the northern parts of Oklahoma, Nebraska, and North and South Dakota. The major species of grasses are the bluestems *(Andropogon spp.)*, porcupinegrass *(Stipa spp.)*, switchgrass *(Pancium spp.)*, Indiangrass *(Sorghastrum spp.)*, and wild rye *(Elymus spp.)*. The average height of these grasses is 4 to 5 feet (1.22 to 1.524 m) with a root depth reaching to 8 feet (2.44 m). The coastal prairie occupies the southern extension of this growth region inland from the coastal marches of Texas and Louisiana (Shelford, 1963).

The mixed-grass prairie

This grass region occupies the area between the tall-grass prairie and the foothills of the Rocky Mountains, extending from Canada to Texas, and expands westward from Texas to Arizona. It is often referred to as the short-grass prairie, but has intermediate-height grass species.

The major species include the western wheat-grass *(Agropyron smithii spp.)*, needle-and-thread *(Stipa comata)*, and buffalo grass *(Buchloe dactyloides)* (Shelford, 1963).

The semidesert grassland

This area extends from central and southwestern Texas to northern Arizona and is the driest of the grassland regions. The species within this group have a short, open growth characteristic and are dominated by black gramma *(Bouteloua eriopoda)*, three-awn grasses *(Aristida spp.)*, and curly mesquite *(Hilaria berlangeri)*. Tobosa grass *(Hilaria mutica)* and alkali sacaton *(Sporobolus airoides)* are characteristic to low sites that become flooded on occasion (Shelford, 1963).

The pacific prairie

This grassland prairie once covered an extensive portion of the valleys and foothills of California, Oregon, and Washington; northern Utah and southern Idaho; south-central Montana, southwestern Wyoming, and northern Nevada; and western Alberta.

Important species of this region include wild oats *(Avena spp.)*, ripgut *(Bromus spp.)*, purple needlegrass *(Stipa pulchra)*, wild ryes *(Elymus spp.)*, Idaho fescue *(Festuca idahoensis)*, Sandbag bluegrass *(Poa secunda)*, and prairie Junegrass *(Koeleria spp.)*.

THE HOT DESERT

The vegetation of this community is adapted to small and irregularly occurring rainfalls, a warm climate, and very hot summers. It consists mostly of brush-covered areas, with a large portion of the soil exposed. The dominant vegetation is creosote.

Western portions stretch from lower California into Arizona; the eastern part reaches from New Mexico into

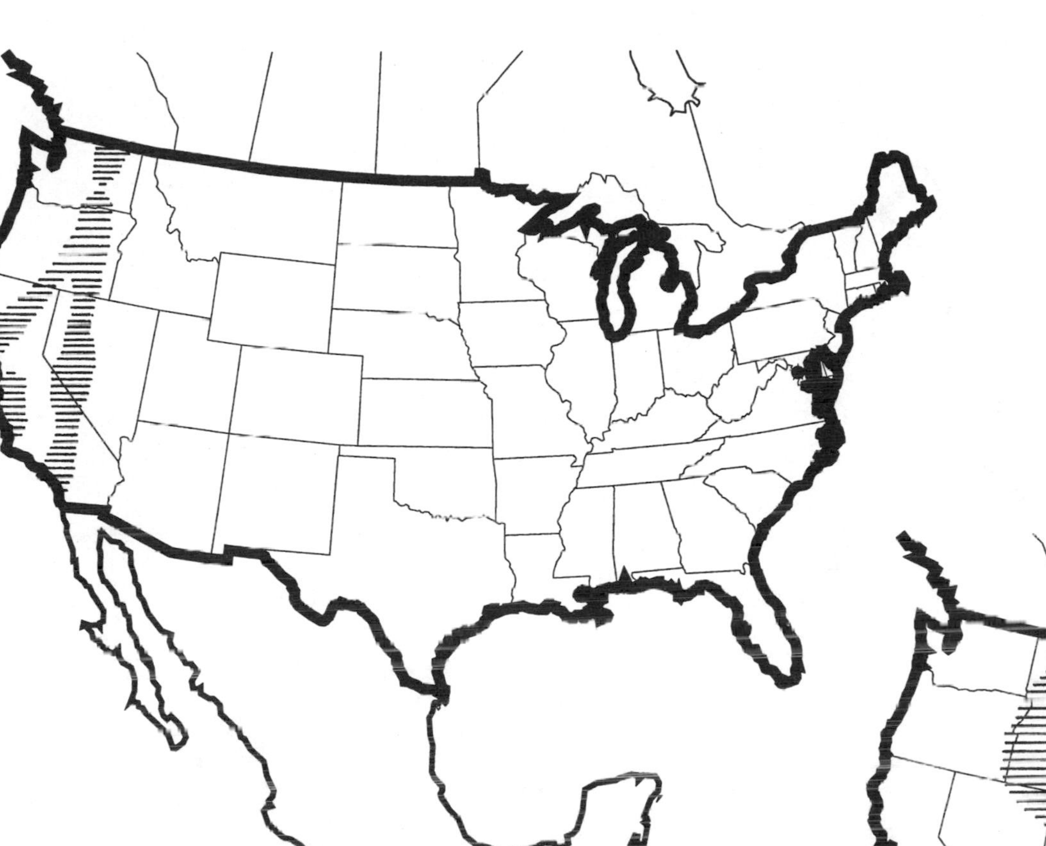

Figure 1-17
The Broad Schlerophyll–Grizzly Bear Region

This region is dominated by evergreen vegetation and has less than 20 percent deciduous plant material.
(U.S. Department of the Interior, Bureau of Land Management.)

Figure 1-18
The Desert and Semidesert Communities

This region has few trees and is dominated by deciduous shrubs and sagebrush.
(U.S. Department of the Interior, Bureau of Land Management.)

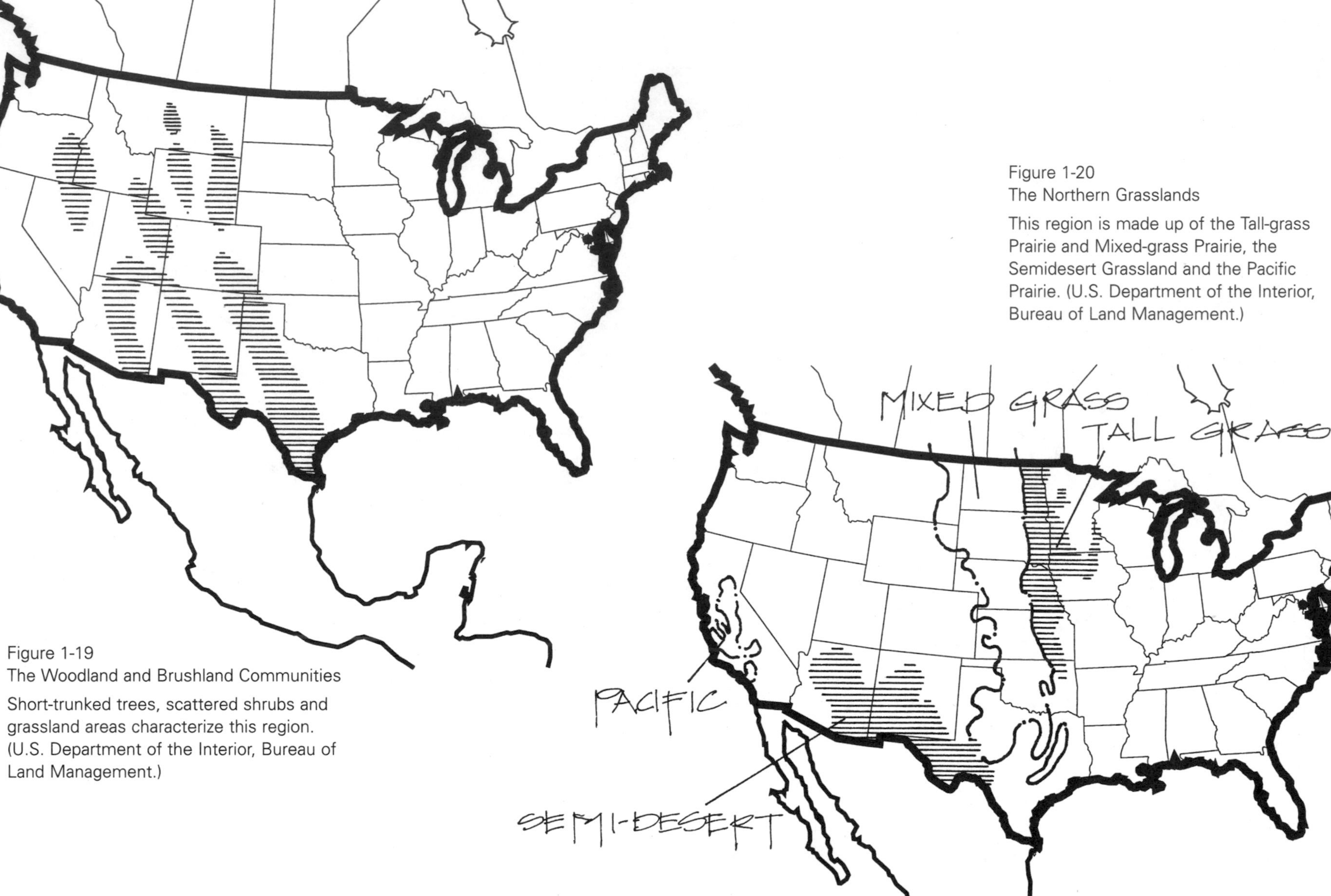

Figure 1-20
The Northern Grasslands

This region is made up of the Tall-grass Prairie and Mixed-grass Prairie, the Semidesert Grassland and the Pacific Prairie. (U.S. Department of the Interior, Bureau of Land Management.)

Figure 1-19
The Woodland and Brushland Communities

Short-trunked trees, scattered shrubs and grassland areas characterize this region. (U.S. Department of the Interior, Bureau of Land Management.)

Texas. Dominant plants are small and rarely exceed 30 feet (9 m) in height; they are widely spaced due to low soil moisture. The diversity of habitat is extensive, with marked differences between slope orientation, sun exposure, and uplands versus lowlands.

The wide variation in habitats causes a complex vegetation distribution and a slow change in site characteristics from one plant type to another. Succession is therefore difficult to distinguish (Fig. 1-21).

SOUTHERN FLORIDA

The vegetation of this area is varied and displays three probable climax stages: subtropical hammocks and a mixture of northern plant varieties; tropical hammocks; and dry and scrubby vegetation on the Keys. Rainfall occurs 12 months a year, with an occasional frost. The tropical and subtropical communities are less than 23 feet (7 m) above sea level (Fig. 1-22) (Shelford, 1963).

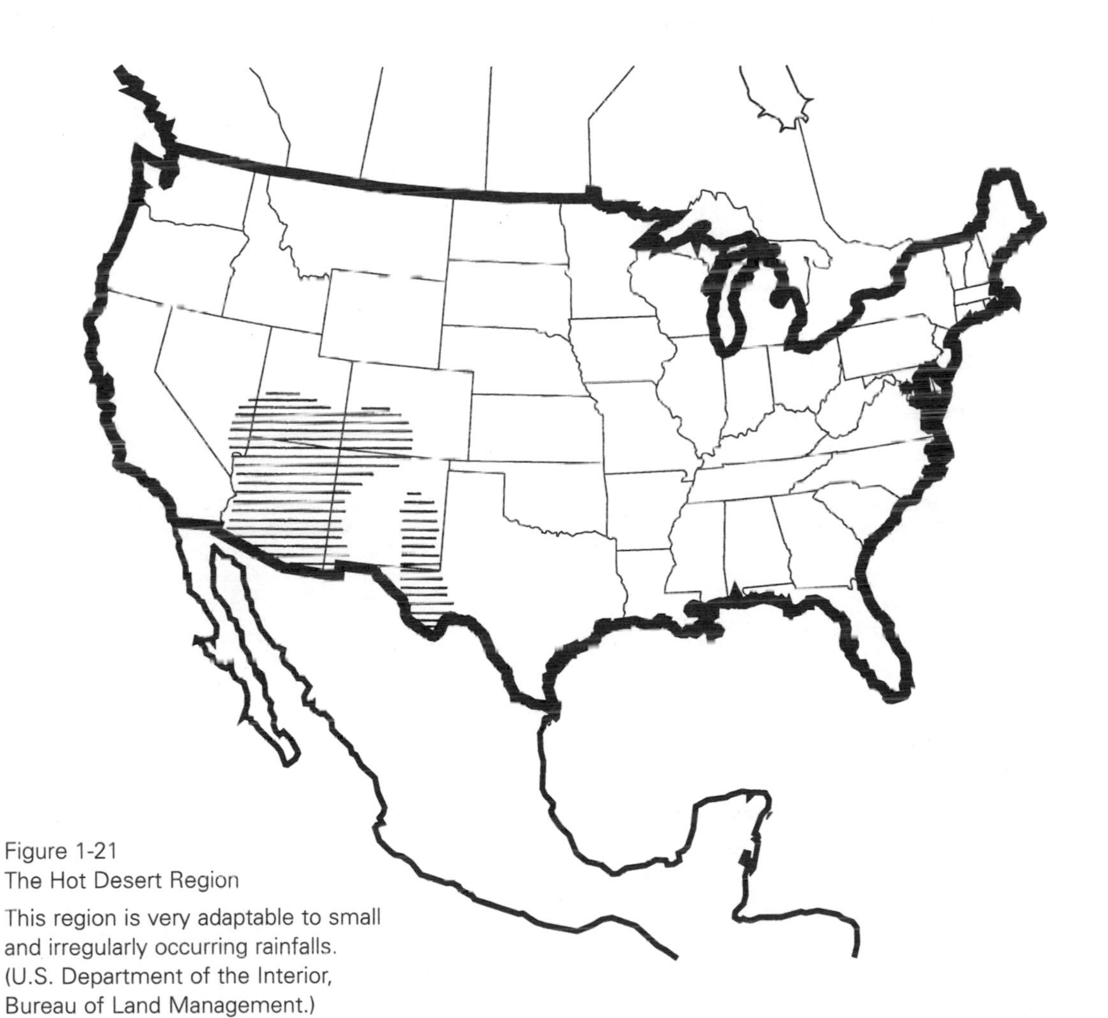

Figure 1-21
The Hot Desert Region
This region is very adaptable to small and irregularly occurring rainfalls. (U.S. Department of the Interior, Bureau of Land Management.)

Figure 1-22
The Southern Florida Region
This region is characterized by three climax stages: subtropical hammocks, tropical hammocks, and dry and shrubby vegetation. (U.S. Department of the Interior, Bureau of Land Management.)

CHAPTER 2

A PROCESS FOR PLANTING DESIGN

In developing a planting composition, the landscape architect pursues a comprehensive solution to a series of related issues that result from the needs and desires of a client or client group. The final outcome should correlate design objectives with site limitations and provide a harmonious living environment.

As wood is to a carpenter or paint to a painter, the living growing plant is to the landscape architect. Issues of design function must be considered before plant material selection and placement can be completed. Without the determination of function at the beginning of the planting-design process, the composition will be nothing more than a disorganized arrangement of growing materials.

To facilitate the orderly and successful attainment of objectives in a planting design, a system of interviews, research, and site evaluations should be developed. This comprehensive system should accommodate original client needs and site limitations while incorporating the creative input of the designer. No process can be fully successful without the vital element of artistic ingression. The following pages describe the preplanning, design, and completion phases of a particular methodology. It is by no means an inclusive arrangement of steps and elements. Adjustments may be necessary to adapt the process to specific design abilities and site, energy, or budget limitations.

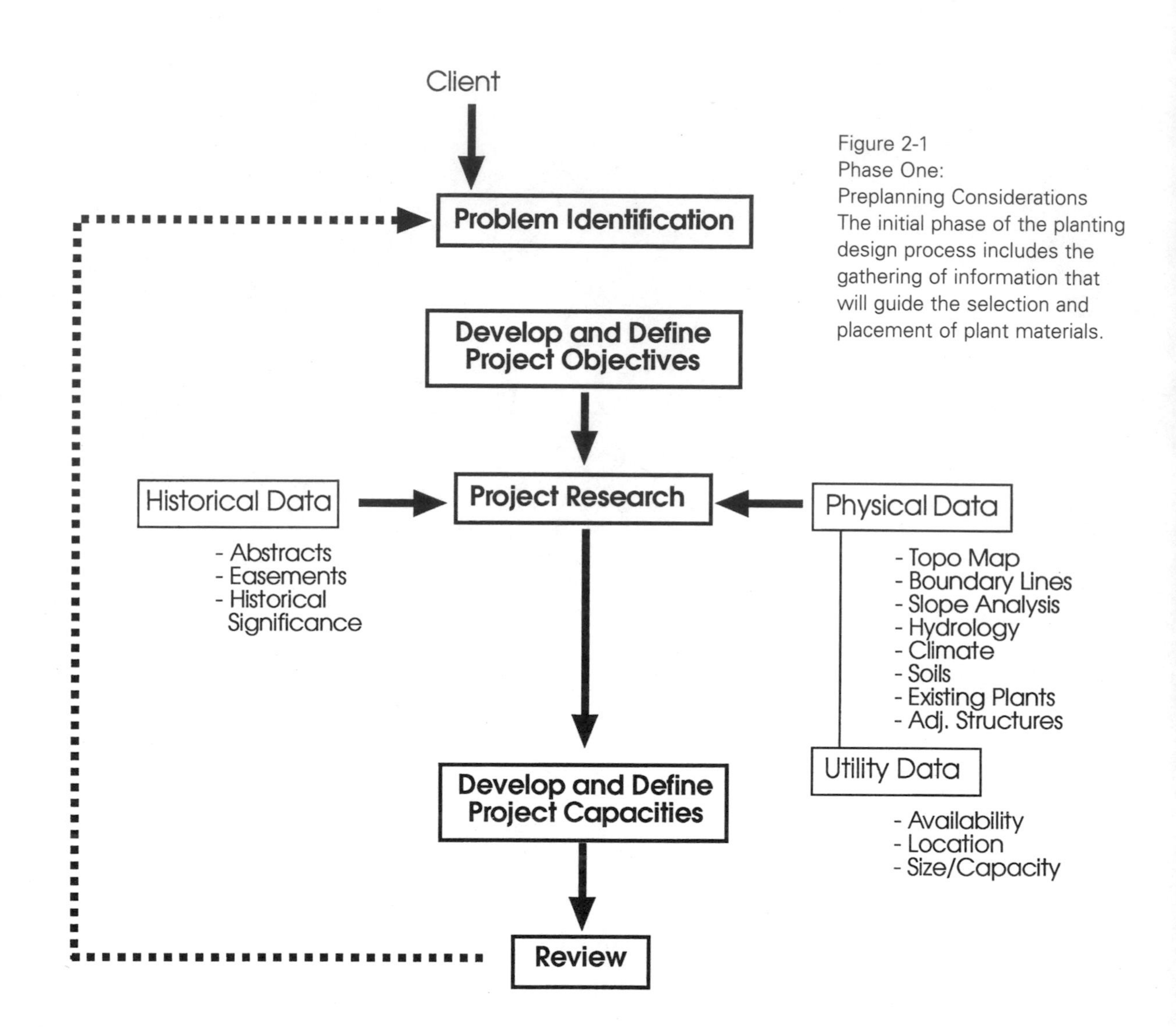

Figure 2-1
Phase One:
Preplanning Considerations
The initial phase of the planting design process includes the gathering of information that will guide the selection and placement of plant materials.

PHASE 1: PREPLANNING CONSIDERATIONS

The initial phase of the process involves gathering information pertinent to the design and planting of the proposed environment. The quality and extent of the information collected during this phase has a direct influence on the analysis and decision-making steps that follow. Care must be taken to collect information that is current and specifically related to the proposed project (Fig. 2-1).

STEP 1: DEVELOP DESIGN OBJECTIVES

The client or client group has specific objectives in mind when contemplating landscape development. Clients may want to develop a formal garden to support a sculpture exposition, for example, or enhance a corporate facility for employee rest and relaxation. They may wish to restore an area to its natural state or reclaim a site damaged by mining. Whatever the goals, the designer must clarify them and translate them into design objectives.

(See Resource Appendix for sample client interview forms.)

STEP 2: EVALUATE SITE CAPACITIES AND EXISTING CONDITIONS

This important research step involves examining the capability of the site to satisfy the client's intent. It includes the investigation of topography, vegetation, water, climate, history, soil, and wildlife. Without this extensive preparation at the beginning, a landscape architect cannot make judgments that will satisfy project objectives. And the most honorable of client goals may have to be abruptly abandoned if the site considered for development cannot support them.

There are basically two important areas of information that must be researched before a design can begin. First, physical information about the site must be collected, analyzed, and evaluated against the objectives of the project. Second, historical information must be collected and evaluated to determine development influences on the site. The following outline summarizes the research needed:

I. PHYSICAL DATA

The various site characteristics considered here are interrelated. They depend on each other for their origin and application to the project. Although they will be discussed individually, they should also be considered in terms of their impact on each other and collective relevance to the development of a planting design project.

A. Property data

It is important to have a complete and accurate description of the proposed project area. A map showing the location of the site in relation to population centers, highways, flood zones, and major utility easements may be helpful in predicting future management strategies (Fig. 2-2).

B. Topography and grades

Land form and structure play an important role in the location and placement of plant materials in a planting design. A complete understanding of this component is mandatory if special effects are desired for spatial environments within the site. Characteristics that should be noted include orientation of slope (north, south, east, west) and the percentage of slope (Fig. 2-3).

The 0 to 3 percent grade is flat to gently sloping and is subject to surface drainage problems. Soil depth for planting is greater in this range. Less site modification may be needed when accommodating structures and circulation facilities. If strong visual experiences are desired, the addition of large plant forms or berms will be needed.

The 3 to 8 percent grade is characterized by gently sloping to rolling terrain, offering a greater variety of interesting visual experiences. Soil often concentrates in low areas, and site modification requirements for circulation and structures will increase.

In the 8 to 15 percent range, hilly, often rocky terrain will expand the visual-experience potential of the site, but will also increase the cost of site modifications. Soil depths are too limited for an extensive introduction of ornamental plant materials.

The severe topographic problems occurring at the 15 to 25 percent range make conventional development almost impossible. Surface drainage is often dangerous and may require water-retention or impoundment facilities. Short-distance visual experiences are easily created with plants and topography. Underground structures work well within this range.

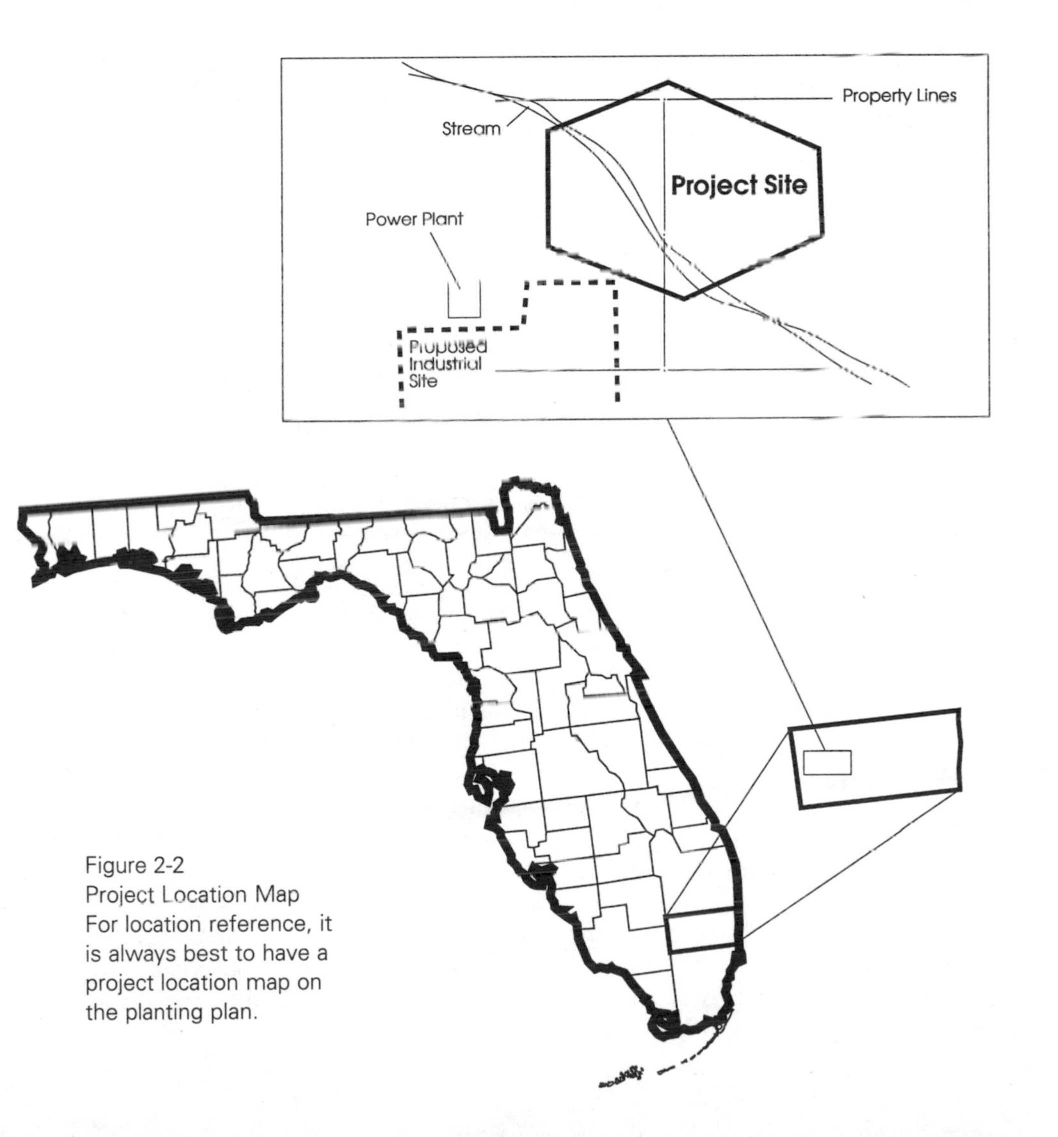

Figure 2-2
Project Location Map
For location reference, it is always best to have a project location map on the planting plan.

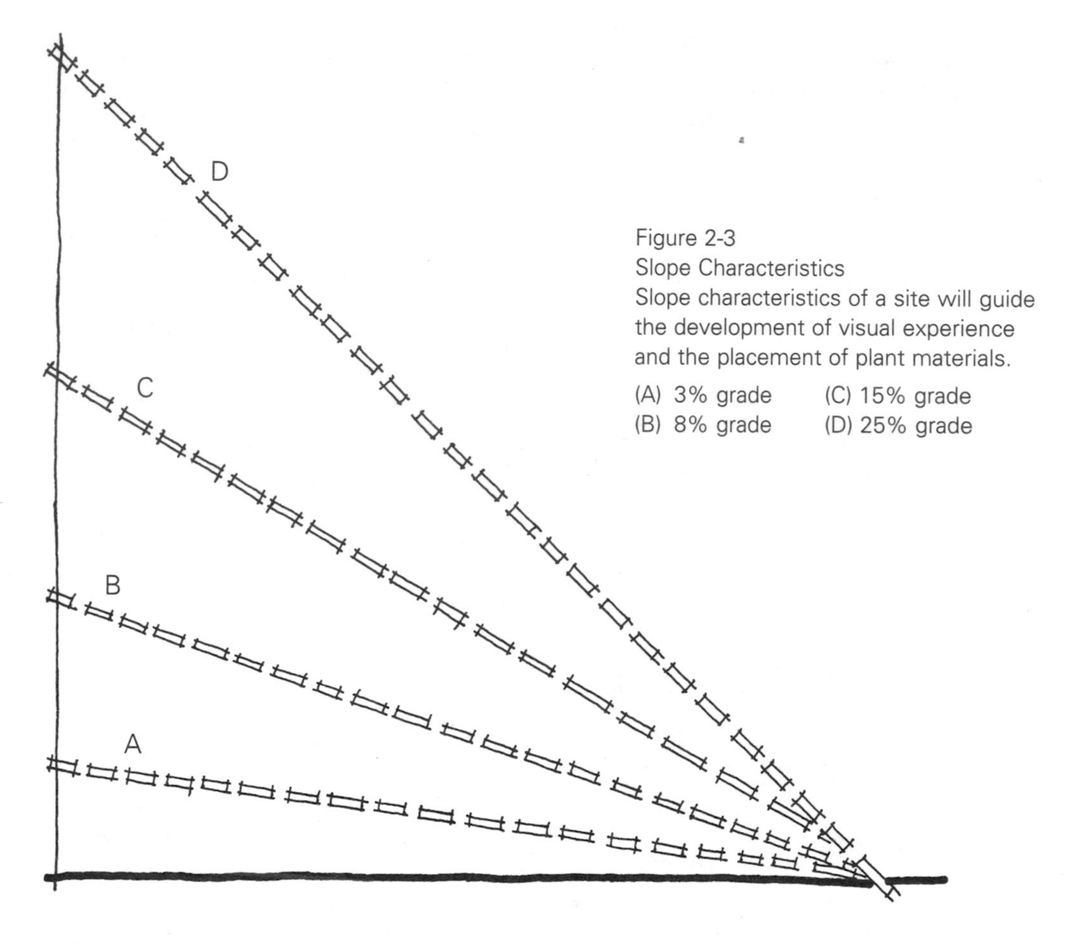

Figure 2-3
Slope Characteristics
Slope characteristics of a site will guide the development of visual experience and the placement of plant materials.
(A) 3% grade (C) 15% grade
(B) 8% grade (D) 25% grade

The topographic analysis of a project should result in a graphic that relates the following grade percentages: 0 to 3; 3 to 8; 8 to 15; 15 to 25; and 25 percent or higher.

The surface features of an area, including the shape of the land and the distribution of water bodies (if present), are its most apparent physical aspects. A topographic map and a soil map are essential documents that portray these features. A standard U.S. Geological Survey 1:24,000-scale topographic quadrangle map may serve as a useful base.

The topography of a site may be classified and the land easily visualized in terms of the landforms that compose it. Among these, for example, may be an association of kinds of soils, valleys, terraces, plains, rolling hills, and subdued or rugged mountains. A small area may consist entirely of one of these landform units or soil associations. A large area, on the other hand, may be divided into various landform types or soil associations that are more homogeneous in vegetative communities, each of which can be developed and managed in different ways.

The percentage of grade for the site is directly associated with soil depth. The more stable the slope, the deeper the soil in most cases. Grade will also influence the location and placement of materials because of exposure to light and air movement. Low areas such as valleys and draws will tend to have higher soil moisture and cooler temperatures

Topography is also related to climate by its orientation. Site temperatures are lower on north- and northeast-facing slopes than on those facing south and west. Cooler temperatures will lower the evaporation of water from plants, resulting in more moisture for plant growth. However, lower temperatures may also reduce the length of the growing season as well as increase the risk of frost damage.

Slope orientation may expose plants to prevailing winds in both summer and winter. Winds increase the availability of water to the plant, both from the soil and in the plants themselves.

c. Geology and soils

Critical to good planting design is good soil, which can be defined as a mixture that has good structure and texture; is loose and friable; is high in organic and nutrient content; retains water but is also well drained and consequently high in oxygen content; and is of a proper pH to allow plant growth.

1. Structure and texture is determined by the particles that make up a soil and how they are related to one another — in what percentages of sand, silt, and clay. A soil with more than 50 percent sand particles and correspondingly smaller percentages of silt and clay would obviously be classified as a sandy soil, but it could still be a good soil if the organic matter content is high enough to aid in water and nutrient retention.

2. Friability refers to the ease of working within a range of moisture conditions. A heavy-clay soil, for example, is difficult to work when wet and impossible to work when dry.

3. Organic and nutrient content affects water retention, aeration, and the supply of binding nutrients.

4. pH content measures the acidity and alkalinity of a soil. Neutral or slightly acid soil is required for optimum growth of most plants.

Light sandy loams are able to support a wide variety of plants for landscape use. Drainage of these soils is good. Medium loams are usually the best type, because particles and drainage are balanced. Heavy loams are not as good as medium or light loams because of the need for extensive conditioning. Clay is usually too heavy for planting operations; drainage is unsatisfactory.

Most soils are a derivative of geologic deposits and occur in layers. These layers, called horizons, provide the planting designer with a record of the properties and growth capabilities of each soil type. The mineral properties of the soil are the most important factors to determine before planting. Minerals should include:

1. *Nitrogen.* The higher the organic-matter content, the better the nitrogen availability. Nitrogen is necessary for fertility, but excess nitrogen depresses the uptake of phosphorus and potassium. Inadequate nitrogen causes yellowing of foliage and weak plant growth.
2. *Phosphorus.* This is the essential element for growth and development. Too little of this material will obstruct the intake of other nutrients.
3. *Potassium.* Large quantities are needed for plant growth. An excess of this element reduces the uptake of magnesium.
4. *Calcium.* This element occurs more often in soil types with a high limestone content. It is useful as a soil conditioner rather than as a nutrient.
5. *Magnesium.* This is easily leached from light soils. A lack of this element may cause early defoliation.
6. *Iron.* High acidity helps break down this element for plants. Yellowing of leaves shows a lack of iron (iron chlorosis).
7. *Manganese.* Most peat and high-organic-content soils are lacking in this element. A lack of manganese is characterized by a yellowing of leaves.
8. *Zinc and copper.* A lack of these elements results in weak plant growth and premature wilting.

To replenish a planting base deficient in any nutrient, the designer adds the various compounds either before, during, or after the planting process. Before planting, nutrients may be applied en masse to an entire site if necessary. During the planting process, the soil mix around the base of the plant may be supplemented. After planting, a periodic application of nutrients may be necessary to maintain plant quality. Since most soil problems are best handled locally, landscape architects should consult the Cooperative Extension Service, a part of the U.S. Department of Agriculture, for specific solutions.

The geologic formations and kinds of soils that underlie an area play a very important role in determining how the area may be designed and the limitations that must be placed on its use. Geologic and soils studies should be undertaken (if they have not already been done) to gather the basic data needed to evaluate the land.

Many kinds of soils and geologic materials are more suitable for some purposes than for others, and a knowledge of the distribution of these characteristics will aid in the selection of suitable plants and in the design and maintenance of management principles that best fit natural conditions. Foundation and excavation conditions, for example, vary with the kind of soil and the depth to bedrock. Clayey soils generally have lower bearing capacity for structures than coarse-grained soils or rocks and are especially hazardous when they become wet; shallow bedrock provides solid foundations but requires more expensive methods of excavation. An evaluation of slope of the ground, soil type or structure, and type of rock provides valuable clues to the stability of the ground and its potential for excavations such as for roads and buildings. Soil wetness, soil flooding, and the ability of the soil to absorb sewage and other wastes can be determined from a knowledge of the kind of soil and of the geologic deposits found in an area.

The depth of the soil surface is a very important factor. The soil surface is the area that is to be occupied by the plant material selected for a design project. Bedrock near the surface will prevent the use of certain species, while a soil susceptible to high water tables during the growing season will limit root growth. A barrier of hard, course soil may limit root penetration for plant expansion.

Some plants require acid soils and some alkaline, while others will tolerate a wide range of pH. Extremely high pH may restrict the availability of nutrients. Extremely low pH may release toxic substances that will limit plant growth or terminate it altogether. Mine spoils are an excellent example of high-risk, toxic soil areas.

Common to arid and semiarid areas is salinity. This will limit plant growth unless sufficient water is available for leaching. Soils derived from magnesium iron silicates are called serpentine and are usually sterile and unproductive. Vegetation that does occur on the serpentine base contrasts strikingly with adjacent species. Regardless of the site, an extensive soil analysis should be made to determine future nutrient requirements for plant growth.

Although basic soil and geologic maps contain the data needed to make evaluations such as those indicated above, information may be more rapidly grasped from more detailed maps that interpret the basic data for specific purposes. Both the Soil Conservation Service and the U.S. Geologic Survey — as well as other groups outside the federal government — have produced such interpretive maps. These maps are made in such a way that they may be readily understood by people without training in geology or soil science. With such maps, designers and managers can avoid designs that are incompatible with the capabilities of a site's soil or rock formations. Listed below are some of the types of maps available. The maps listed need not all be used for any one project area. The types selected would depend on the specific project under consideration. Some are essentially different versions of the same map, with emphases appropriate to the characteristics of different areas.

Depth of bedrock (thickness of soil and unconsolidated deposits)

Elevation of bedrock surface

Thickness of clay
Lithology (rock type)
Texture of soil (particle size)
Clay content of soil
Stoniness of soil
Droughtiness of soil (indicative of need for irrigation)
Permeability of soil and/or rocks
Soil wetness
Soil productivity for different plants
Soil limitations for specific recreation uses
Absorptive capacity (suitability for waste disposal)
Suitability for impounding water
Shrink pressure potential of soil (expansive clays)
Soil susceptibility to frost heave
Soil bearing qualities
Limitation for excavation
Geologic hazards
Steepness of slope and slope stability
Susceptibility to landscaping
Erodibility of soils and/or geologic materials
Seismic susceptibility
pH rating

D. Hydrology

Water is a key to the success or failure of a planting composition. Using a plant or plants that require an unusual amount of water taxes the supply source as well as the often limited patience of the client. Before beginning any planting operation, it is important to determine the following:

1. Exact location, size, and capacity of the sources of water.
2. Quality of the water for the support of plant growth.
3. Potential cost of obtaining the water on the site.
4. Location of all sources of existing surface water such as lakes, ponds, and streams (these may be sources for irrigation).
5. Direction of the water flow and the extent of any watershed area (design should not interrupt natural flows).
6. Presence of natural water sources such as springs, artesian wells, and streams (for natural planting areas).

In the design and management of planting composition, it is essential to have an inventory of the quantity and quality of the water resources in or available to the area, as these will influence significantly the carrying capacity of the site. The size, depth, location, and quality of surface bodies of water directly influence the choice of vegetation types. Irrigation can improve natural vegetation and, as a result, increase the tolerance thresholds of some vegetative species. Introduction of available water, however, can also fundamentally change the quality and character of the existing vegetation.

Data, including maps as appropriate, should be obtained on the following factors:

Drainage areas
Potential for flooding, including frequency and duration
Low flow of streams
Sediment load of streams
Maximum concentration of dissolved solids in surface water
Amount and quality of surface runoff
Depth of surface water bodies
Potential reservoir sites
Availability of ground water
Location of wells and test holes
Depth to water table
Elevation of water table
Elevation of piezometric surface (level to which water in wells will rise, seasonal water table)
Thickness of saturated materials
Quality of ground water
Ground-water recharge areas

E. Climate

Site climate is obviously related to plant growth and to the quantity of the existing vegetative cover. The amount and duration of precipitation and the fluctuations of temperature are critical. Plant species are genetically adapted to their site by these factors, and the changing of the climate may limit or extend a specific plant's use as a design element.

Basic climate data that influence the site carrying capacity include:

Average monthly temperature and precipitation
Maximum daily, monthly, and annual temperature range
Number of days with snow cover
Number of frost-free days
Annual flood cycles and flood levels
Likelihood of tornadoes, hurricanes, other intense storms and fog
Average monthly humidity and wind velocity
Number of days per month when the sky is clear, partly cloudy, or cloudy

Short-term climatic trends should also be taken into account. Some specific hazards to natural vegetation that are related to climate are flash floods, polluted air, and the fire risks of very dry conditions.

Light and heat are two of the most important climate factors that are directly available to the plant. Light is the source of energy for photosynthesis, while heat is the energy source for the plants' metabolic processes.

The quality of light that will reach the understory will depend upon the density of the canopy. Growth in plants is directly related to their rate of photosynthesis. The failure of seedlings under the existing canopy of a site may be associated with low light levels, which may lead to a fungal attack even in shade-tolerant species.

Root growth in larger plantings will be greatly impaired by poor light situations and is affected by the structure of the overall plant canopy. Too much shade during important periods of development may cause the plant to be easily damaged during severe ice or windstorms.

Temperature is a factor when it fluctuates radically, causing injury to plant tissue. Topography and the direction of the winds will influence the temperature of the site. Some plants may require one temperature at night and another during the day. Some planted seedlings are able to withstand lower temperatures and avoid injury because of lowered transpiration.

Atmospheric pollutants will quickly destroy any existing or introduced plant material. Damage can be noticed in inhibited sexual reproduction, revegetation following a fire, poor seedling growth, or even death.

Damage from ice, windstorms, and lightning are factors that must be considered in design. These conditions can terminate the life of a plant or make it vulnerable to diseases or insects. Large exposed trees on a site may become ground terminals of lightning discharges, damaging plants nearby.

F. Physiography

The physiographic elements are those natural features that may inhibit certain types of management programs. Earthquake faults, flash-flood zones, areas susceptible to violent storms, areas of unusually high water table, and critical wildlife habitats are just a few elements to look out for before developing the site.

G. Existing vegetative spectrum

The location, size, condition, and potential for design should be determined for each plant or plant mass that exists on a site. The location should be accurately marked on a base map, and the distance to other major features of the site recorded. Vegetation size should be defined in terms of the width, length, and height of the material. For an individual tree, the caliper (the diameter of the trunk one foot above the ground) should be measured and recorded, and for a shrub the width at the base is important. The crown dimension (width of tree top) is referred to as the drip line and should be sketched on the plan for an individual plant as well as for a plant mass. The condition of the plant or plant mass relates to its potential for continued use. Storm, insect, or disease damage will limit its ability to satisfy its intended function. If destruction is obvious and excessive, the designer will have to decide whether to repair or replace the material. A plant's potential for design depends on the assessment of all the other factors. Design function is the criterion for determining if removal is necessary. A review of the natural systems and conditions of existing materials is important. Existing vegetation is dependent on soil types, climates, and topography. Adverse planting conditions must be corrected before development can be successful.

The type, species, location, size, and density of existing vegetation have a tremendous effect on the selection of design materials and the future carrying capacity of the site. A designer should make a careful analysis of all existing vegetation in a project area. The abundance of species, their size, and their location will indicate the very nature of the systems.

Because trees are long-lived and easily identifiable in all seasons, they are the first that should be studied. Some species, such as the black walnut, the white ash, and the yellow poplar, grow best on moist, well-drained soil. Understory species often have a more restricted ecological tolerance than does the canopy layer and may prove useful in site studies.

In all cases, plants should be related to their requirements for moisture, soil, light, and association with the successional stage. Remember, however, that competition and past events such as drought, fire, and insect damage will influence the quantity and size of the materials.

Specific events or stages of vegetative development should be noted, with a careful on-site analysis of the following:

1. *Pioneer or invader species.* These plant types are usually the first to become established on a disturbed site. They are the more aggressive of the varieties and can grow on a soil less capable of supporting stronger plants. If extensive soil restoration is not possible immediately, these materials make excellent choices for an initial planting program.
2. *Transitional species.* These plants follow the pioneer varieties and will remain until a more dominant material emerges.
3. *Subclimax and climax species.* These plants represent the final stage in the successional process. They require a more nutritious soil and a more stable climate.
4. *Adjacent site vegetation.* The vegetative types on opposite ends of a site may indicate a "direction" for the establishment of new vegetative communities. The direction of winds and the movement of surface water may allow seeds to be dispensed to the area, allowing for natural revegetative techniques. If this natural technique is used, however, a great amount of time will be needed to reach the final objective.

H. Wildlife considerations

An important and often overlooked factor in planting design is that of wildlife populations within the project area. How will the proposed design intent and planting operations relate to existing wildlife habitats? Some animal species are in danger of extinction primarily due to the loss of food sources. The planting designer can provide a valuable service with the introduction or protection of plant materials that will support and enhance the animals that may live within the spaces of the design area.

Birds and small mammals — even rodents — will greatly expand the enjoyment of a designed space. The sounds of birds and the activities of other animals create experiences that cannot be achieved from any other source. The ecological support of a zoological garden cannot be achieved without correct selection and placement of plant materials by the landscape designer.

It is important to consider the type, location, and habitat of the existing wildlife of a site. Existing species and those that may be attracted to the finished site will influence the overall carrying capacity of the vegetative communities. For example, the number of deer on or near a project depends upon the abundance of suitable food and cover plants within their habitat range. If a planting program increases the food and cover materials, the deer population may increase or be attracted to the new site. This may in turn exert new pressures on the tolerance thresholds of the vegetation components.

Aerial photographs, notes from on-site inspections, vegetation maps, and wildlife species range maps may be utilized in the evaluation of wildlife components. The primary objective should be to preserve (or to attract back) a representative segment of the area's natural fauna and maintain the habitat critical to its continued existence. Important considerations should be planting that influences diversity and abundance of food supplies; presence of water; and availability of den and nest sites and cover.

II. HISTORICAL INFORMATION

The success or failure of any planting project will depend in part on the past uses of the site. Whether the proposed project site was previously a landfill, a chemical dump, an orchard, or a landscape nursery can have a profound effect on the way it can be used in a later design. Were there any historic structures that conditioned its use? Good sources for research on these issues are local and state historical societies.

A. Past and present land use

Knowing the location and extent of the different uses, past and present, of a site is important for evaluating the present and potential carrying capacity of the site. Maps showing the location of these uses can be part of the first step in evaluating design considerations for specific sites. Delineation of boundary lines, property lines and the limits of the design project are important factors in this research step.

B. Existing man-made facilities

To determine the capacity of an area to support vegetation, it is essential that an inventory be made of present facilities. This includes the number, size, and capacity of utilities (especially those underground), roads, buildings, recreational facilities, and structures. Such elements as farm dwellings, residences, railway facilities, and overhead transmission lines should be graphically portrayed for consideration during the design process.

C. Aesthetics

The aesthetic appeal of a site usually depends upon landform diversity, vegetative pattern, spatial definition, views, vistas, and overall site image. Specific consideration during the design process should be given to existing scenic vistas; orientation vistas; and overall scenic quality.

The primary objective is to preserve existing areas of natural scenic beauty within the project site. Information used to evaluate the aesthetics may be obtained from aerial photographs, color slides, and detailed on-site inspections. Although each member of a planning team may have different interpretations of the aesthetic quality of a project, the following criteria may be used:

High aesthetic quality. These are portions of the site that possess unique beauty in their immediate proximity.

Medium aesthetic quality. From these portions of the site scenic views or vistas may be seen.

Low aesthetic quality. These portions of the site appear scenic when seen from a distance but may not have unique beauty when viewed up close.

Historical attributes. Almost every project area has significant historical features. Knowing the exact location of these features and their importance is a major consideration for the design team. Historical features might include trails, passageways, structures, or sites located within the project boundaries.

STEP 3: DETERMINE DEVELOPMENT LIMITATIONS

Given the design intent and estimated site capacity research, the designer should be able to set forth specific site-development limitations and suggest alternatives that would satisfy the objectives of the project. Present these limitations to the client and suggest development strategies.

Three alternatives can be envisioned at this step:

1. all of the client objectives can be satisfied by the site;
2. a portion of the objectives can be met with minor alterations in either the client program or the site features;
3. none of the objectives can be met without major and costly modifications of the program or the site features. It is at this phase of the process that the designer and/or the client should determine whether or not the project should be continued or abandoned.

PHASE 2:
DEVELOP A PRELIMINARY PLAN

This phase consists of the arrangement of basic design elements into a preliminary set of design concepts that will fulfill the intended program. With continued input from the client, the designer begins to make specific decisions necessary to the development of the planting plan (Fig. 2-4).

STEP 1:
DETERMINE FUNCTIONAL REQUIREMENTS OF PLANT MATERIALS

Establish the shape of the planned environment based on the program intent. The basic architectural forms of the plant materials (walls, ceilings, floors, canopies, barriers, baffles, screens, and ground covers) should be considered.

STEP 2:
DEVELOP PRELIMINARY CONCEPTS

Using the planting design elements — color, form, texture, and the like — determine the features within the space. These features, or small-scale environments, supported by the elements and controlled by the sculptured macroenvironment, should reflect your planting design concepts.

STEP 3
SELECT PLANT MATERIALS

Plants should now be selected to meet design requirements. If a specific element is needed, such as a frame for an attractive view, a specific plant should be selected to fulfill that need.

STEP 4
DEVELOP A PRELIMINARY PLAN

Summarize your research, reviews, and design concepts in a preliminary development plan. Review it with the client, modify if necessary, and obtain approval.

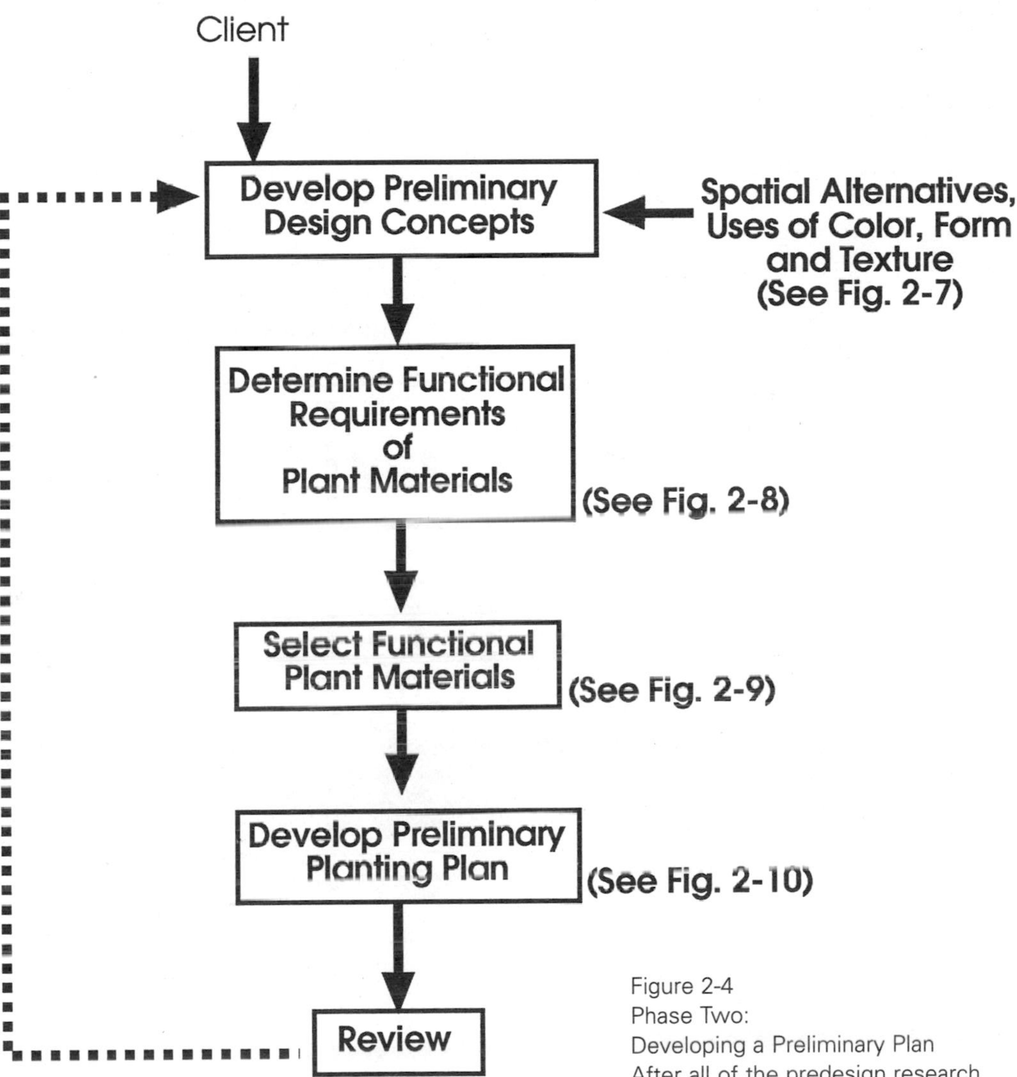

Figure 2-4
Phase Two:
Developing a Preliminary Plan
After all of the predesign research has been completed, the basic design elements should be incorporated into a preliminary set of planting concepts.

PHASE 3
DEVELOP THE FINAL PLANTING PLAN

STEP 1
PREPARE THE FINAL PLANTING PLAN

If all the alternatives have been discussed and a preliminary plan has been completed, develop the final plan based upon a summary of all the preceding steps. Client input should be continually maintained even though this is the final phase of the design process (Fig. 2-5).

STEP 2
PREPARE SUPPORT AND IMPLEMENTATION DOCUMENTS

Develop the planting and construction details, installation and planting specifications, and maintenance requirements of the plan. The elements of your design may need to be communicated to a third party such as a government agency for approval. Make sure that you have presented all the necessary data.

STEP 3
PREPARE FOR IMPLEMENTATION

Develop the necessary documents to advertise the bidding process. Select the most comprehensive bid package to develop the planting design. Remember to review the steps to eliminate mistakes or evaluate alternatives.

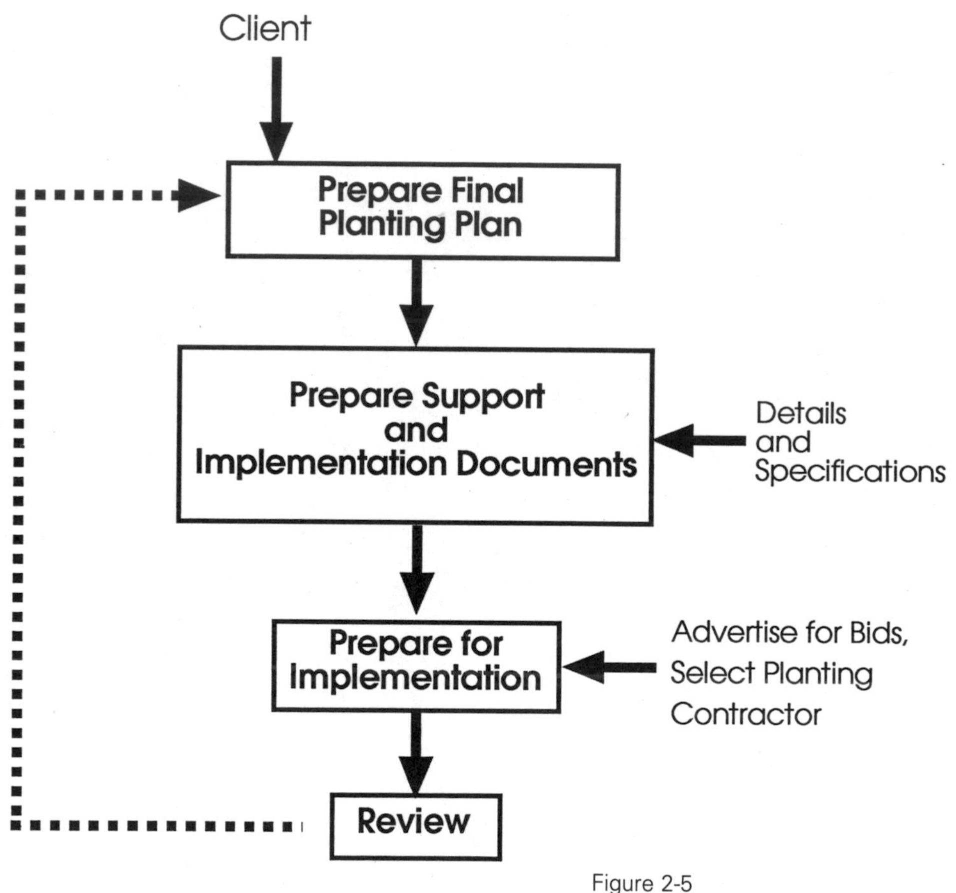

Figure 2-5
Phase Three:
Developing a Final Plan

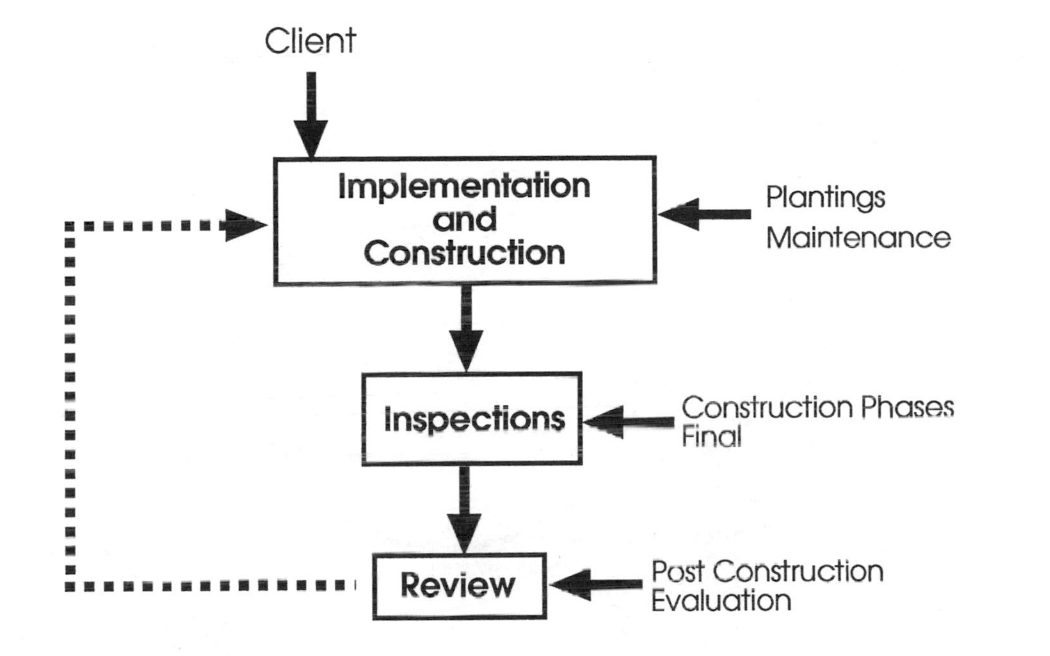

Figure 2-6
Phase Four:
Completion

PHASE 4
COMPLETION

STEP 1
IMPLEMENTATION/CONSTRUCTION

Although the basic design phases have been completed, changes may be required to adjust for unforeseen hazards at the site. Periodically review the procedures selected and employed to achieve the design (Fig. 2-6).

STEP 2
INSPECTION

During this final phase of the planting design process, inspect each area of construction and conduct a final inspection to assure total compliance with the planting program.

STEP 3
EVALUATION

The plant's you have selected may be growing and prospering in their new home, but your function as a designer has not ended. As plants grow and mature, so does their relationship to the environment. Evaluate these changes and learn from mistakes of selection and judgment. Constant testing of design results will make you a better planting designer (Fig. 2-7 to Fig. 2-10).

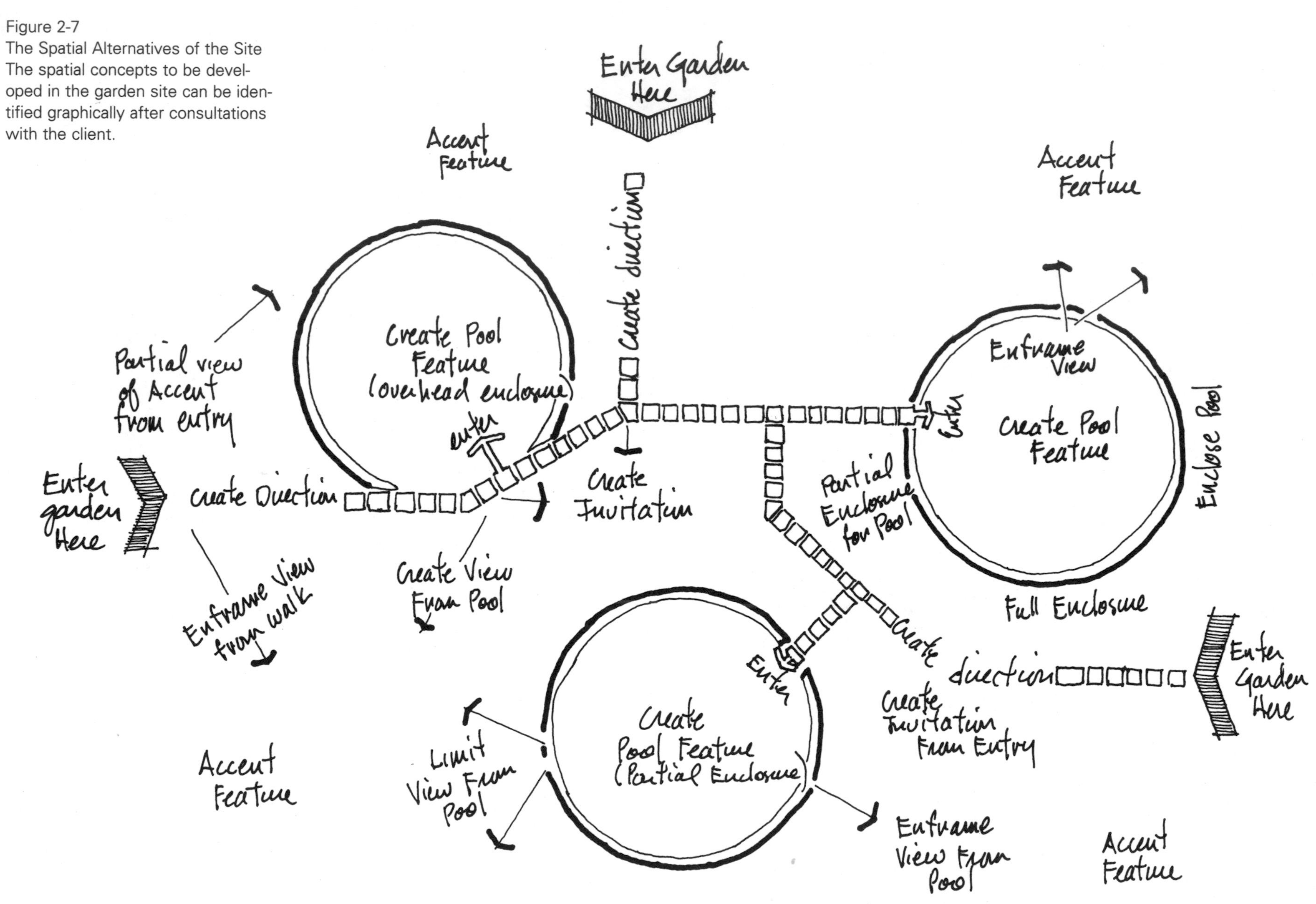

Figure 2-7
The Spatial Alternatives of the Site
The spatial concepts to be developed in the garden site can be identified graphically after consultations with the client.

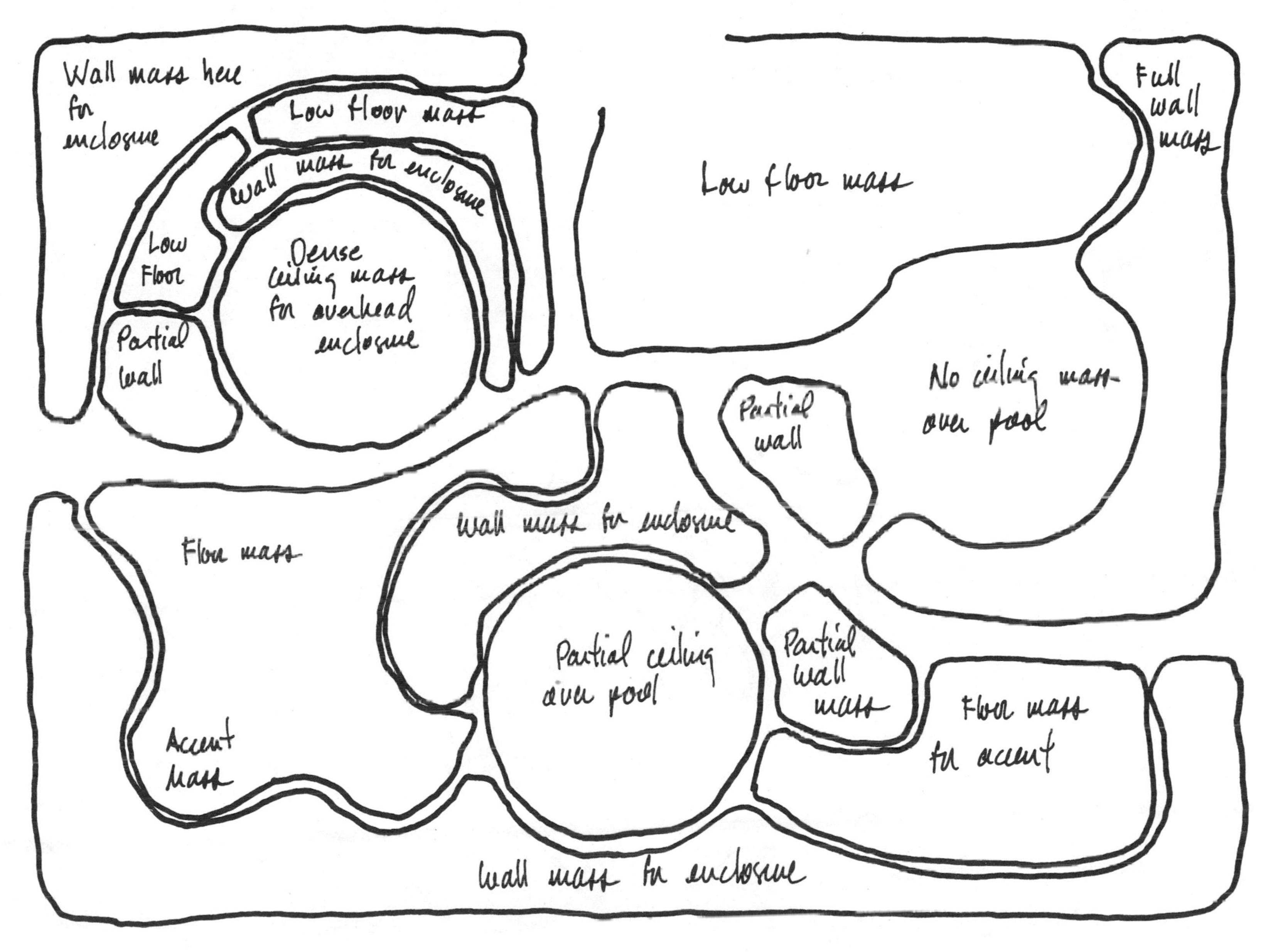

Figure 2-8
The Functional Requirements of the Space

Figure 2-9
Selection of the plant materials follows the determination of their design function.

A. Dense screen to support the enclosure of the pool
B. Low-height ground cover for viewing the accent feature
C. Medium-height ground cover as an accent element for the entry positions
D. Narrow screen to enclose and obstruct the accent feature from within the pool
E. Baffle to allow the viewing of the accent feature from the pathway
F. Dense canopy for overhead enclosure
G. Low-growing ground cover for an "open" feeling
H. Small, bright accent shrub
I. Dense screen to enclose the pool
J. Baffle for partial enclosure of the pool
K. Dense screen for more complete enclosure of the pool
L. Low-growing ground cover
M. Dense screen for enclosure of the pool
N. Medium-height accent
O. Partial canopy for pool enclosure
P. Accent shrub for visitation
Q. Low-growing ground cover
R. Low accent shrub

Figure 2-10
The Final Planting Plan
The first step is to identify the spatial areas and visual experience to be created in the space (Figure 2-7). Next, the functional requirements of the plants and plant masses can be identified (Figure 2-8).

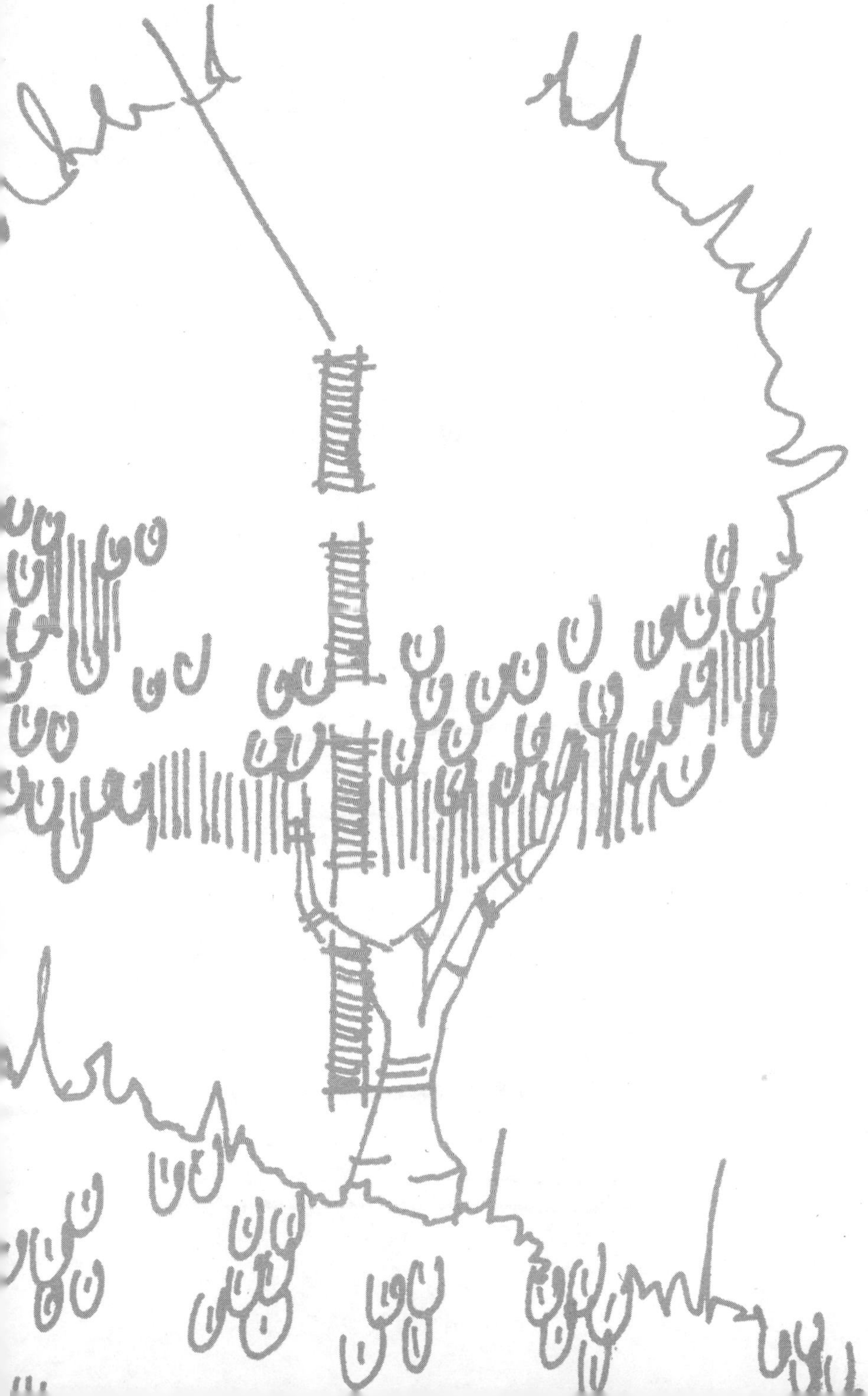

CHAPTER 3

DESIGNING WITH PLANTS

The Physical Characteristics of Plants

Color

The color of a plant or plant mass is the visual property that is dependent on the wavelength of the light reflected from it. It is the most striking of all the planting-design elements. It can attract attention, influence emotions, create atmosphere, or produce specific effects in a composition. Harmonious colors often produce satisfying designs even if visual contrast is lacking.

The psychological effect of color is generally the same for most people, although color preference and impact vary among individuals. For example, bright colors tend to excite or stimulate, while subdued or cool colors are more conducive to restfulness and relaxation. Color is the result of a stimulus (light) reacting on the retina of the eye. This response is transmitted to the brain, which registers the stimulus. Each individual reacts to color in a personal way, and it is this response that lends originality to a landscape design, allowing designers to create many different visually pleasing experiences.

There are basically two types of color used in planting design. The first is background or basic color, used as a gentle wash to harmonize a view. It should be uniform throughout the composition so it will be smooth and pleasing to the eyes. The second is accent color, which is used to emphasize certain features of composition. The use of color in planting design may be further classified into three types of compositions: monochromatic, using the same tone or color (green or brown) throughout the design; complementary, using washes of a dominant color with accents and mixtures of complementary colors; and variegated, using colors at random and painting a colorful picture with them.

The way a color will appear within a landscape is influenced by the distance at which it is viewed, the amount of direct or indirect light, the amount of shade, and the soil conditions of the planting area (Fig. 3-1).

Viewing distance affects the impact of colors. Don't place important colors too far away from the viewer. Any color can become diffused by lights and shadows, creating an unwanted muddiness in a planting composition.

Direct or indirect light may cause a plant color to dominate a composition and cause an unwanted glare. It may be necessary to diffuse the light reaching the plants by an overhead plant form or architectural feature. Full or partial shade will soften glaring colors and allow a greater range of experiences for the viewer.

Soil conditions will affect the colors of both foliage and flowers. The acidity level is the most important factor and can be easily controlled mechanically.

The following principles should be remembered when using color in a composition.

People have a psychological tendency to lean toward light and vivid colors.

Subdued light and cool colors are more conducive to reflections.

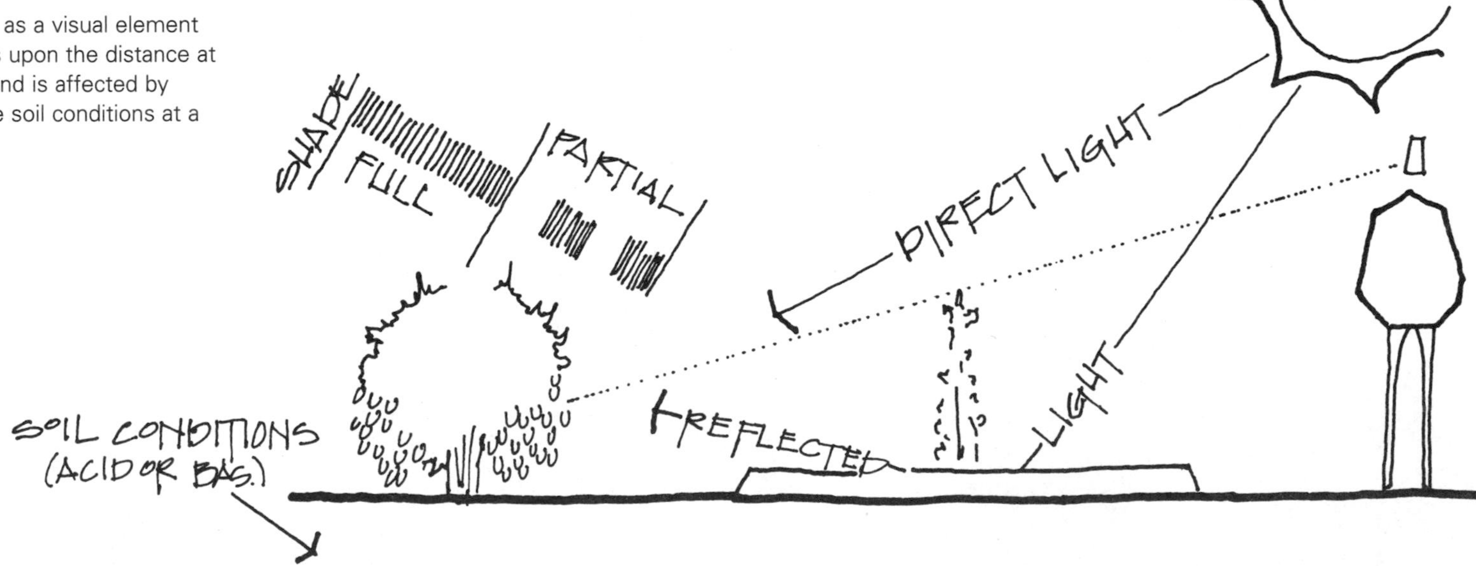

Figure 3-1
The value of a plant as a visual element in a design depends upon the distance at which it is viewed and is affected by light, shade, and the soil conditions at a site.

Bright light and warm colors tend to excite and may lead the viewer to move through a landscape.

Each plant or plant mass must blend with its surroundings.

Color changes should be graduated so as not to break continuity.

Warm colors such as reds, yellows, and oranges have a tendency to appear nearer to the observer or to advance, while cool colors such as blues and greens tend to appear farther away or to recede.

Colors and textures are related in that delicate colors (tints and pastels) have a fine textural appearance, while harsher or brighter colors suggest a coarse texture.

FORM

Form refers to the shape and structure of a plant or plant mass. It is used to indicate two-dimensional shapes (shapes that have only length and width) as well as three-dimensional shapes (those that have length, width, and thickness). Landscape architects, when completing a planting design, think primarily in three-dimensional forms (Fig. 3-2 to 3-6).

Every plant in the landscape has a distinct form that establishes its functional characteristics. General plant forms are rounded or globular, oval, conical or pyramidal, upright, weeping or drooping, spreading or horizontal, or irregular.

The basic form of any plant depends upon undisturbed growth. If left alone, most plants acquire their characteristic appearance at maturity, if not sooner. To alter the natural form of a plant and use a modified form in a composition, it is necessary to clip or shear the plant into the desired shape. A designer must remember, however, that such alteration can require excessive amounts of energy to develop and maintain.

Vertical forms can be used to create strong accents as well as to add height to a composition. Horizontal and spreading forms add width to tall structures. Weeping or drooping forms tend to create soft lines and also provide a tie to

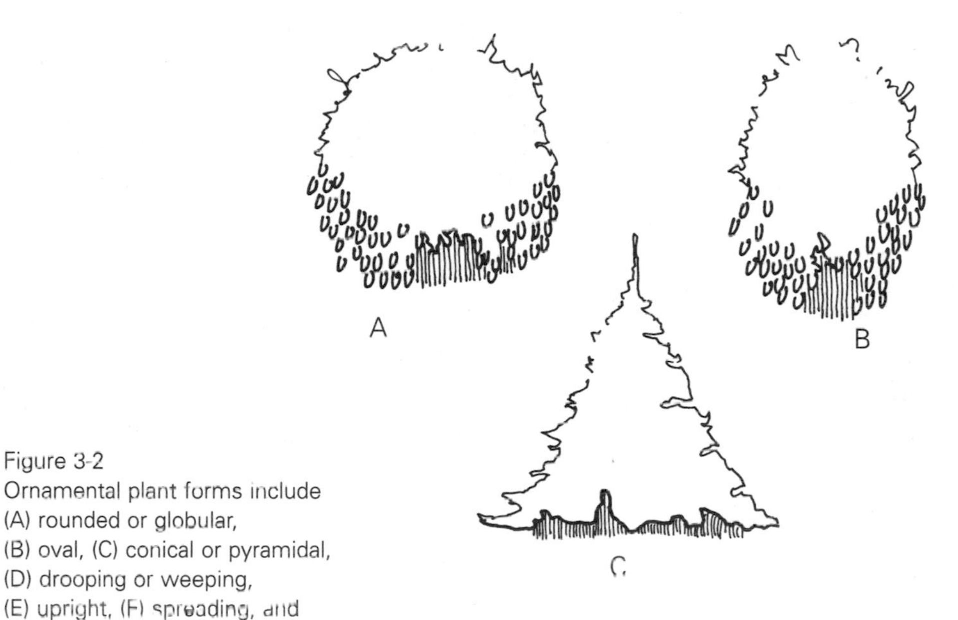

Figure 3-2
Ornamental plant forms include (A) rounded or globular, (B) oval, (C) conical or pyramidal, (D) drooping or weeping, (E) upright, (F) spreading, and (G) irregular.

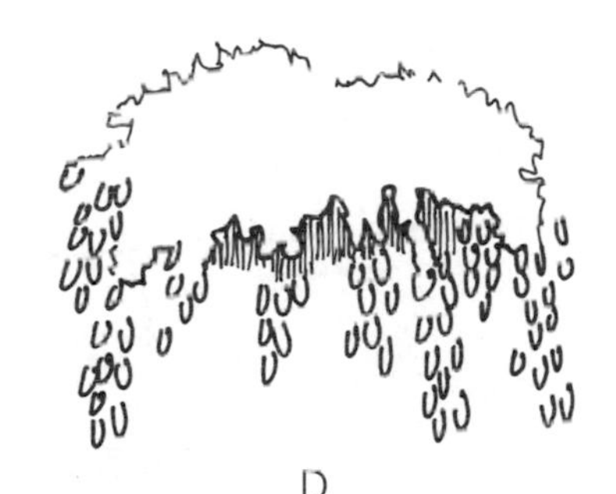

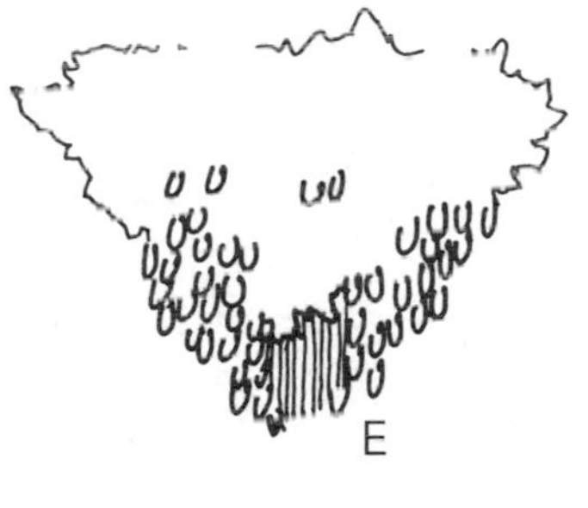

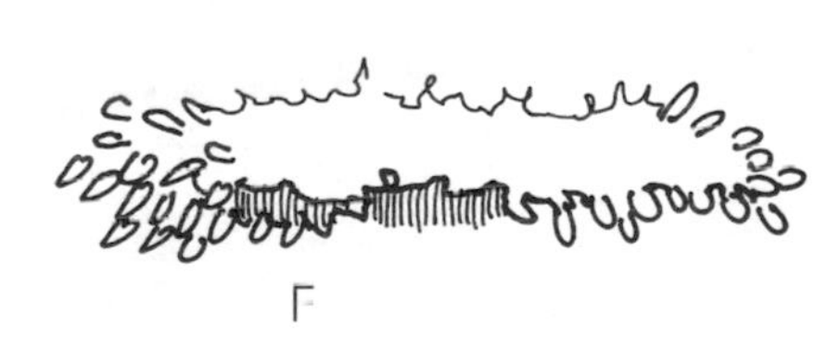

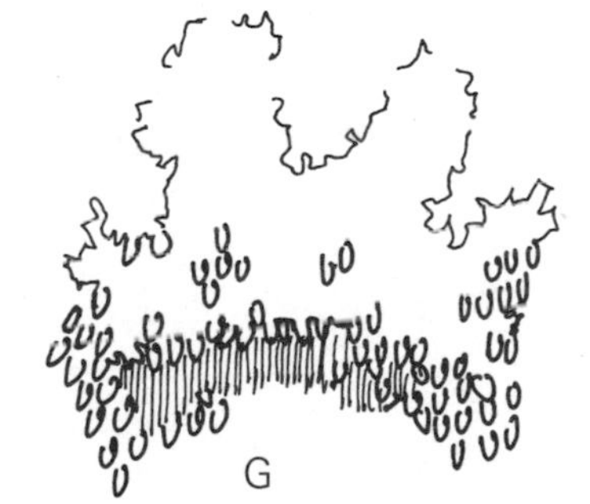

Figure 3-3
Ornamental deciduous plants tend to be rounded.

Figure 3-4
Evergreen plants tend to be pyramidal.

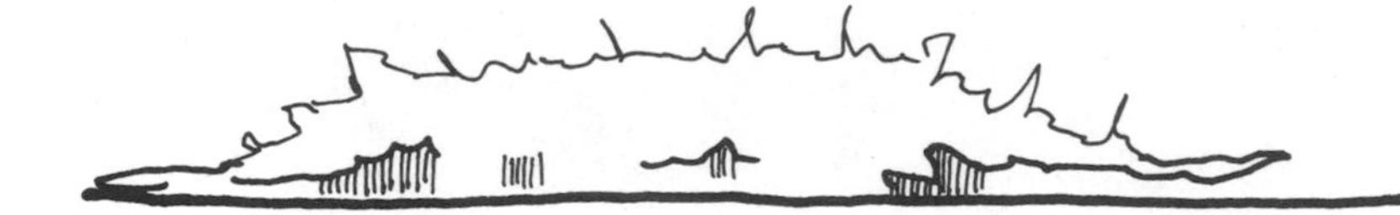

Figure 3-5
Evergreen shrubs tend to be \spreading.

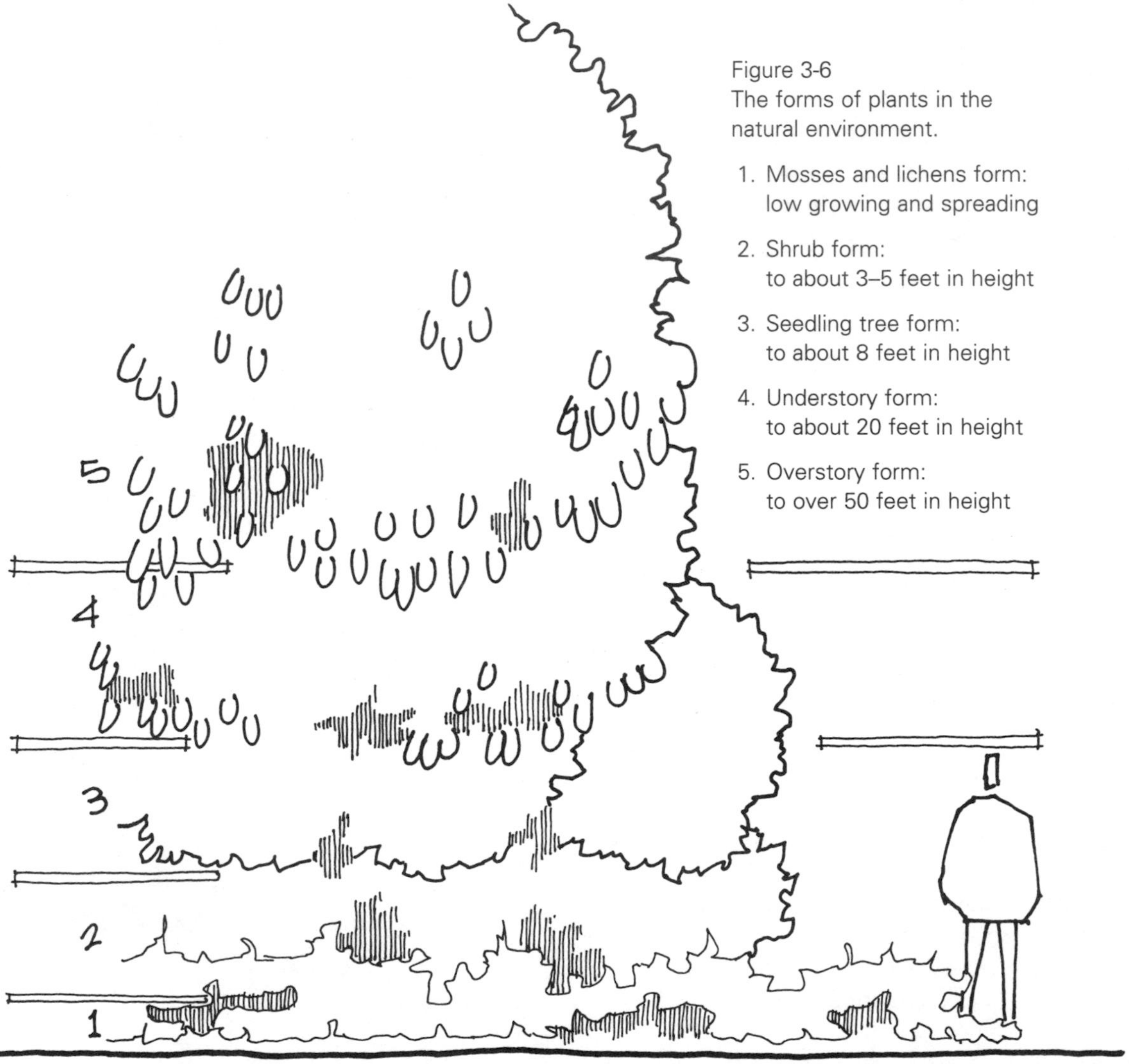

Figure 3-6
The forms of plants in the natural environment.

1. Mosses and lichens form: low growing and spreading
2. Shrub form: to about 3–5 feet in height
3. Seedling tree form: to about 8 feet in height
4. Understory form: to about 20 feet in height
5. Overstory form: to over 50 feet in height

the ground plane. Rounded and globular forms are useful for creating large plant masses for borders and enclosures. These forms can be accented with contrasting shapes and materials to prevent monotony of composition (Fig. 3-7).

Plants that are similar in form always seem to belong together. They create harmonious planting compositions themselves and with the group. Planting design can be unified by using one dominant form throughout a composition.

A variety of plant forms are used to create, define, enhance, and mold exterior spaces and to govern the way a viewer perceives the designed space. Two-dimensional form is flat and lacks depth. A convex three-dimensional form is experienced from without as the observer moves around it to various vantage points. A concave three-dimensional form creates vantage points for visual experiences within the form itself (Fig. 3-8).

Figure 3-7
Plant size variation is an important tool in creating accent.

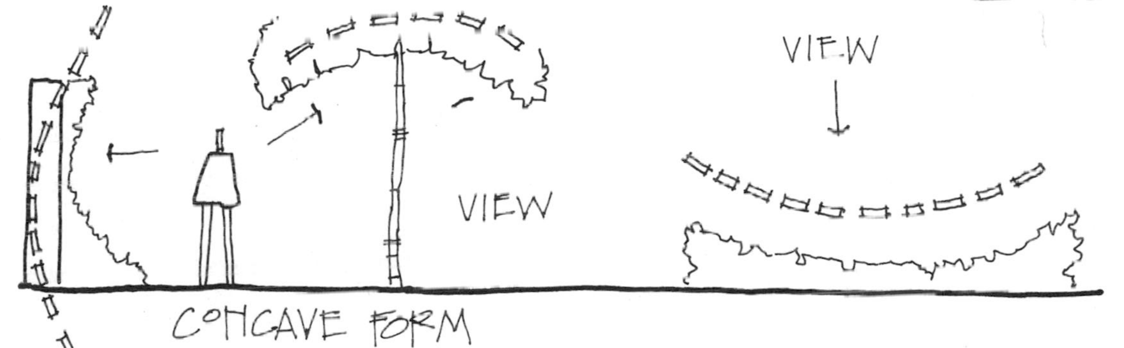

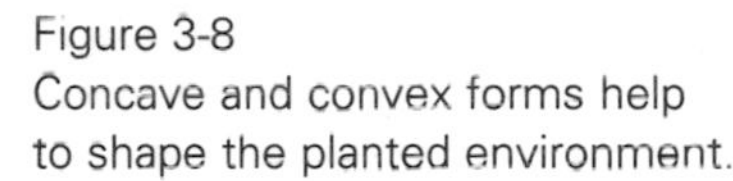
Figure 3-8
Concave and convex forms help to shape the planted environment.

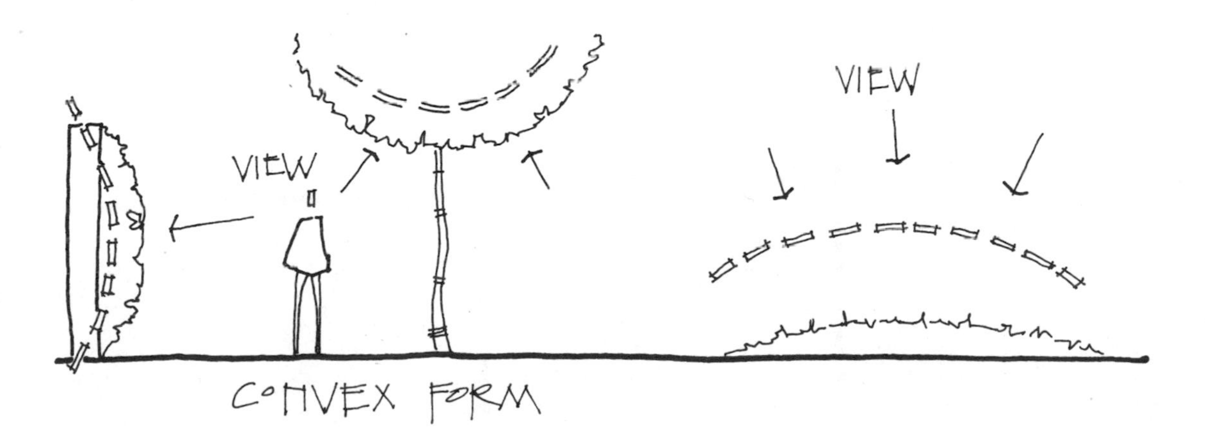

Three-dimensional form can be positive or negative. Positive space has a limited (enclosed) field of vision and is usually focused inward. Negative space is the "leftover" (open) space and has an unlimited field of vision (Fig. 3-9 and 3-10).

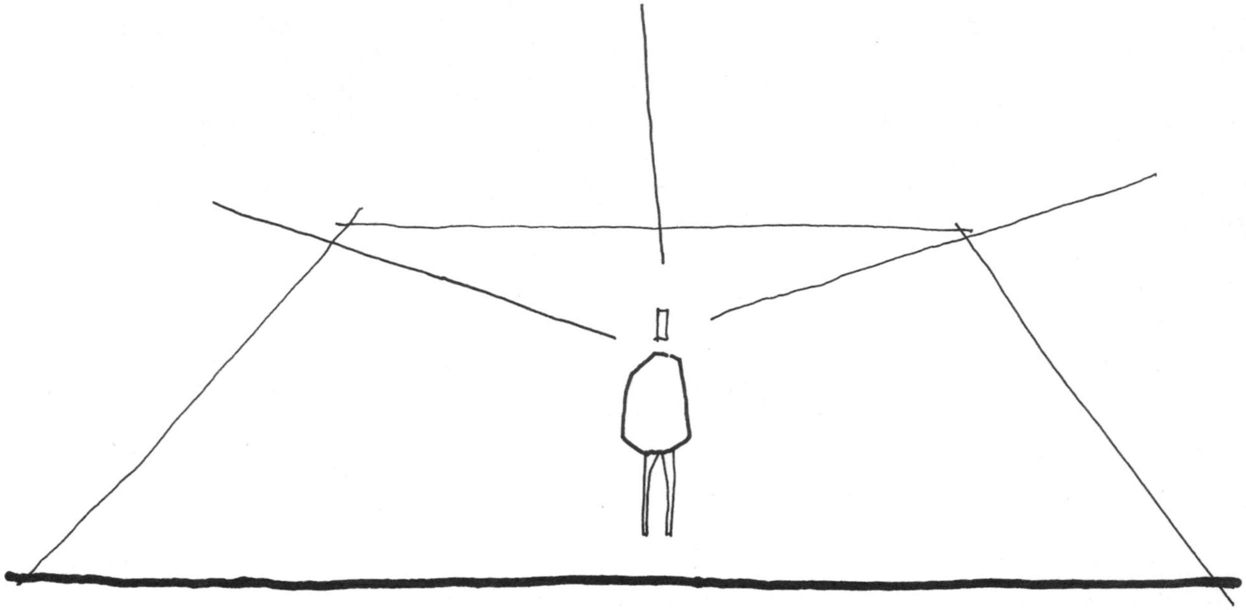

Figure 3-9
Until a planted space has definition, it is termed negative space.

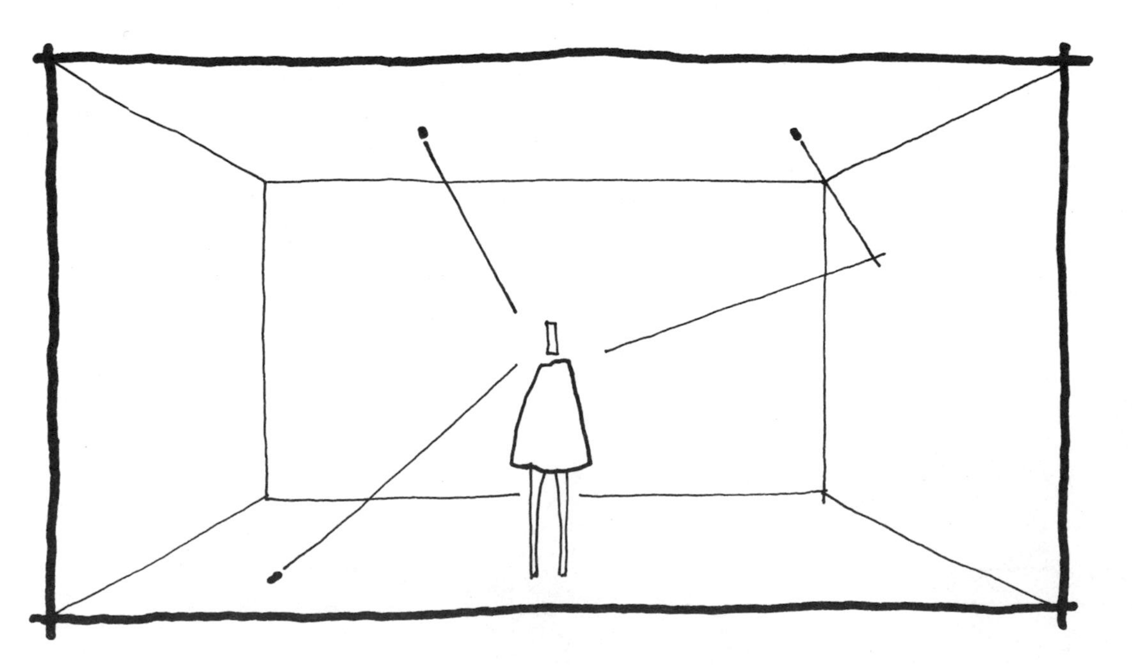

Figure 3-10
Once there is physical definition of a space through its walls, ceiling and floors, it becomes positive space.

In using form as a landscape design element, a landscape architect should go beyond the shape of an individual plant (single form) and use groups of plants (combined form) to accomplish the goals of a planting composition. The choice of a dominant form will establish the overall character of the exterior space and, when combined with the other design elements, determine the total quality of the plantings (Fig. 3-11 to 3-18).

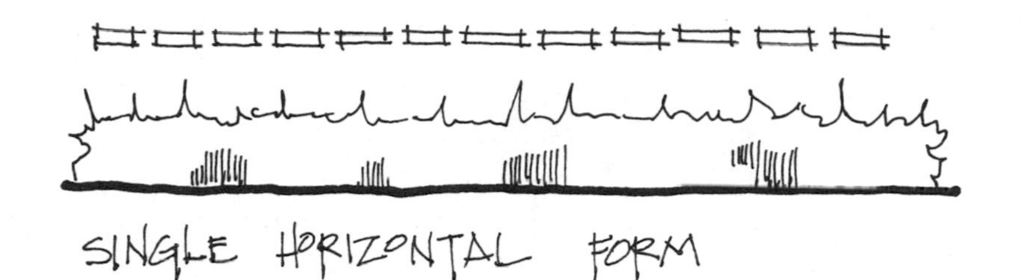

Figure 3-11
A row of small shrubs can create horizontal form.

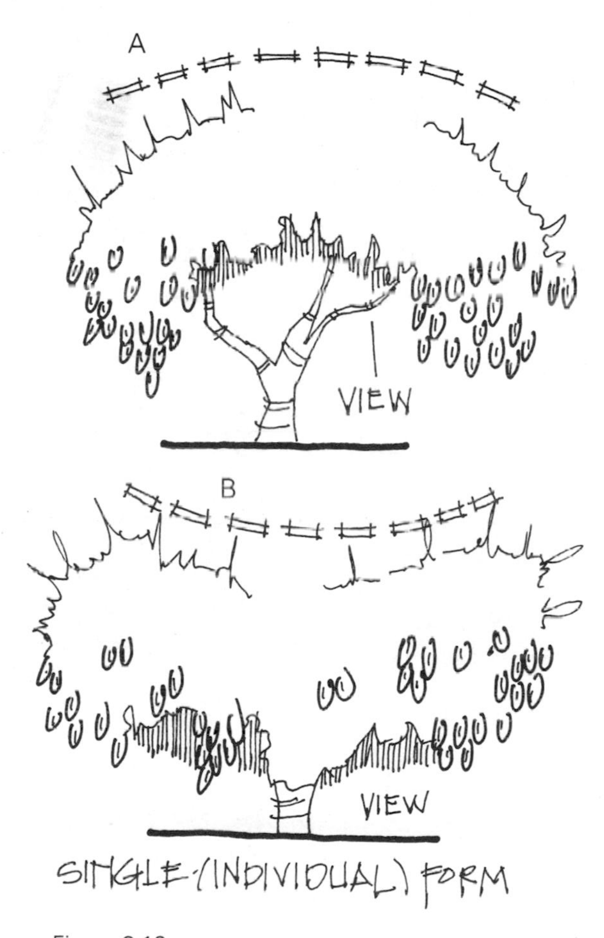

Figure 3-12
A single plant can be perceived as a concave form (A) or a convex form (B).

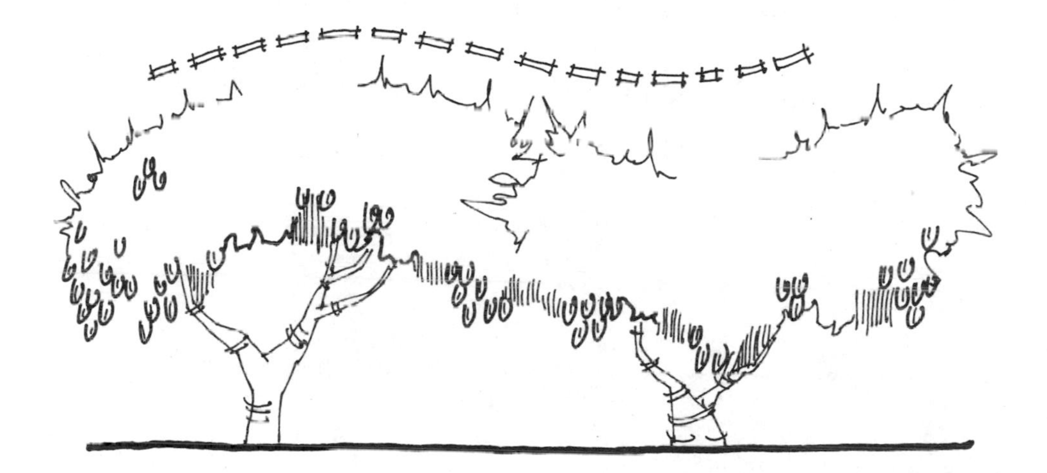

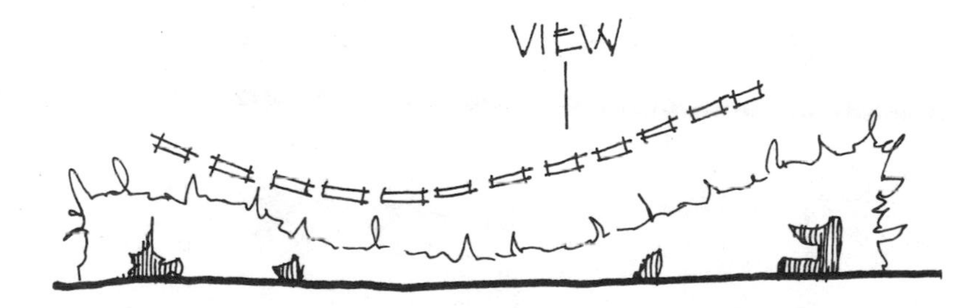

Figure 3-13
Concave and convex forms can also be viewed in combination.

Figure 3-15
Rounded forms in a mass can create an interesting affect.

Figure 3-14
Unique and creative forms can be used as accents in a composition.

Figure 3-16 (right)
A natural pyramidal form in a composition.

Figure 3-17 (far right)
Some evergreen materials have been developed into a more rounded form for specimen accents.

Figure 3-18 (below)
Rounded forms can become large masses to function as a screen.

Texture

Texture is the surface quality of plant material. Although often overlooked or discounted, it is a design tool that can add dimension, variety, and interest to a planting composition. Texture can be defined as the tactile and visual character of the physical surface as determined by the form, size, and aggregation of the units of which a plant is composed (Fig. 3-19).

Texture should be considered in terms of comparison between plants in the design. A honey locust, for instance, may seem to have a somewhat fine texture when compared to a burr oak; but when compared to a smooth stucco or concrete wall, it may appear rather coarse. Slender elm twigs seem to have a lacy texture when compared to the stubby branches of oaks, and ferns have a more delicate visual texture than hackberries (Fig. 3-20).

Texture may also be qualified by the distance from which the plant is viewed. The perceived size of the units depends on viewing distance. When we are close enough to touch an oak tree, we are able to see the form of the individual leaves and the texture of the leaf surfaces. At a distance of a hundred yards, we see the leaves of the same oak only in the aggregate, not as individual units. Texture then becomes the entire mass of the plants in the design (Fig. 3-21 to 3-23).

In planting design, texture is created by the arrangement and size of leaves, twigs, or branches and is described in terms of of coarseness or fineness, roughness or smoothness, heaviness or lightness, and thickness or thinness, which vary somewhat with the season of the year. The texture of a deciduous tree in winter is determined by the size, number, and position of its twigs and branches (thick or thin, numerous or sparse, congregated or scattered). When the tree is in leaf, its texture is primarily determined by the size, shape, number, and arrangement of leaves (Fig. 3-22).

For texture to be used effectively in planting design, each part of the plant must be so related that it blends with its neighbor. If textures change, they must do so in a logical and graduated manner. They should generally proceed in a sequence and not break continuity (Fig. 3-23 to 3-29).

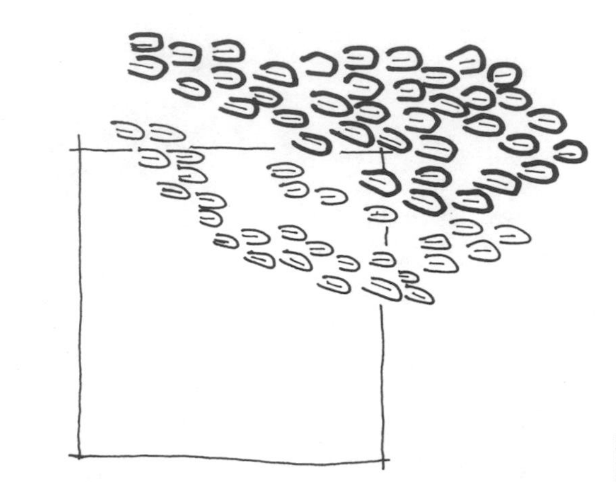

Figure 3-19
The texture of a plant can depend upon its surroundings and what is adjacent to it.

Figure 3-20
A yucca may look fine-textured unless it is planted next to a fine-textured pine tree.

Figure 3-21
Boston ivy on a cedar fence can create an interesting texture.

Figure 3-22
At a distance, this oak tree may look fine-textured.

Figure 3-23
As you move closer, the same tree begins to change in its textural appearance.

Figure 3-24
The leaves of the same oak tree can be a coarse element if viewed from close up.

Figure 3-25
During the winter months, the branching structure of a small tree can add an interesting texture to a composition.

Figure 3-26
Texture can also be effective when viewed from underneath a large tree.

Figure 3-27
Even different evergreen materials can provide a contrast in texture.

Figure 3-28
The soft texture of this pine can be very beneficial to a composition.

Figure 3-29
Fine-textured ground covers can offer a contrast in a composition.

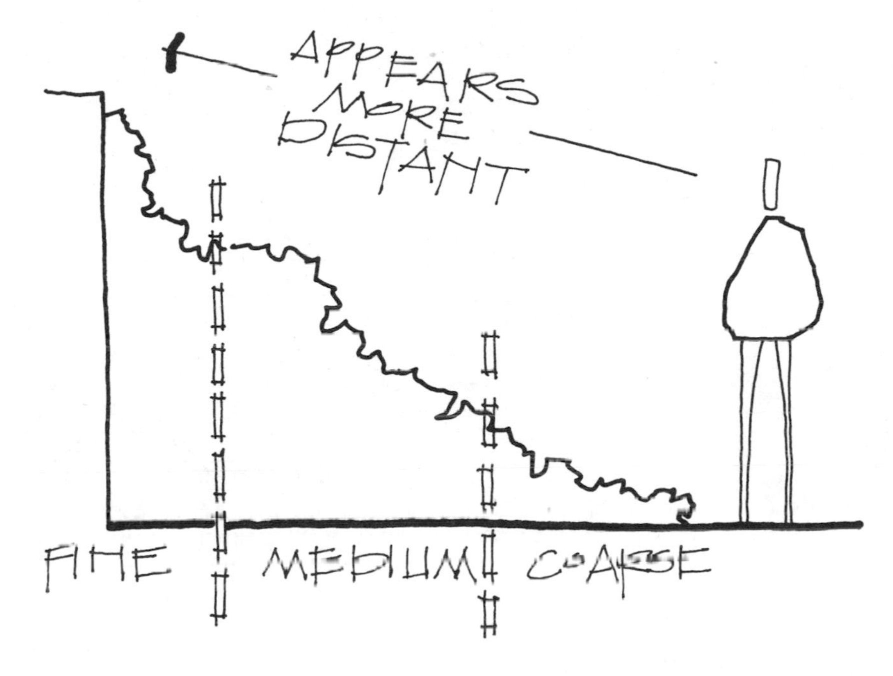

Figure 3-30
A space can be made to appear larger when fine texture is placed farther from the eye.

Texture also has certain psychological and physical effects upon the viewer. For example, textures can change in a sequence from fine to medium to coarse or the reverse. A coarse-to-fine sequence can expand the composition, causing it to appear farther away, while a sequence from fine to coarse contracts the composition. It must also be remembered that fine textures reflect more light than do coarse textures; this causes fine textures to appear brighter. Glossy foliage also reflects more light than does rough foliage (Fig. 3-30 and 3-31).

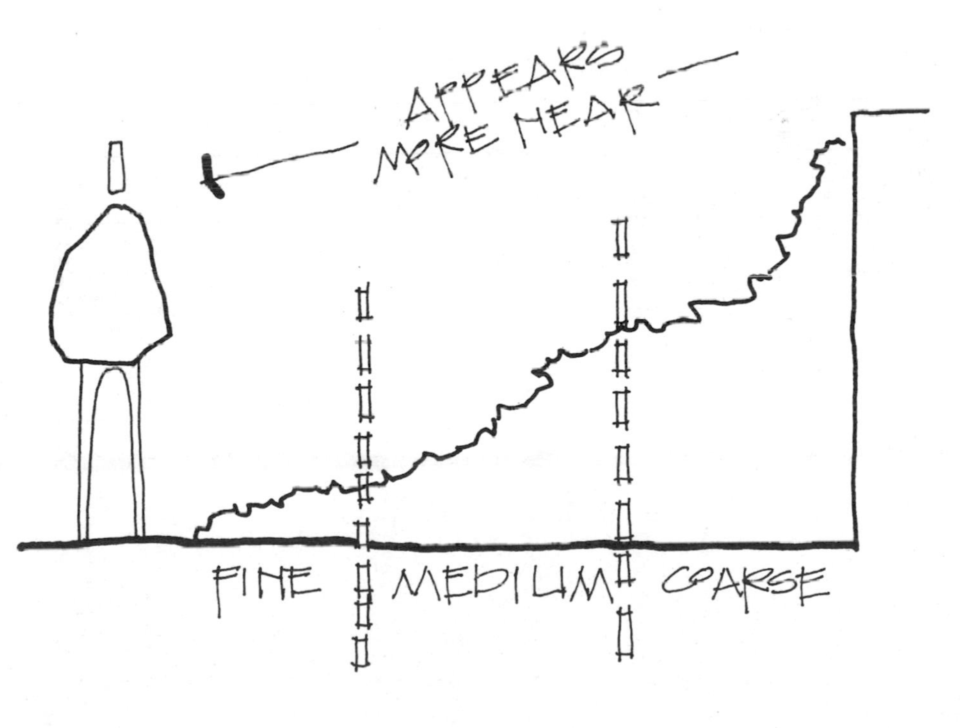

Figure 3-31
Using the reverse strategy, a space can be made to appear smaller.

The Visual Characteristics of Plants

Accent

An accent is a visual break in a sequence or pattern of plant materials. It has a dramatic effect on the appearance of a planting environment, concentrating attention on a specific portion of the design. Unlike other art forms, a landscape is usually viewed while walking through a space, with attention moving to different elements from minute to minute. The use of an accent in a planting design can capture the attention of the viewer and control how the composition is seen.

For accents to be effective, they must be eye-catching. The human eye, with its ability to see peripherally, tends to wander aimlessly. Accents, therefore help capture attention and allow the visual experience to be controlled more easily (Fig. 3-32).

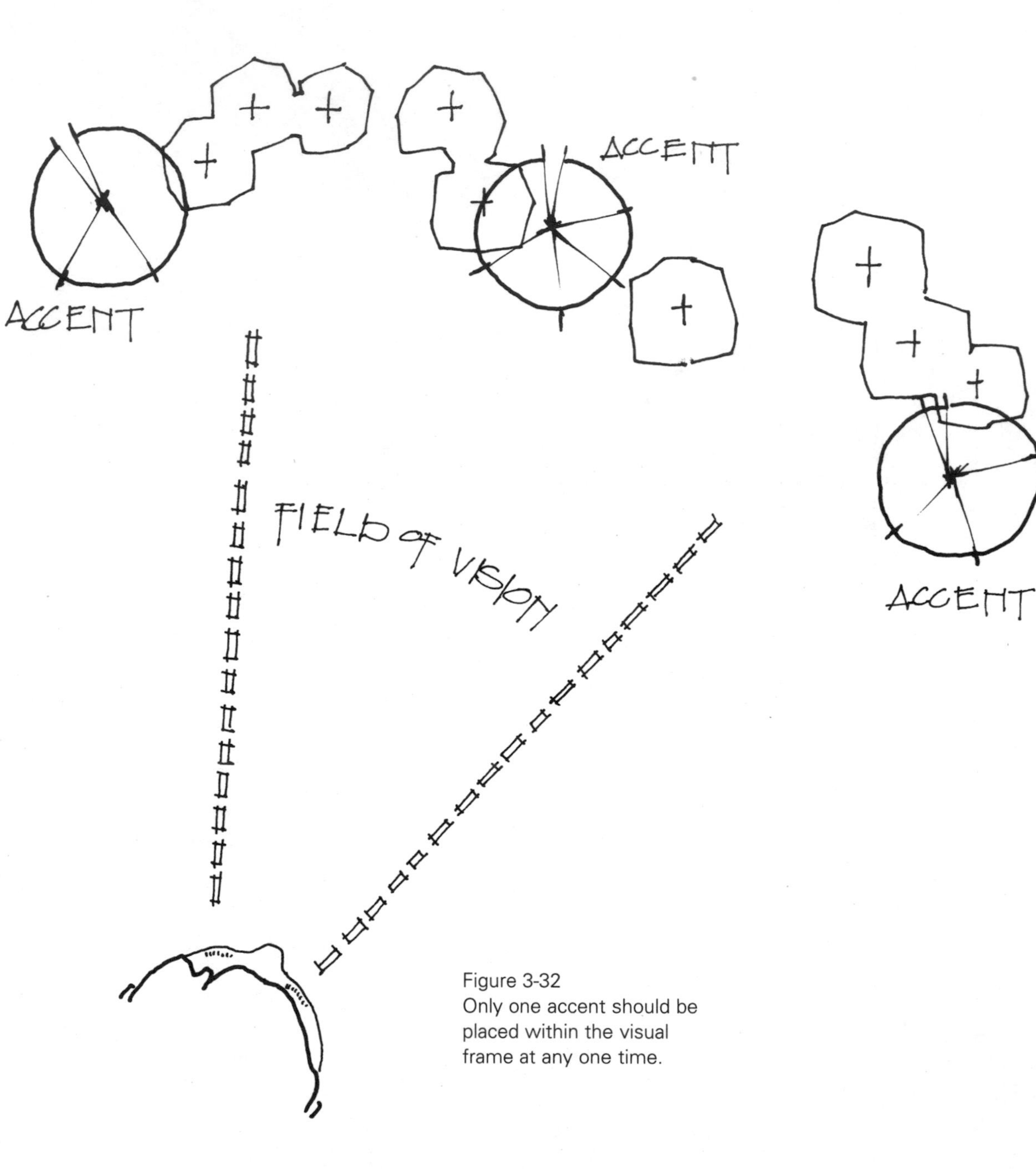

Figure 3-32
Only one accent should be placed within the visual frame at any one time.

Be careful in the placement of accents, however. Too many accents within the visual field will confuse the viewer. Whenever possible, accents should be visually framed. This can be accomplished by placing the feature of emphasis in a proper position to be viewed through a visual "window" or natural opening.

Accents may also be created with texture. If the dominant plant pattern has a fine texture, another plant with a medium or coarse texture will stand out as an accent.

If one plant form is used predominantly throughout the design, it can be relieved by the introduction of a contrasting form. This accent can be another type of plant, a piece of garden sculpture, or even an architectural structure or backdrop (Fig. 3-33).

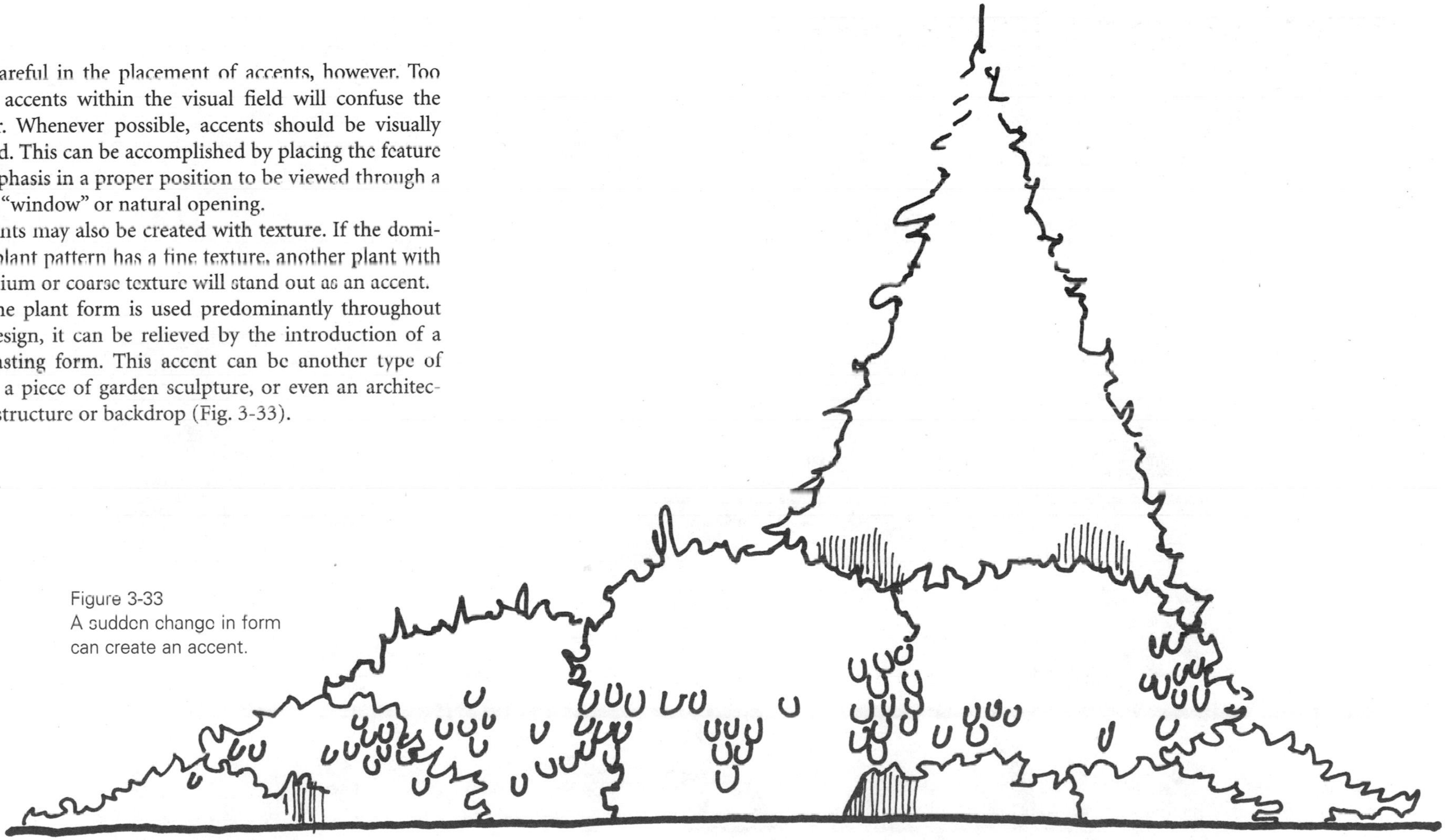

Figure 3-33
A sudden change in form can create an accent.

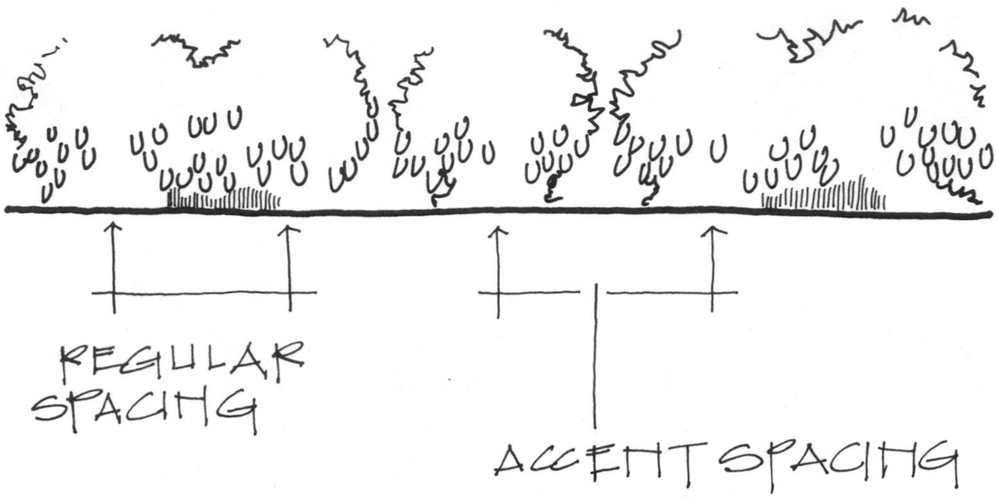

A contrast in the spacing of plants within a composition can also serve as an accent. Plant materials placed in sequential order never attract attention until one of the units disappears. This "gap" is eye-catching and will serve as a good planting-design accent. You can also create an accent by varying the size of one of the objects in a sequence (Fig. 3-34 to 3-38).

Figure 3-34
A change in spacing can create accent.

Figure 3-35
A gradual change in plant size can create a subtle accent.

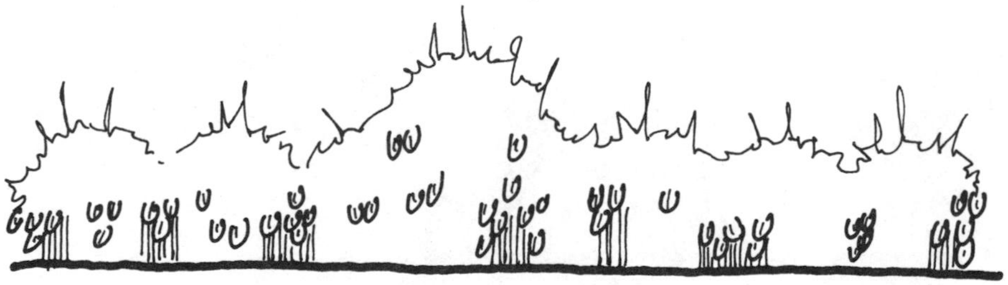

Figure 3-36
A dramatic change in plant size can create a stronger accent.

The most vivid impact upon our senses is made by an accent of color. It is created simply by providing an abrupt color change in the plant-material sequence.

Line can capture the eye as well. For example, a designer can use lines that lead to or converge upon a single point in the distance. With the use of plant walls or screens, vision can be physically limited or moved toward a focal point. This method is often used to enhance another accent.

Accents may be created by grouping objects within a design composition. Plants of the same type may be planted en masse for greater visual impact.

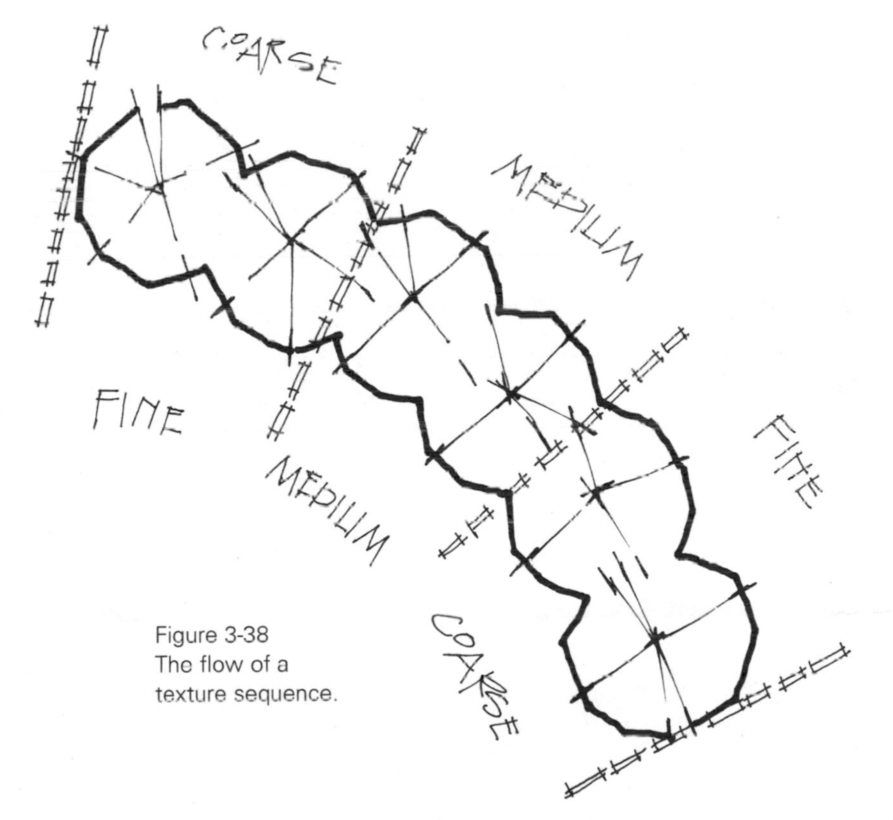

Figure 3-38
The flow of a texture sequence.

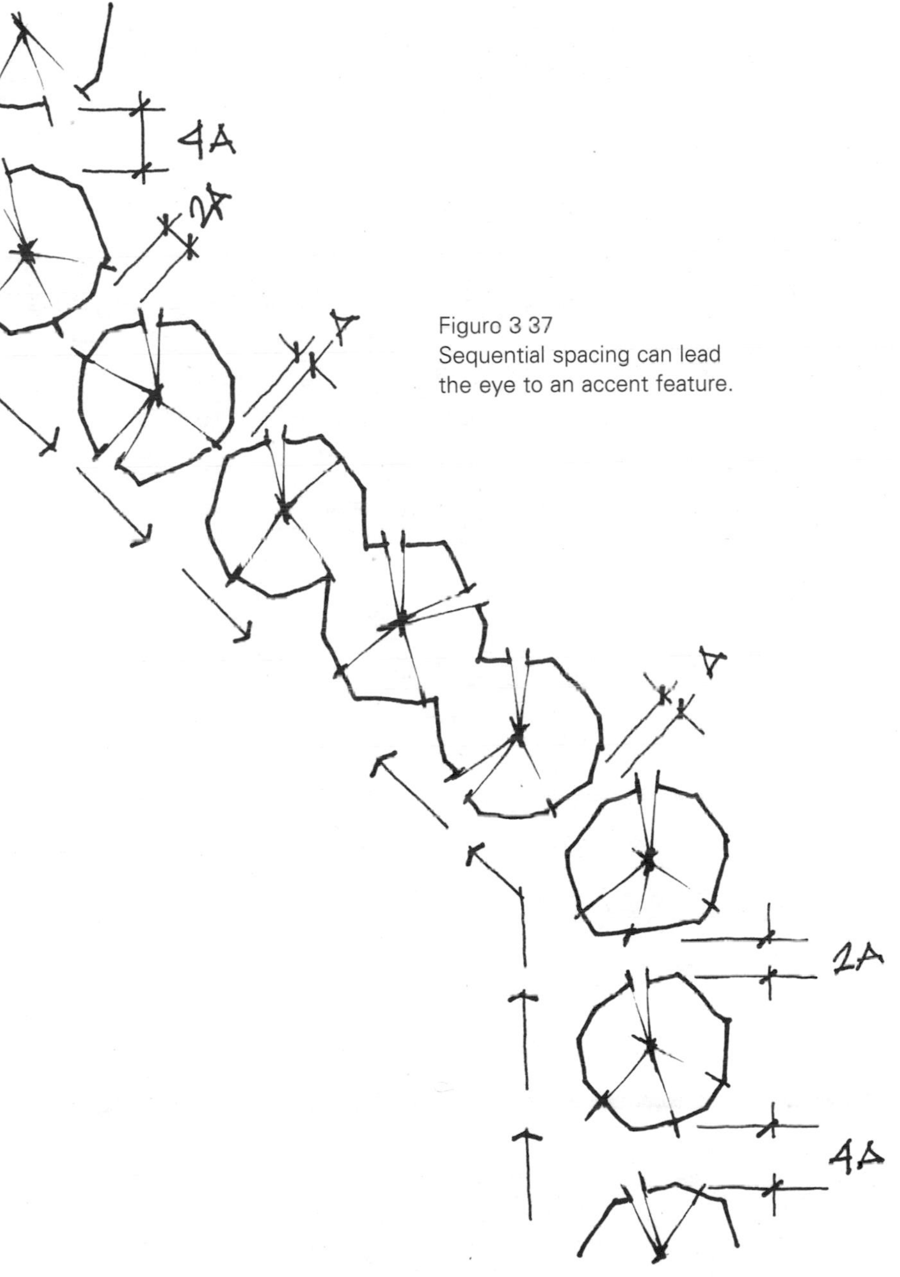

Figure 3-37
Sequential spacing can lead the eye to an accent feature.

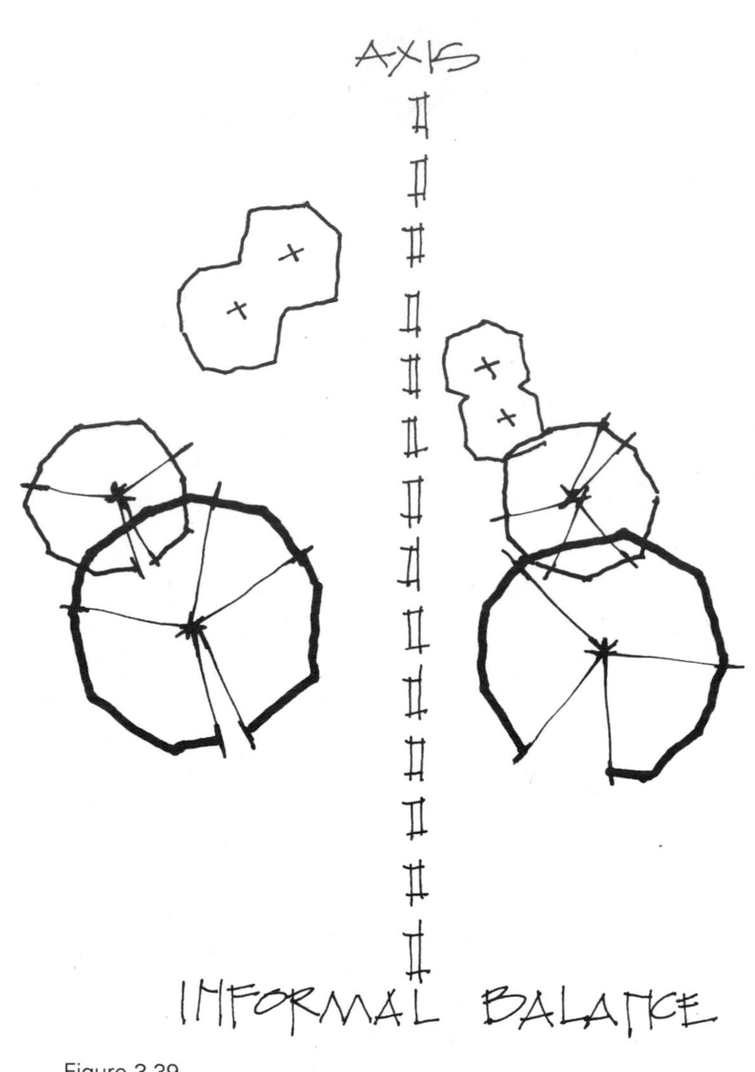

Figure 3-39
The visual sense of a space is created in an informal composition.

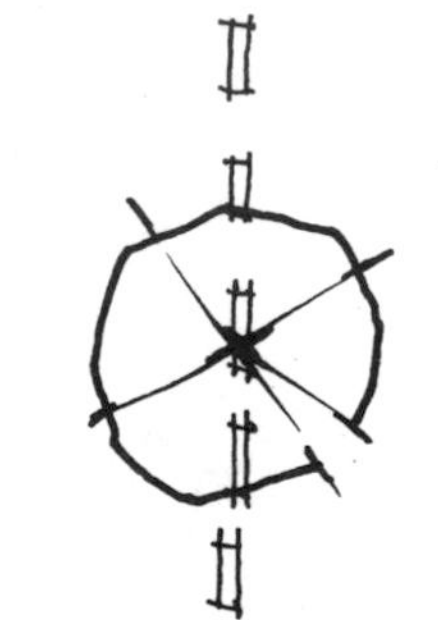

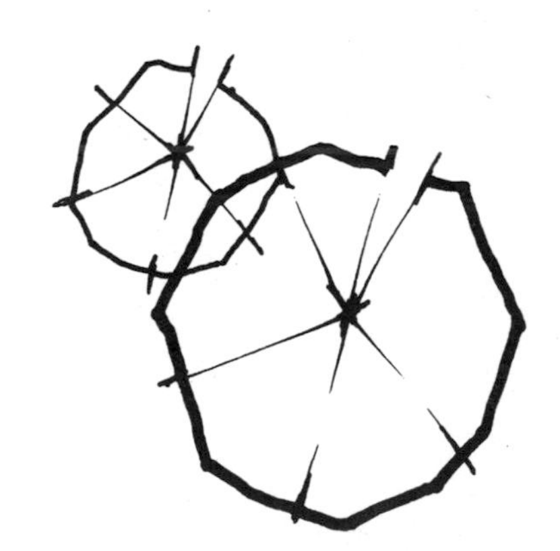

Figure 3-40
Elements on each side of the axis should be balanced in a formal composition.

Scale

Scale, or proportion, concerns the relationship of a plant to other plants and to the planted space as a whole. In establishing scale within the composition, the human subject is the standard of measurement. All aspects of the composition must be in scale with its users. Several considerations should be made in establishing scale.

First, scale is relative to the perception of the viewer. That perception may vary from individual to individual, but harmony between the parts and the whole within the composition must exist in order for the viewer to feel comfortable.

Second, because scale is relative to perception, it can be manipulated psychologically within the space. The following points should be considered when manipulating scale within the planted space:

1. The size of the total space will offer certain limitations or advantages. Space in this context is relative to the lines of sight. Our sight is ordinarily limited only by physical barriers. Interior spaces are closed, with limiting boundaries; thus the ability to sculpture that space is also limited. In landscape design, however, there are virtually no boundaries. The limits that do exist fall into two basic categories: primary, which are immediate barriers such as the ground, architectural structures, and on-site foliage; and secondary, which are far-off boundaries such as distant mountains, the sky, or foliage located off the site. These limitations serve as the basis for introducing scale in the design. If the area to be designed is open and relatively free of scenic barriers, the designer is left with many alternatives. On the other hand, a site that is confined visually by topography, neighboring structures, or existing foliage must be carefully analyzed to determine how the space is affected.
2. A designer can cause certain planes or surfaces within a space to appear either close or far in relation to the viewer through the selection of textures. A fine texture appears more distant than a coarse texture. Texture is created by several factors, including size of units within a space; number of units within a space; and space between units.
3. Color has an effect on our perception of scale. Darker colors seems to recede and to be more distant, while lighter colors appear to be near. The human eye is unable to focus on adjacent colors when those colors are opposites on the color wheel. For example, a mass of red flowers placed within a predominantly green environment has minimal effect unless another color is planted between them.

Sequence

Sequence is characterized by continuity and connection from one element to another. It is imperative to any art form and is especially important in planting design. The proper sequence of color or texture will allow a viewer's eye to move within the space in an orderly fashion and heighten the visual experience.

Using color or texture in a rhythmic pattern adds harmony to the arrangement of plant materials. A fine-textured tree, shrub, or ground cover should blend into a medium-textured plant, which in turn should blend into a coarse-textured plant — or that sequence can be reversed. This is not to say that all three textures must be represented in every arrangement. Fine or coarse textures may need to flow only into medium textures; but fine textures should never be placed next to coarse textures without the buffer of a medium pattern to maintain the transitional illusion.

A designer can support a textural sequence with a harmonious color sequence. Color supports design harmony when there is a blending of colors from dark to medium to light, or light to medium to dark.

Spacing, which should be related to the plant's capacity for growth, should also have transitional order. Undefined spacing patterns cause dramatic breaks in the visual harmony of a planting arrangement. To achieve sequence with spacing, a designer must pay attention to the spacing of a mass of plants as well as the spacing of individual materials.

Balance

Balance is the state of equipoise between planting design elements. It is the "visual sense" you have as a planting designer: how you use masses, colors, lines, and textures, and how they appear to the viewer within a space.

Planting design involves two basic types of balance: formal or symmetrical, which is the repetition of features on each side of the central axis, often called mirror-image design; and informal or asymmetrical, the variation of plant type, quantity, or position on either side of the central axis (Fig. 3-39 and 3-40).

Implementing a Planting Design

The Architectural Forms of Plants

Plants can be used to create many architectural design forms. The primary design forms are walls, ceilings, and floors. The secondary forms are screens, canopies, barriers, baffles, and ground covers (Fig. 3-41 and 3-42).

The primary wall form may consist of a screen, barrier, baffle, or a combination of these. The ceiling form is reinforced by a canopy, and the floor form is supported by the ground cover.

A wall functions as a shield against outside influences, both visual and physical. It obstructs objectionable views, blocks undesirable winds, creates privacy, and protects the individual within a space. A ceiling occupies the overhead space and gives us shade, shelter, and protection from above. A floor connects the other primary features, providing continuity (Fig. 3-43 to 3-45).

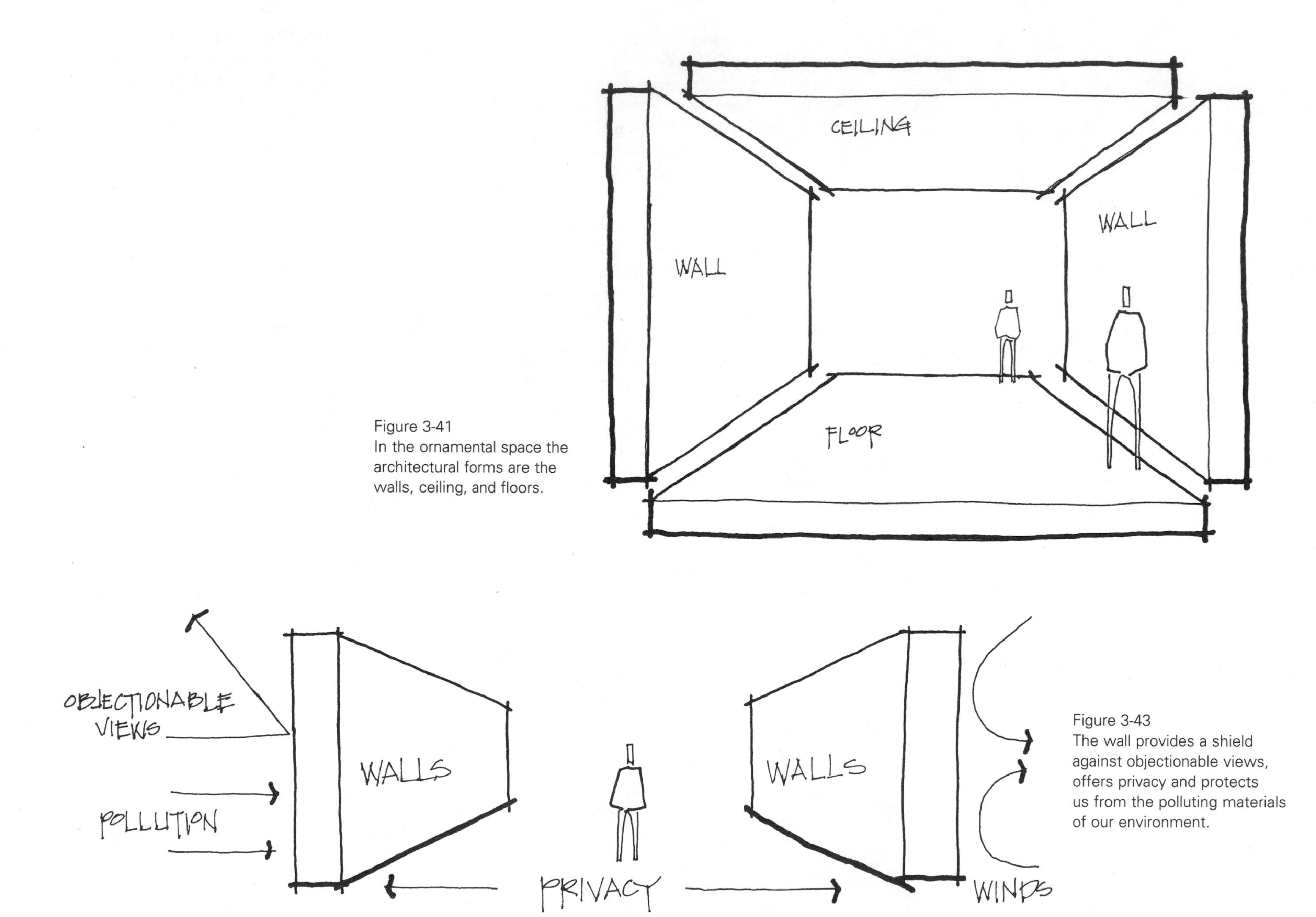

Figure 3-41
In the ornamental space the architectural forms are the walls, ceiling, and floors.

Figure 3-43
The wall provides a shield against objectionable views, offers privacy and protects us from the polluting materials of our environment.

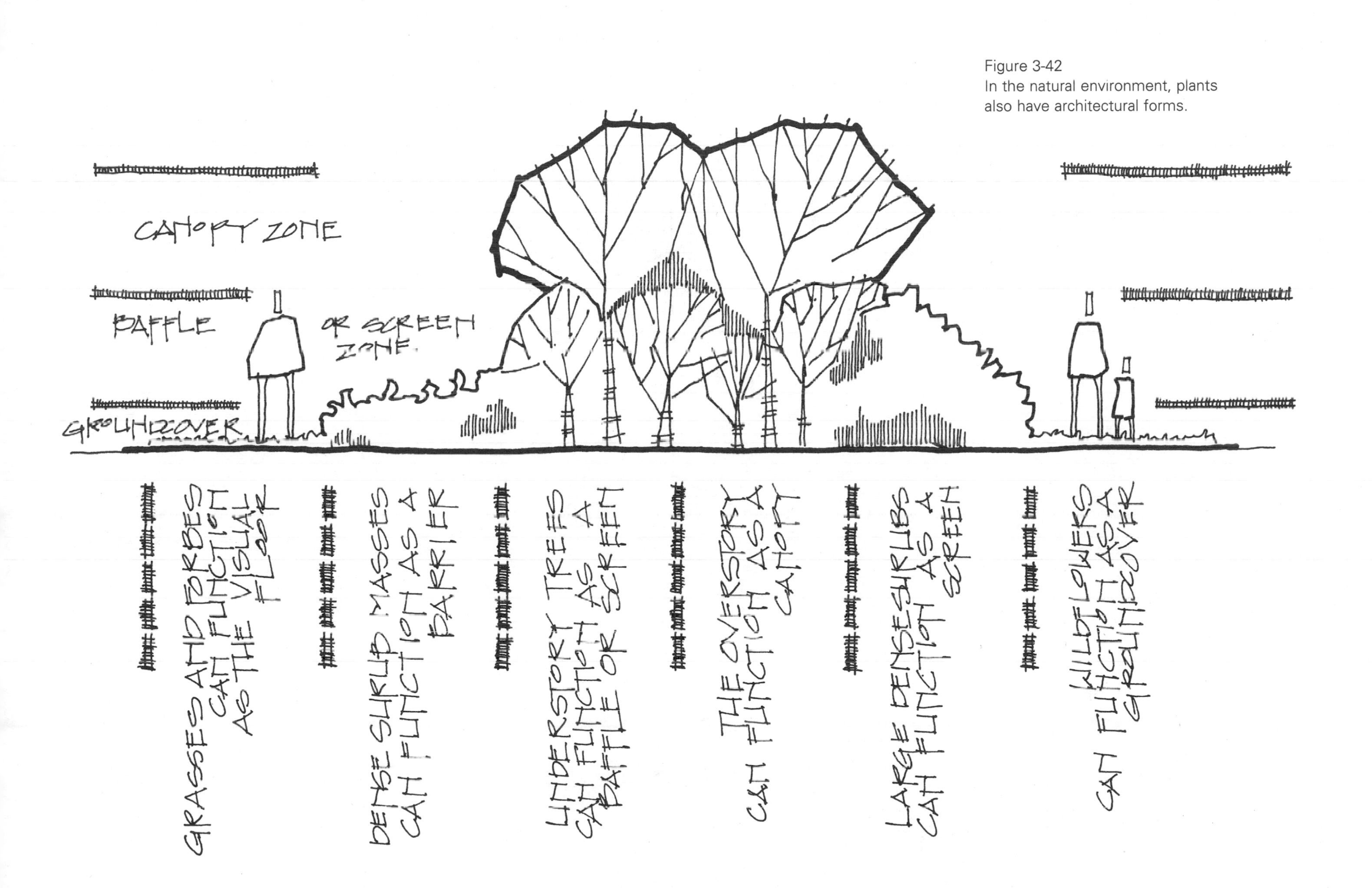

Figure 3-42
In the natural environment, plants also have architectural forms.

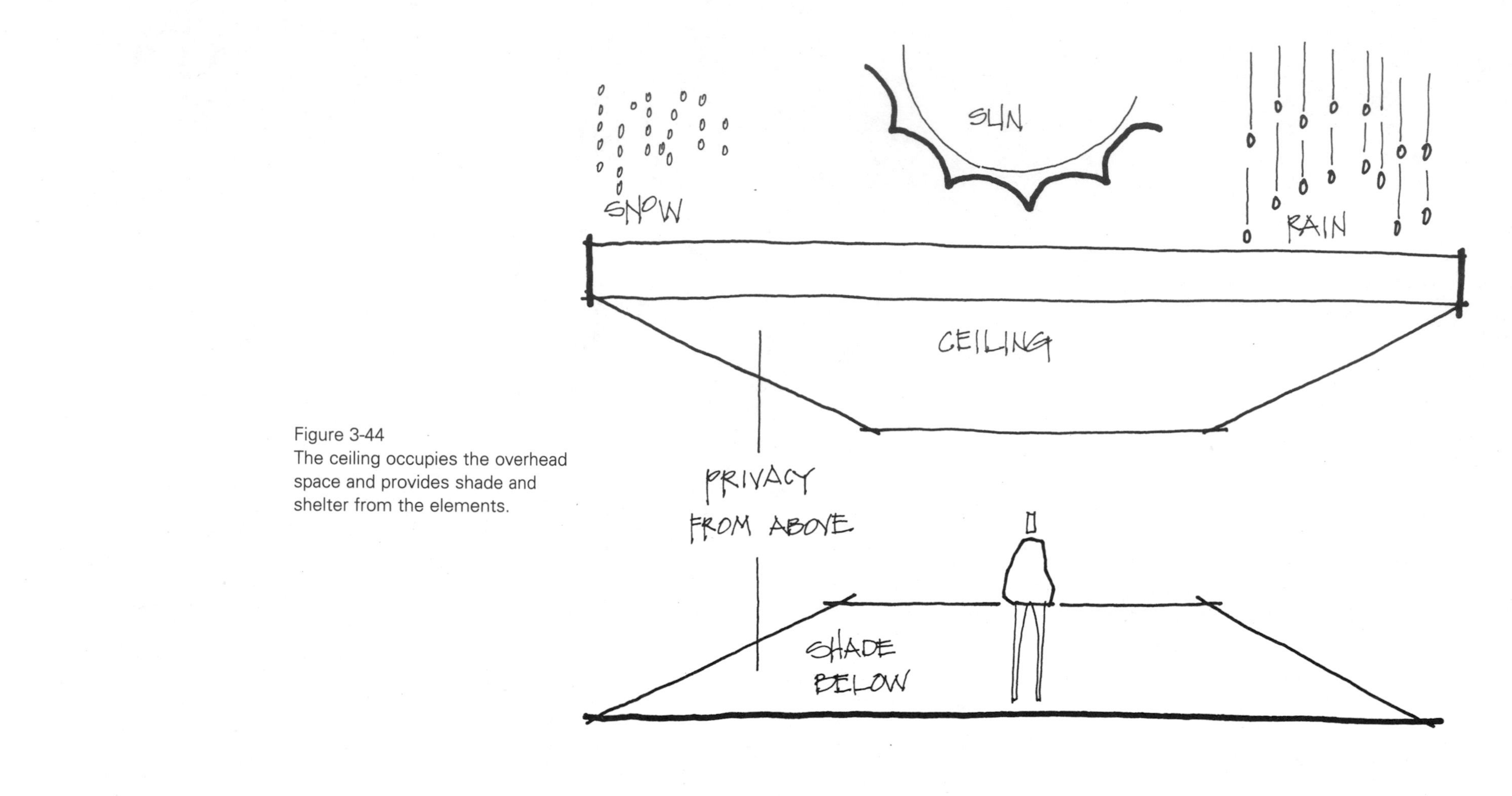

Figure 3-44
The ceiling occupies the overhead space and provides shade and shelter from the elements.

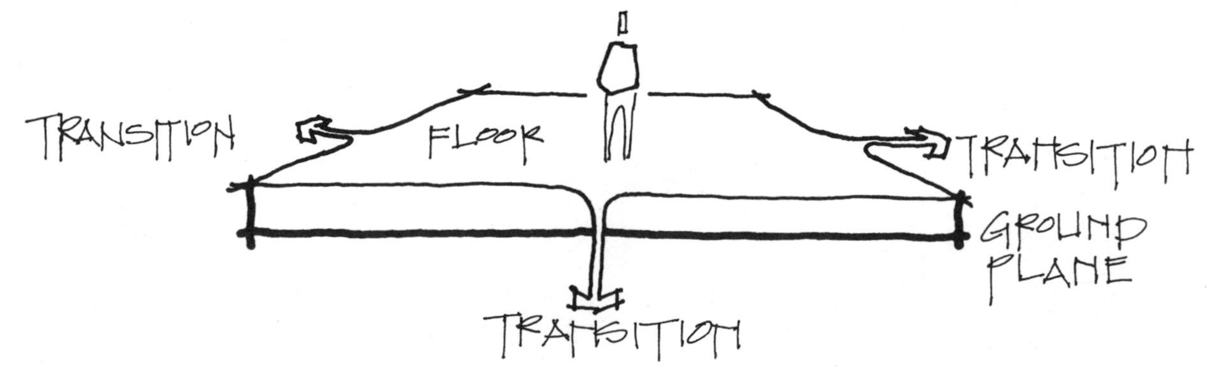

Figure 3-45
The floor is the ground plane of the planted space and connects plants and plant masses.

The secondary architectural forms may be defined as follows:

1. A screen is a plant or plant mass used for the total enclosure of a landscape space. A person within the space cannot walk or see through this form. A screen may be created with a single plant, a plant mass, or a combination of plants with other landscape elements (Fig. 3-46 to 3-51).
2. A canopy is a plant or plant mass with a branching height of seven feet or more that will allow an individual to walk underneath. Its most important design characteristic is that it occupies only the overhead plane. A canopy may be created by using a plant type that will occupy this spatial zone (Fig. 3-52 to 3-57).
3. A barrier is a plant or plant mass used for a partial enclosure or to control the circulation within a landscape space. A person may see over this feature but not pass through it. A barrier is usually created with a plant mass bewtween two feet and five feet in height (Fig. 3-58 to 3-60).
4. A baffle is a plant or plant mass that is used to control visual experiences within a landscape. An individual within the space may see through but cannot walk through it. A baffle may be created by a plant or plant mass that does not interrupt the visual experience but does act as a physical barrier (Fig. 3-61 and 3-63).
5. The ground cover is a plant or plant mass used as a visual floor, usually reaching a maximum height of 18 inches. This should be kept below the eye level of the individual within the space (Fig. 3-64 to 3-66).

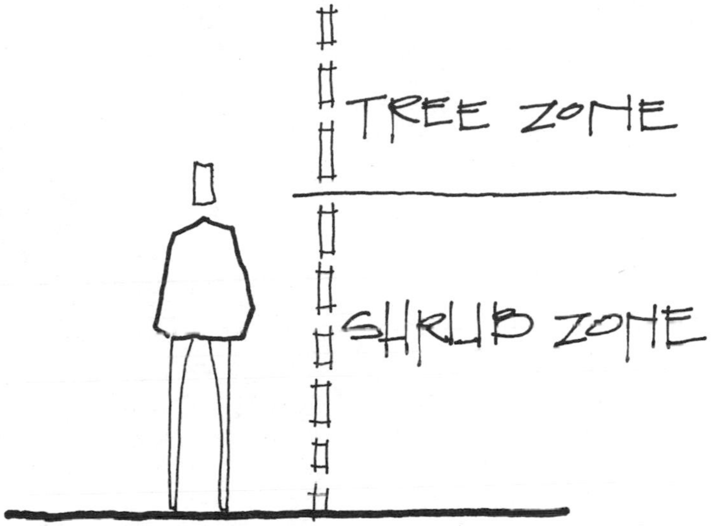

Figure 3-46
To function as a screen, a plant must be within the tree zone.

Figure 3-47
A small shrub and a berm can function as a screen.

Figure 3-48
A small plant mass can create a screen.

Figure 3-49
A small shrub at the top of a stone wall can create a screen.

Figure 3-50
An attempt to screen this site feature may be ineffective until these plants are more mature.

Figure 3-51
Large shrubs need to reach maturity to function as a screen

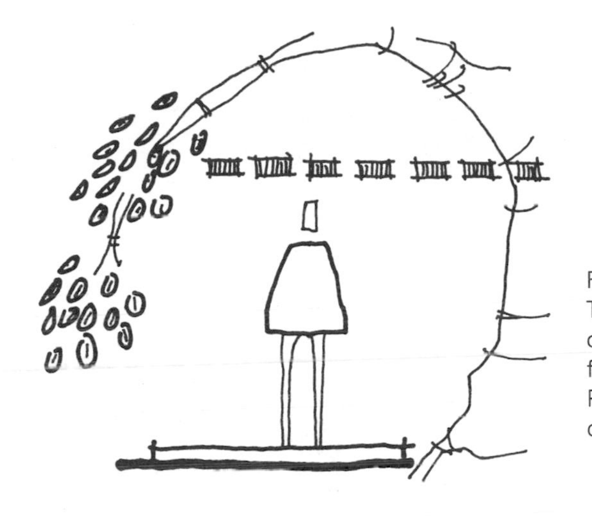

Figure 3-52
The ceiling dominates the overhead space with either full or partial enclosure. Plants with drooping branches can create a canopy.

Figure 3-54
The branching height of this small tree is too low to form a ceiling.

Figure 3-53
A ceiling can be created by trimming the branches of an evergreen tree, allowing users to walk beneath it.

Figure 3-55
Users need to be able to walk under a plant for it to function as a canopy.

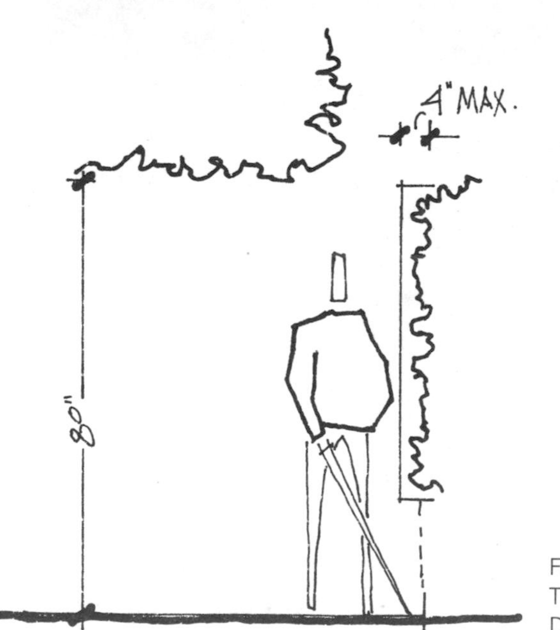

Figure 3-57
The Americans with Disabilities Act requires an overhead clearance of 80 inches.

Figure 3-56
Small trees at two different levels function as a canopy for this entry planting.

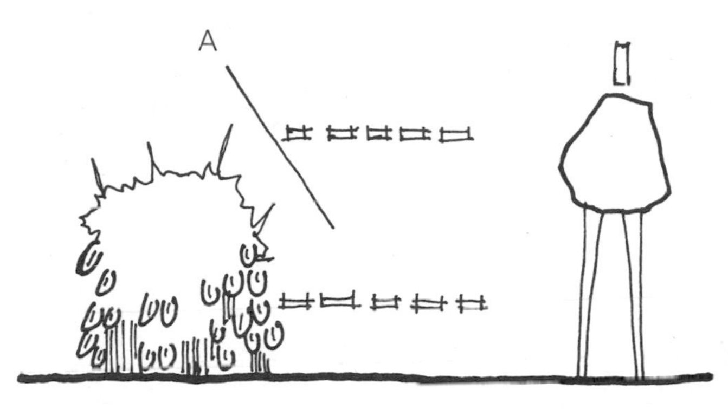

Figure 3-58
A barrier zone (A) may be seen over, but not passed through.

Figure 3-60
Users can see over this barrier, but cannot pass through it to the space behind.

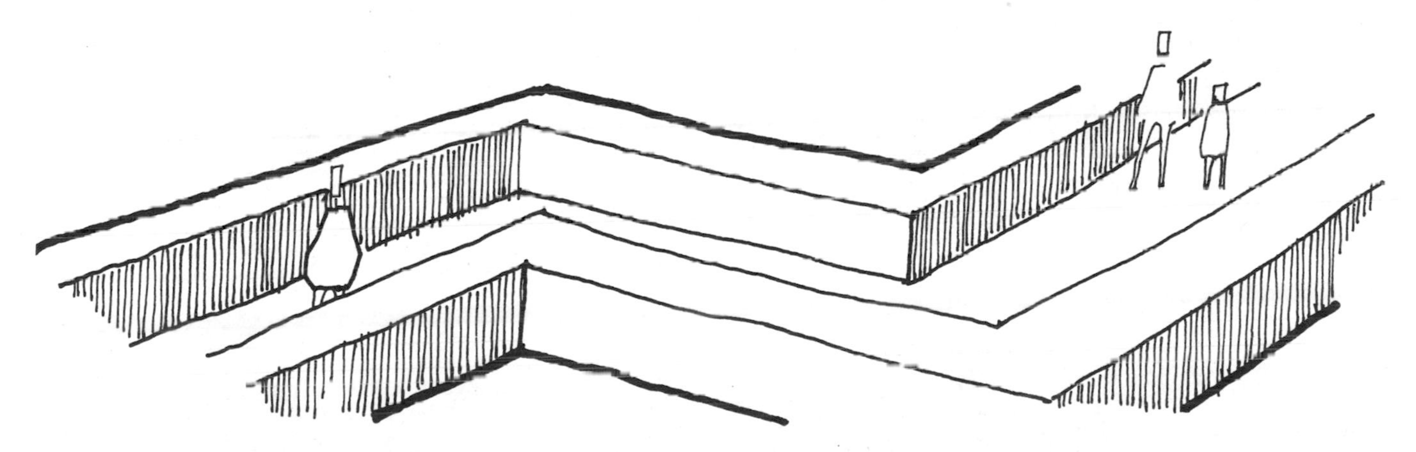

Figure 3-59
A barrier defines and controls the direction of movement through a planted space.

Figure 3-61
A baffle is a partial screen that can be seen through, but not passed through.

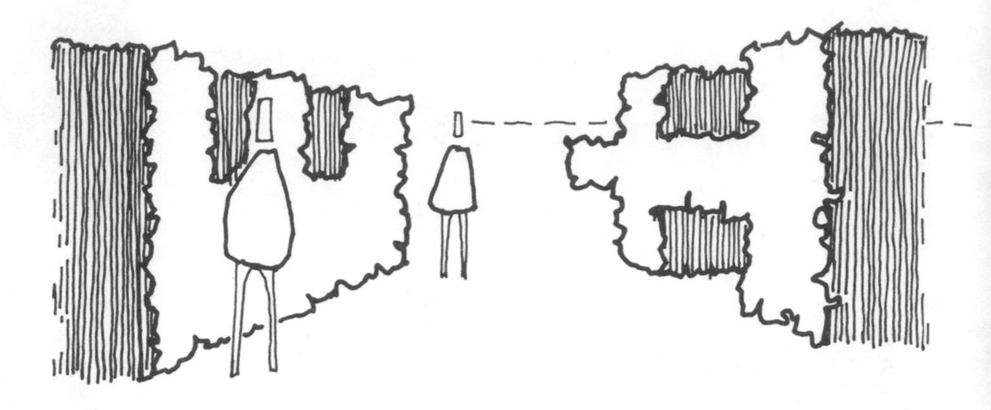

Figure 3-62
A baffle can create an interesting visual experience.

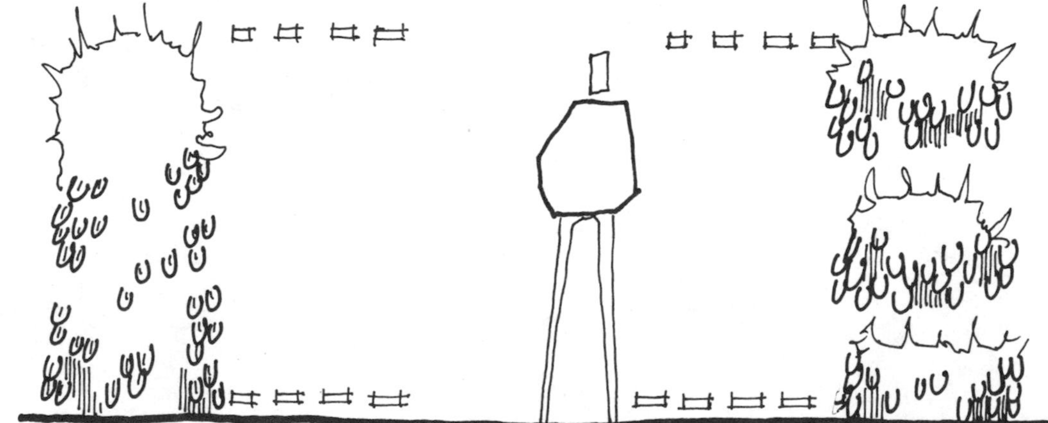

Figure 3-63
The screen and the baffle occupy the wall zone.

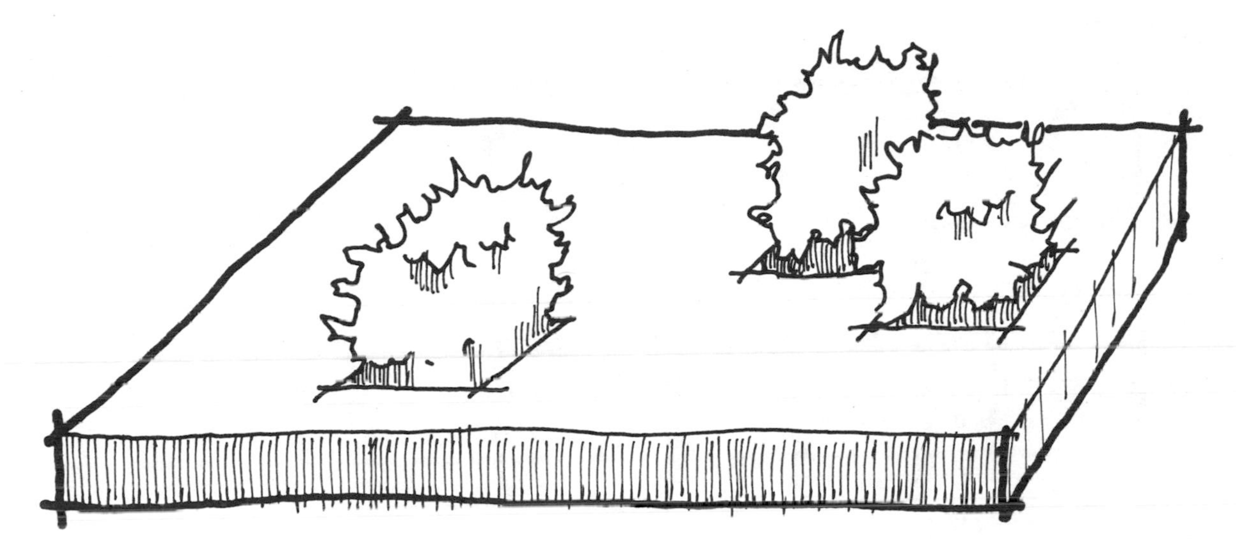

Figure 3-64
The floor is the ground plane of the planted space. This element helps connect one plant material type to another.

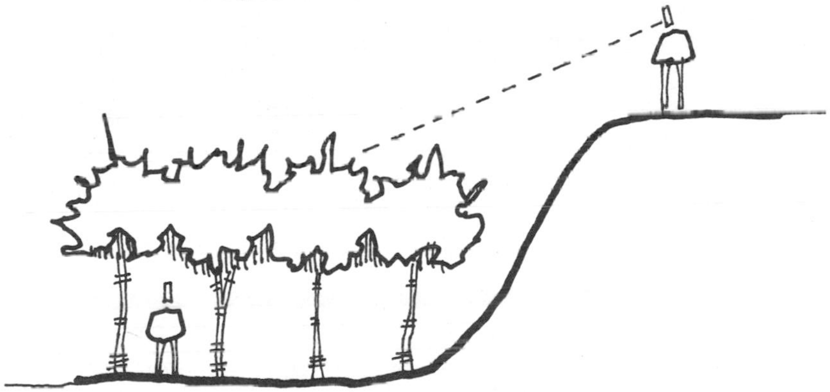

Figure 3-66
From above, a tree mass can look like a ground cover.

Figure 3-65
Ground cover can replace a grass lawn for an almost maintenance-free planting.

Primary and secondary architectural forms may be used by a planting designer to create numerous and varied landscape compositions. The constraints for their effectiveness as a design feature, however, are as follows:

1. The type, age and condition of the plant materials
2. The spacing of the plants, which determines the opacity, translucency, or transparency of the form
3. The form and grown rate of the individual plants, which affect the density of the total form. (Density is affected by the shape and size of the leaves, branching patterns, branching heights, and the height and width of the plant when planted and when mature.)

The Design Components

As a designer considers the effects of a single plant or plant mass on the rest of the environment, additional thought must be given to the way in which the viewer will react within the composition. The elements of color, form, texture, accent, scale, and sequence are the basic considerations in the application of various design components to a finished landscape. Combined with the architectural forms, the design components magnify the character of the molded space and allow the designer to control the way in which the space is both seen and felt by the viewer.

The primary design components are the physical units that support the design:

1. *Direction* moderates the physical movement within a landscape space. A designer may control the visual experiences within the composition by allowing movement only in a specific direction or area (Fig. 3-67 to 3-71)
2. *Pooling* divides the space into outdoor rooms. As viewers are directed throughout a composition, it may be desirable to expand the perceived space or alter available experiences (Fig. 3-72 to 3-75).

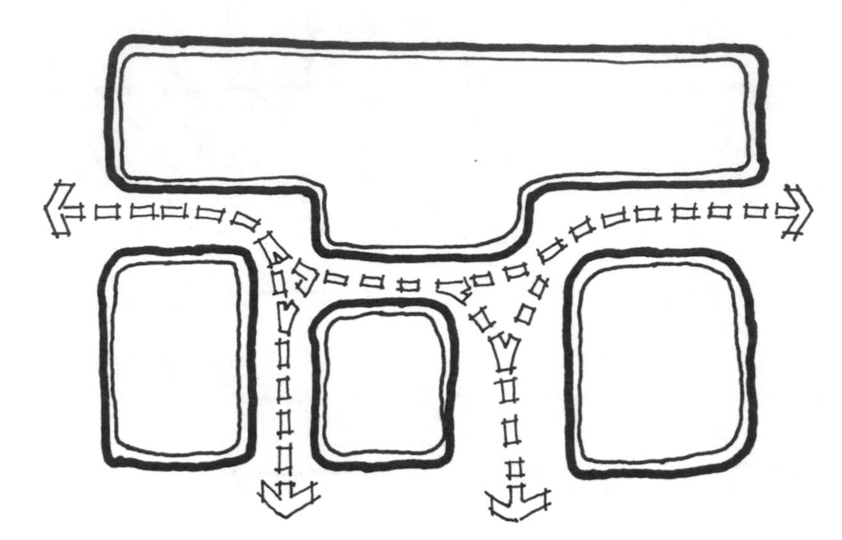

Figure 3-67
Direction moderates physical movement within a planted space.

Figure 3-68
Edge plantings can reinforce direction in the space.

Figure 3-71
Direction through this space is less defined.

Figure 3-69
A low-growing barrier can help define circulation.

Figure 3-70
Screens can help control direction through a space.

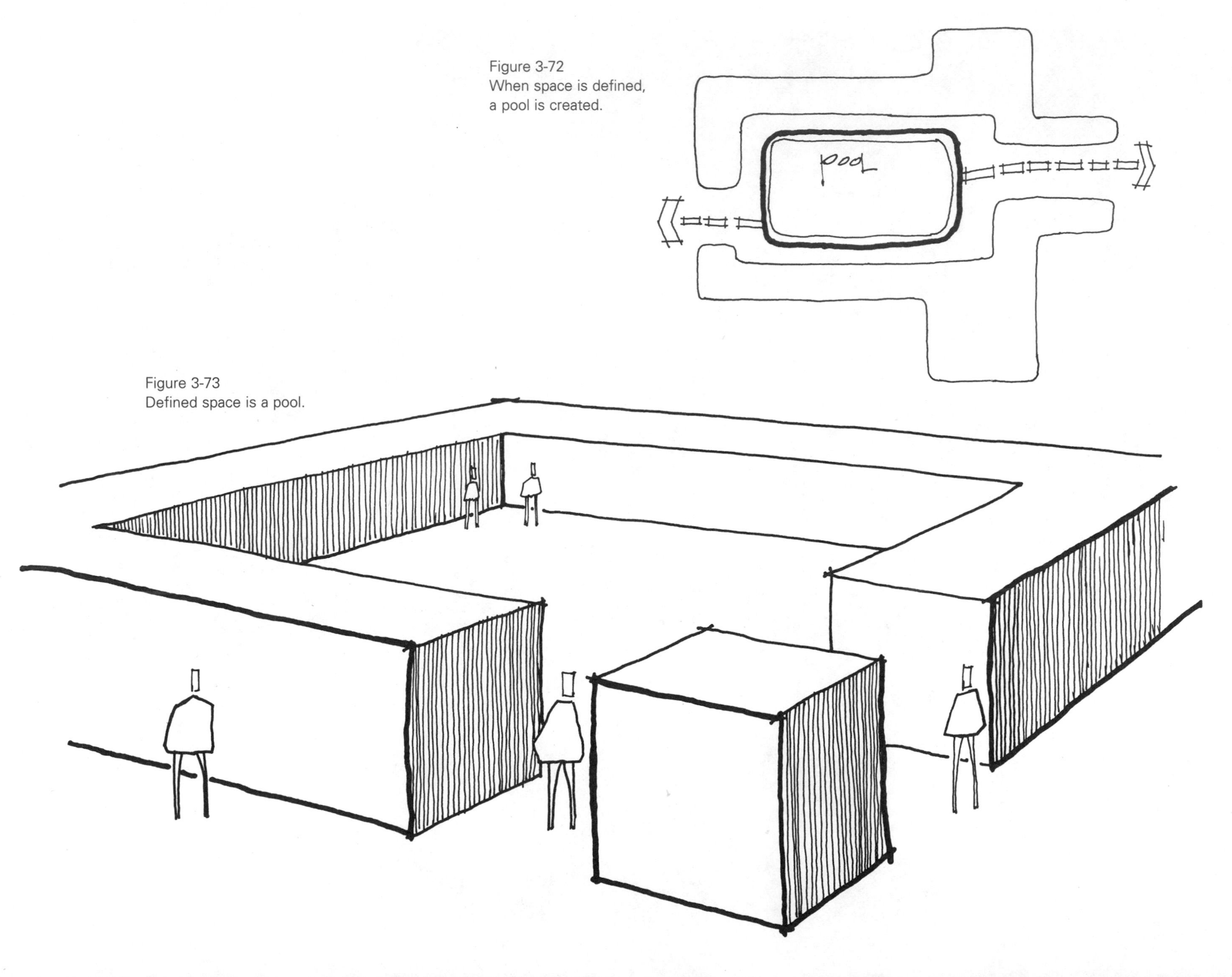

Figure 3-72
When space is defined, a pool is created.

Figure 3-73
Defined space is a pool.

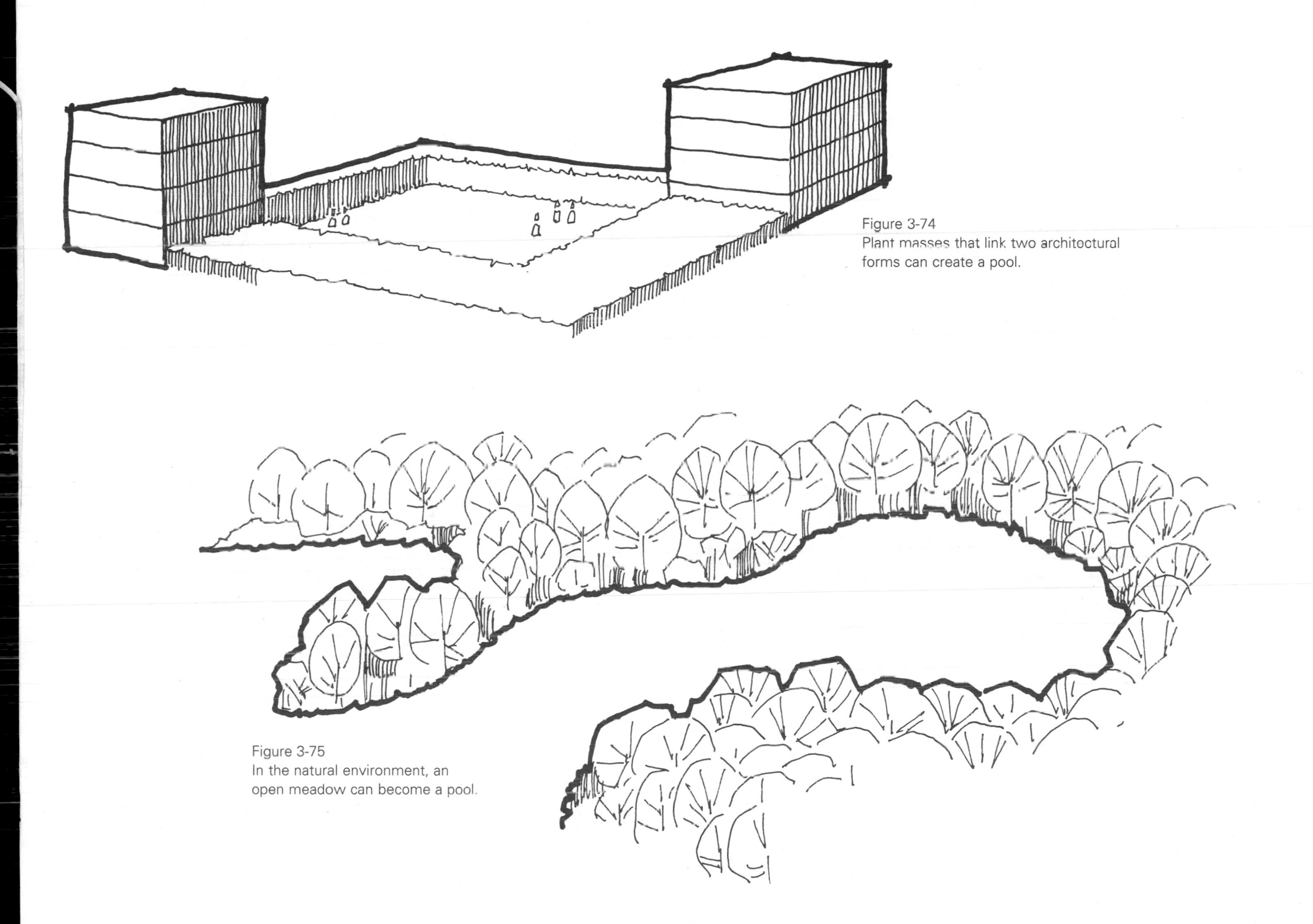

Figure 3-74
Plant masses that link two architectural forms can create a pool.

Figure 3-75
In the natural environment, an open meadow can become a pool.

The secondary components are the visual units that support the design:

1. *Enframement* draws attention to a focal area or view within the composition or to an off-site feature. It may be accomplished by using trees or shrubs that project into the visual plane (Fig. 3-76).
2. *Linkage* visually joins one space or object to another space or object (Fig. 3-77).
3. *Enlargement* or *reduction* is the ability to change the apparent size of a composition. It may be accomplished by varying the degree of enclosure of the space (Fig. 3-78 and 3-79).
4. *Invitation* involves the use of stimulation, suggestion, or curiosity to pull a viewer into or through a space. It may be accomplished with moving objects or with bright, sudden changes of color (Fig. 3-80).
5. *Subdivision* is the use of plant materials to divide a large space into smaller components or to create a small space within a large one (Fig. 3-81).

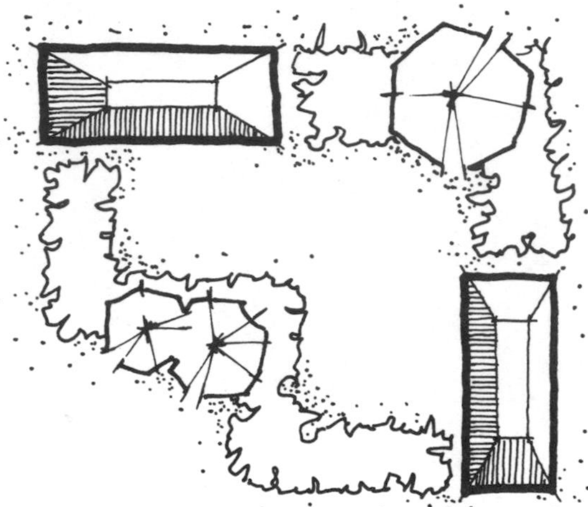

Figure 3-77
Plant masses can link architectural forms.

Figure 3-76
These two trees planted on each side of the patio space frame the view out of the windows and doors.

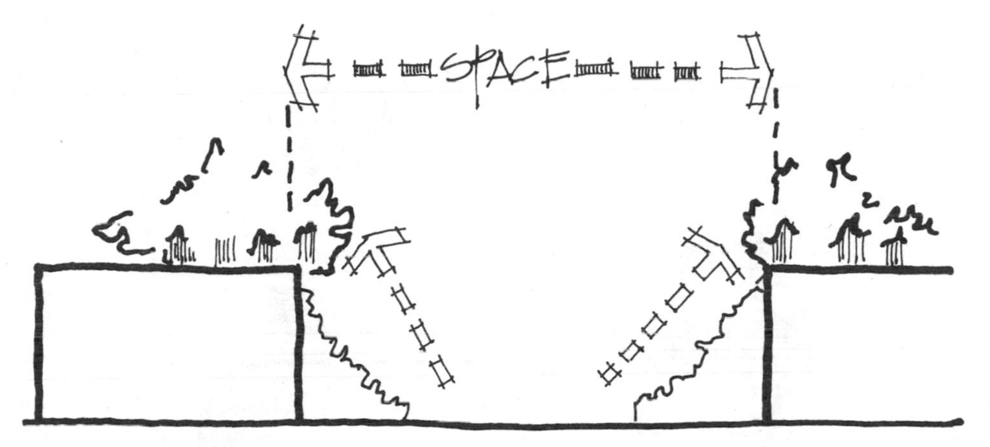

Figure 3-78
Plants can be placed in a space so as to make it appear larger.

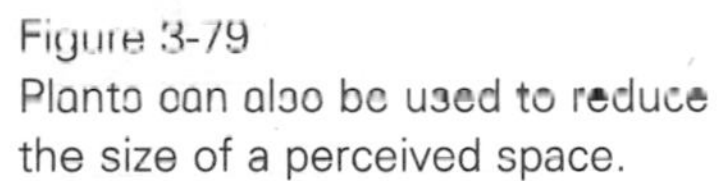

Figure 3-79
Plants can also be used to reduce the size of a perceived space.

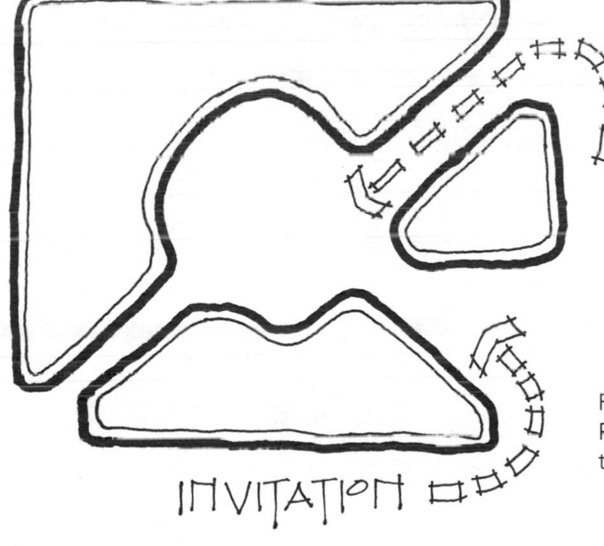

Figure 3-80
Plant masses can be positioned to help invite users into a space.

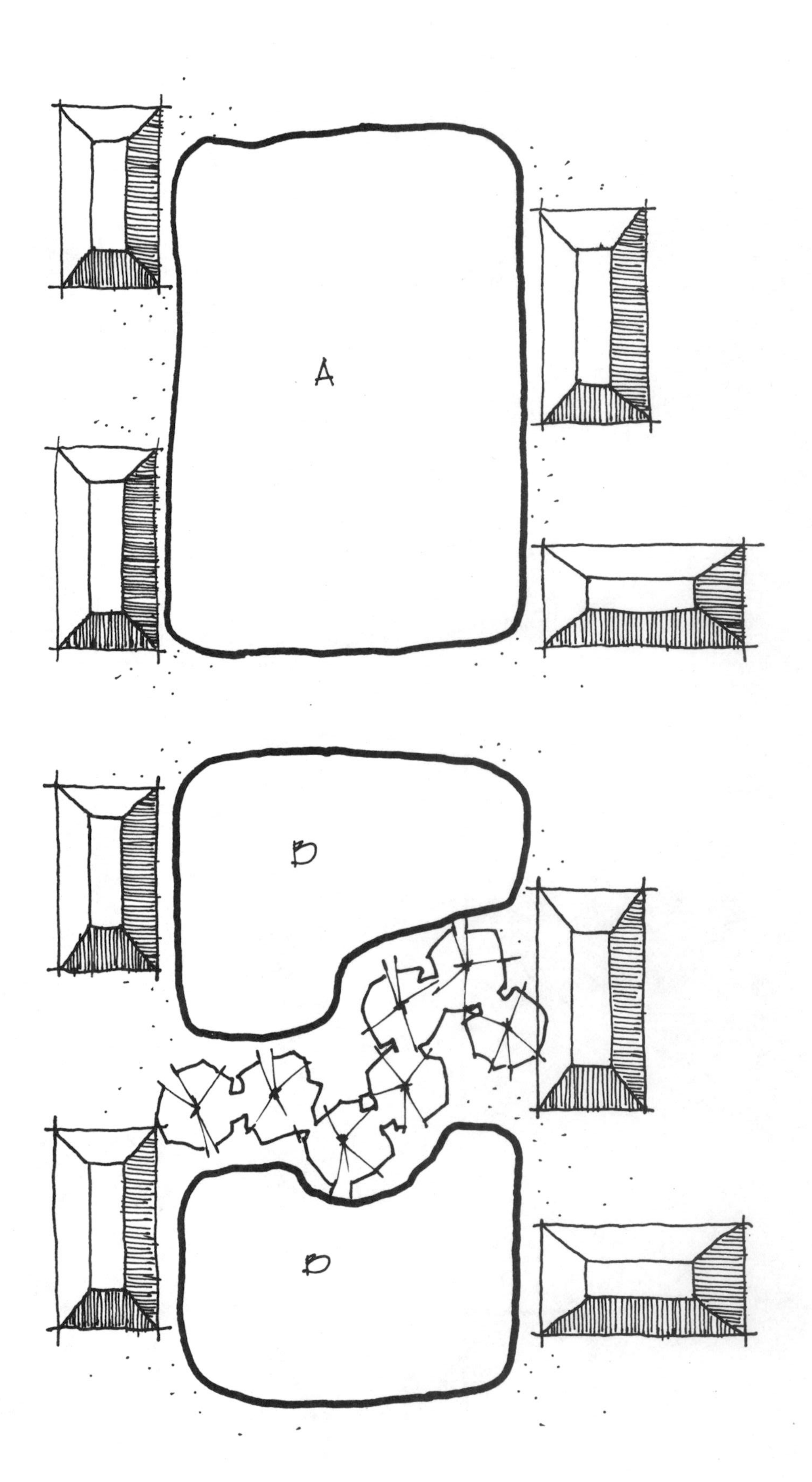

Figure 3-81
Area A is open and undefined.
Area B has been divided with
plant masses.

Developing a Preliminary Planting Plan

The development of the final concept for a planting environment begins in the preliminary phase of the design process. In developing the planting plan we must first establish the design function of the materials. The selection of a plant for a landscape composition should first be based upon its design function and then upon its horticultural characteristics. Too often, landscapes exhibit the reverse, containing materials that are awkward for their location and seem out of place. Although both considerations are of critical importance to the success of a composition, focusing on function will allow a designer to adapt the design to almost any geographic region.

The following procedures can be used to determine the design function of the plants and plant masses to be selected for a space:

1. Determine the general design components of the composition. Based on the client's design intent, establish the primary design components by planning specific pools of space and a specific direction for pedestrian movement. Determine the views that need to be framed from various vantage points. Select the features that should be linked together with plant masses and locate special materials that will invite the viewer's attention. If the site is composed of one large space, propose plant masses that will subdivide the composition into smaller areas (Fig. 2-7).
2. Shape the space to create primary architectural forms. Plan for the use of walls, ceilings, and floors to shape the composition. This is the beginning of the sculpturing process, where the designer establishes control over the planting environment (Fig. 2-8).
3. Refine the space with secondary architectural forms. Select plants or plant masses that will create the spaces and effects called for by the design intent. Use color, form, texture, accent, scale, sequence, and balance to support the composition (Fig. 2-9).
4. Select design elements that will reinforce spatial objectives. Develop a preliminary planting plan that meets the client's needs and allows full creative input from the designer (Fig. 2-10).

These steps should govern plant selection for the given space. For example, it may now be determined that a dark green (foliage color), rounded (form), fine-textured, accent canopy is needed for a particular location within the composition.

Plant Applications

Trees

Trees are the most fundamental element in any planting environment. Because of their long life and high value in the landscape, which increases with age, careful attention should be given to their function, selection, and placement. Properly selected trees may be more permanent than most building structures, and if care is taken during the planning process, they will add a great deal to the beauty and value of the space being developed.

One of the most important points to remember is that no single tree species can perform all the functions necessary for a successful landscape development. Trees should be planted to solve various problems and to fulfill several purposes. When selecting a tree, consider these uses:

1. *Shade.* Plant shade trees in the area where they will do the most good. The stronger-branched varieties may be planted closer to an architectural structure without fear of breakage. Fast-growing, weaker-branched trees should never be planted too near a structure because of possible damage during severe ice or windstorms.
2. *Enframement.* Some varieties of trees may be used to frame an area or structure. Such trees may be placed just off the front corners or to the sides of a lawn to give the space or its architectural features a specific accent (Fig. 3-76) (Robinette, 1972).
3. *Screening.* Trees are useful for screening out undesirable views. When arranged in natural-looking clumps, they become objects of beauty in color for form and draw attention away from undesirable objects. They may also provide protection from summer or winter winds. Dense plantings of deciduous trees and perhaps some evergreen varieties are also effective barriers against harsh environmental elements such as cold winds and blowing dust. (See previous section on screens.) Every tree variety has a characteristic growth rate. Slow-growing trees usually have less than 18 inches of new growth each year. Medium-growing trees produce up to three feet of new shoots in a growing season. The fast-growing varieties, which produce more than three feet of growth a year, are the trees most often planted in residential landscapes because they produce quick shade and add value more rapidly. However, do not make the mistake of planting only fast growing varieties. Think of the environment's appearance in ten or fifteen years. The correct tree size to use in an environment is determined by the height and spread of the plant at maturity and the amount of space with which you have to work. Small trees are generally 30 feet or less in height at maturity and work best in small gardens and miniature landscape settings. They include most of the ornamental flowering trees and many of the "patio" varieties. Medium trees most often attain a height between 30 and 70 feet at maturity and look attractive in an urban landscape setting. Medium trees do not become too tall for inner-city gardens or for landscapes around single-story homes. Large trees reach a mature height of 70 feet or more. They should be planted only in large spaces, such as extensive parks, where their branches will not interfere with each other. The width of a tree varies with the individual species; this factor should be checked against its height before a selection is made (Fig. 3-82).

Figure 3-82
The correct tree size to use in an environment is determined by the height and spread at maturity.

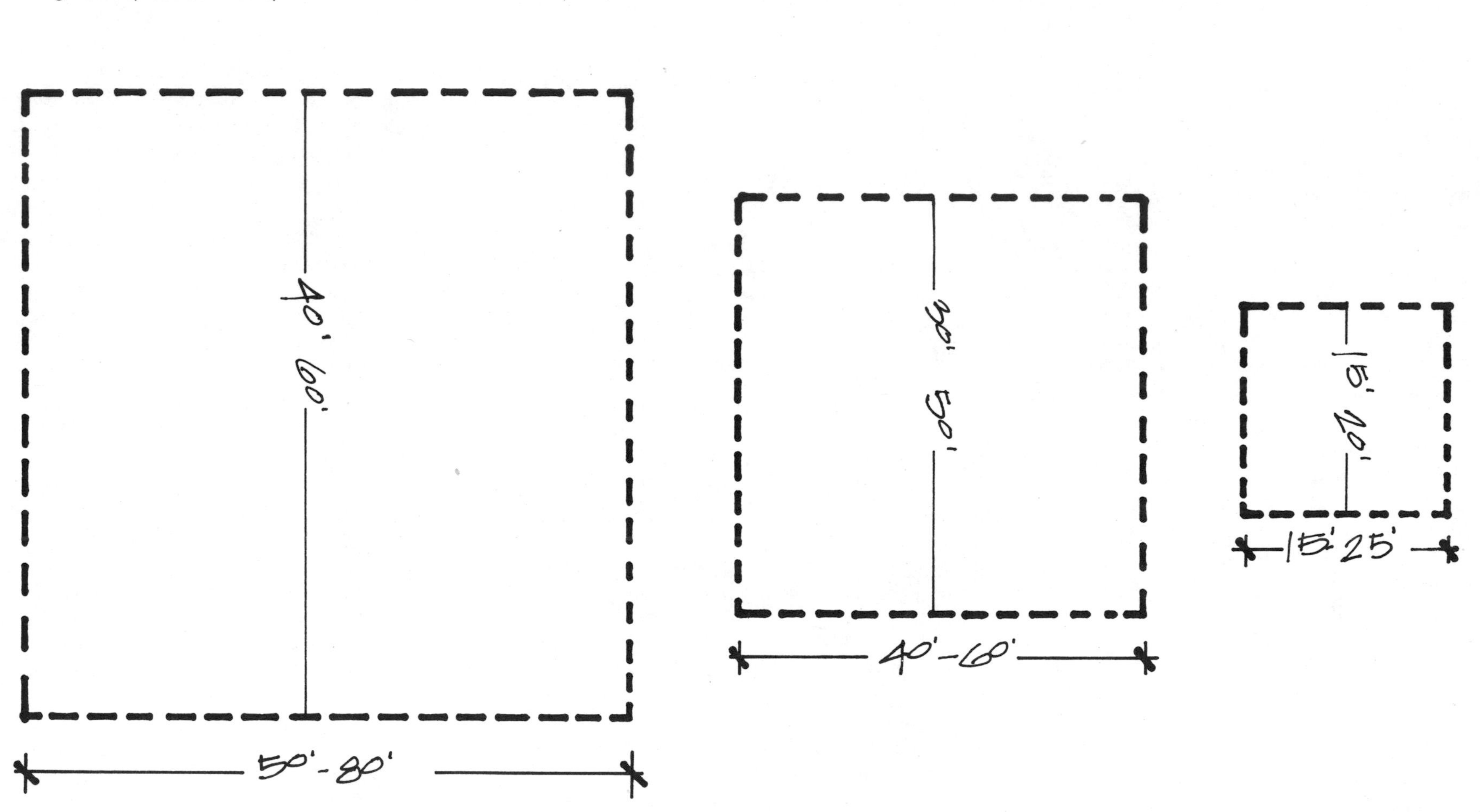

SHRUBS

Shrubs provide many of the same design functions as trees, but on a different spatial scale. For all practical purposes, the shrub's particular application lies in the space between the overhead canopy and the ground plant. A large shrub that can grow as high as an overhead plant should be considered a small tree. A small shrub growing horizontally along the ground should be used as a ground cover instead of as an individual plant. When selecting a shrub, consider these uses (Robinette, 1972):

1. *Enframement*. A shrub can frame a special view into or away from a landscape space. However, because of its modest size, it may require support from a landform or construction feature. Place the shrub on either side of the intended accent and frame it as if it were a picture (Fig. 3-76).
2. *Screening*. Large shrubs can screen undesirable views or provide a visual corridor into a landscape space. The object of the screen is to obstruct a view from one area into another. A small or medium shrub can also act as a screen if combined with a landform or construction feature (Fig. 3-47).
3. *Accent*. Shrubs are very often used as accents within a landscape space. This is one of the most demanding functions, so the species should be chosen and used with caution. Too many accents, or one that is too strong, will confuse the viewer and create disharmony in the composition.

GROUND COVERS

The term *ground cover* can be used to describe almost any plant in the landscape. However, it refers primarily to plants under 18 inches in height that tend to spread or creep, and that are used to hide unsightly areas of exposed ground.

The value of this plant feature can be easily measured in greatly reduced maintenance costs. With a mass of groundcover, less weeding will be required under trees and shrubs, erosion can be controlled along steep banks, and the loss of water from soil due to sun exposure can be halted (Fig. 3-83).

There are two functional classes of ground covers. The first is the lawn substitute, used to cover a large expanse of ground and give the general appearance of a lawn. It requires the same careful soil preparation, the same initial weeding requirements, and often the same winter hardiness as grass. Therefore little if any energy conservation can be found by using this type of ground cover. The second class is ornamental ground cover. It can decorate walks with borders, cover the ground where grass will not grow, and add beauty and accent to shrub masses.

A vine can be a ground cover or a cover for a mechanical structure. When combined with a trellis, decorative fence, or wire frame, this plant element can be used where space is limited or as a canopy, baffle, screen, or barrier.

Vines climb in very specific patterns, and each pattern should be understood before it is used in an environment. Vines climb in the following ways:

1. *Twining* is characterized by a vertical, twisting growth pattern as plants grasp small posts or other plants. Both vertical and top supports are needed. These types of vines tend to become top-heavy.
2. *Clinging* is a habit of growth that allows the plant to adhere to flat surfaces.
3. *Waving* is exhibited by a vine with younger, growing shoots that wrap through older branches.
4. *Leaning* is shown by a vine that grows against a structure or a tree trunk.A shrub with climbing shoots may also lean.

APPLICATION OF DESIGN ELEMENTS

When using any tree, shrub, ground cover, or vine, it is important to remember these elements of design.

FLOWER AND FOLIAGE COLORS

Flowering materials add interest to any planting design, and care should be taken in their selection. Use different flowering plants together to extend the blooming season and to maintain the visual effect of the total composition.

Foliage color is often considered when selecting a tree or a shrub. However, some ground cover and vine species are also brilliant in the spring and fall and should not be overlooked. (Do not expect all plants to produce bright red or gold colorations every autumn. The pigments that produce the hues and tints are dependent upon proper light and temperature combinations during the early autumn months.)

FORM

The shape of a plant at maturity should be considered before a selection is made. Rounded or broadly spreading trees provide the best shade. Shrubs with this shape also produce a more dramatic effect when allowed to grow without competition from other plants.

Oval-shaped trees are best arranged in groups if the desired effect is shade, because they produce a less abundant sunscreen than do the round forms. Pyramidal plants are narrowest at the top and cast a pointed shadow with only a small amount of shade. Columnar plants can provide a screen or fill in a narrow planting space. They often soften the lines of a building or home. Weeping or drooping forms provide dramatic accents in a design space and can act as a visual link between an overhead canopy and a ground plane.

LOCATION CONSIDERATIONS

Proper planning of each location will allow many years of trouble-free maintenance. Here are some situations that should be avoided whenever possible:

Figure 3-83
While maintenance costs may have been reduced here, the result is a substantial loss of aesthetic appeal.

1. Do not plant trees closer than four to five feet from drives or walks. As they grow to maturity, the root system may cause cracks and separations in the paving.
2. Do not plant trees or large shrubs under overhead wires. Utility companies have the right to prune the branches without the owner's permission (in most cases) and the results may not meet your design objectives.
3. Do not plant weak, fast-growing trees closer than 30 to 40 feet from a structure. These trees are easily damaged by winds and ice storms, and the branches may fall and cause damage.
4. Do not overplant. A few good specimens in a mass arrangement are better than a large number of overcrowded, single-species arrangements.
5. Do not plant trees or large shrubs closer than one to one-and-a-half times their spread from sewer, water, or septic lines.
6. Do not plant trees or large shrubs too close to windows or doors or directly in front of a structure. If you do, you may hide attractive architectural features (Fig. 3-84 to 3-90).

Figure 3-84
Allow plenty of room next to a parking lot for plants to grow and mature.

Figure 3-85
Do not allow large shrubs to protrude onto the walkway.

Figure 3-86
Even small shrubs can be a hazard when allowed to grow onto a walk.

Figure 3-87
A temporary traffic barrier may be needed until plants reach a more mature height.

Figure 3-89
A landscape timber provides a mowing strip between a lawn and a bed of mulch.

Figure 3-88
Gravel next to a plant pit provides a mulch.

Figure 3-90
A steel edge provides a mowing barrier.

Planting Suggestions

The planting techniques chosen determine the success or failure of the materials used in a design. A plant will not reach its full potential if placed incorrectly in the composition. Follow these general rules in order to reach optimum growing conditions:

1. Select a location where a plant has enough room to reach maturity. Crowding plants may cause excessive competition for light, soil nutrients, and growing space. When planting, use the measurements of the mature spread of plants to determine location.
2. Choose the time of planting carefully. Some deciduous trees are best planted while dormant. Most evergreen materials can be planted during any season as long as care is taken to maintain a soil ball around the root system.
3. Excavate a generous planting pit and add soil amendments as required by the geographic area. If the soil is too heavy or too sandy, it will benefit from a healthy addition of organic matter such as peat or humus (Fig. 3-91 and 3-92).
4. Plant as soon as the material is purchased from the nursery or collected from the field. Waiting too long may increase the "shock" a plant experiences when moved.
5. Trees more than two inches in caliper (diameter) should be supported with guy wires. This allows the growing position to be corrected as the soil around the root system settles (Fig. 3-93 to 3-96).

Figure 3-91
Plants should never
be planted without
adequate soil coverage.

Figure 3-92
Covering the root ball
will not prevent damage
to the plant.

Figure 3-93
Small stakes will help keep the plant upright as it settles after planting.

Figure 3-94
A single tree staking arrangement.

Figure 3-95
A double staking arrangement.

Figure 3-96
Do not allow wire to touch the trunk of the tree.

ENVIRONMENTAL INSULATION

One form of insulation that has been overlooked by many designers is that provided by plant materials. The plants that you choose for your environment can serve not only aesthetic and food-supplement purposes but also that of energy conservation.

Insulation is now recognized as an essential link in the chain of comprehensive energy conservation and an important factor in the establishment of a desirable living environment (Fig. 3-97 to 3-99).

As humans, we receive and emit heat. We absorb it either from a direct temperature source, from a reflected source, or by conduction (the transmission of heat from particle to particle). We radiate heat in much the same fashion. Our comfort is reached when there is a balance of heat emission and heat absorption.

Plant materials can act as a supplementary insulation resource supporting the attainment and maintenance of our comfort requirements. Plants can be the first line of defense in absorbing, reflecting, or filtering extreme temperatures, allowing cellulose or synthetic materials to perform at their highest efficiency.

The heat we receive in our day-to-day living begins some 90 million miles away on the surface of the sun. As this solar radiation begins its journey to the surface of the earth, it comes into contact with high-level clouds, causing some of it to be reflected back into space. Other rays strike small air particles and become diffused, while even more rays are absorbed by carbon dioxide and water vapor. The remaining radiation, approximately one-fifth of the initial amount, reaches us and affects the way we live.

Plants are the best first-line barriers against solar radiation. We have only to look at the natural organization of plants to support this claim. In hot tropical climates, where the sun can be oppressive, large and thick plants that provide shade to animals unadapted to living in the extreme heat predominate. In colder climates, plants shed their leaves in order to allow increased radiation to reach the earth's surface during the colder periods.

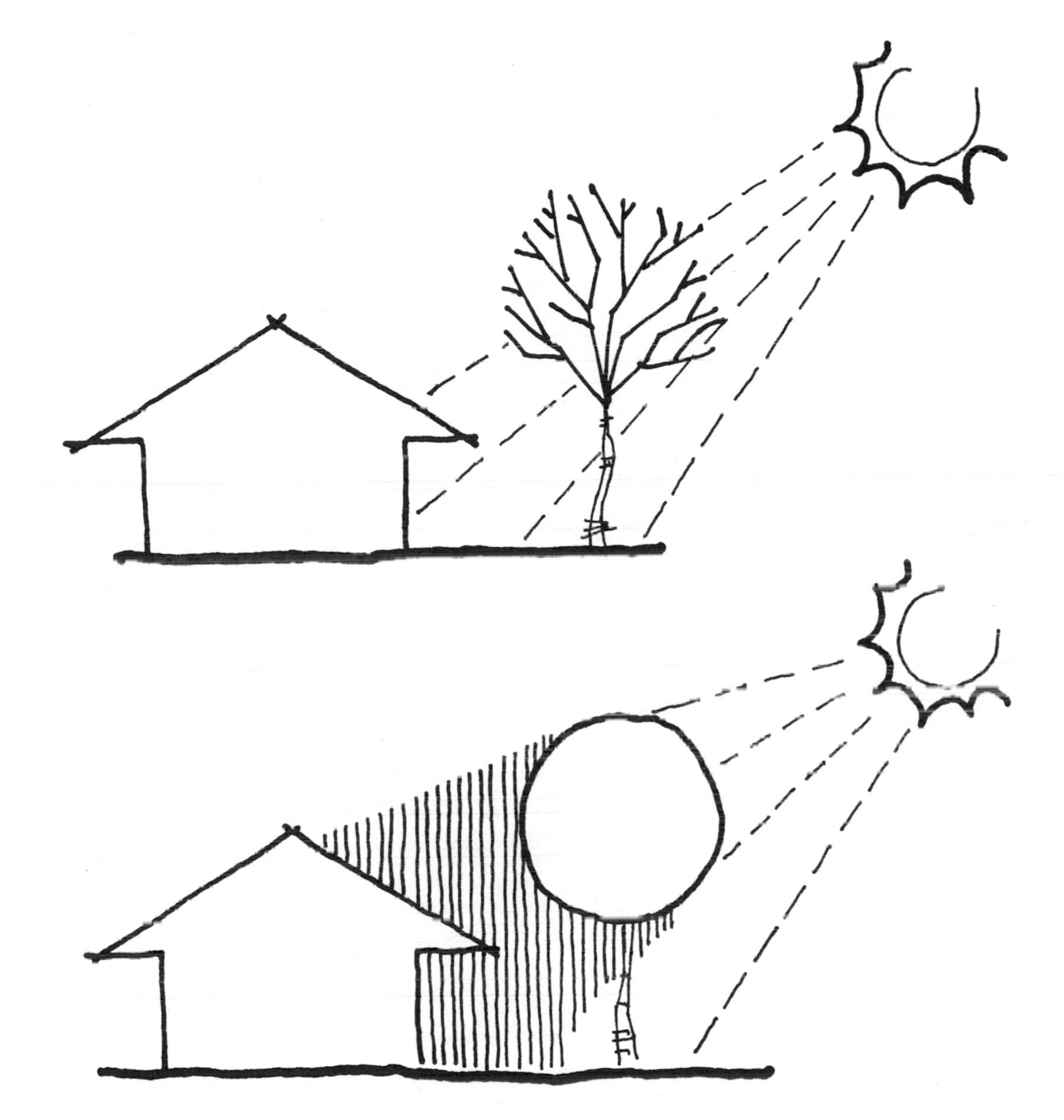

Figure 3-97
The fundamental insulation value of plants is felt in the cold of the winter and the heat of the summer.

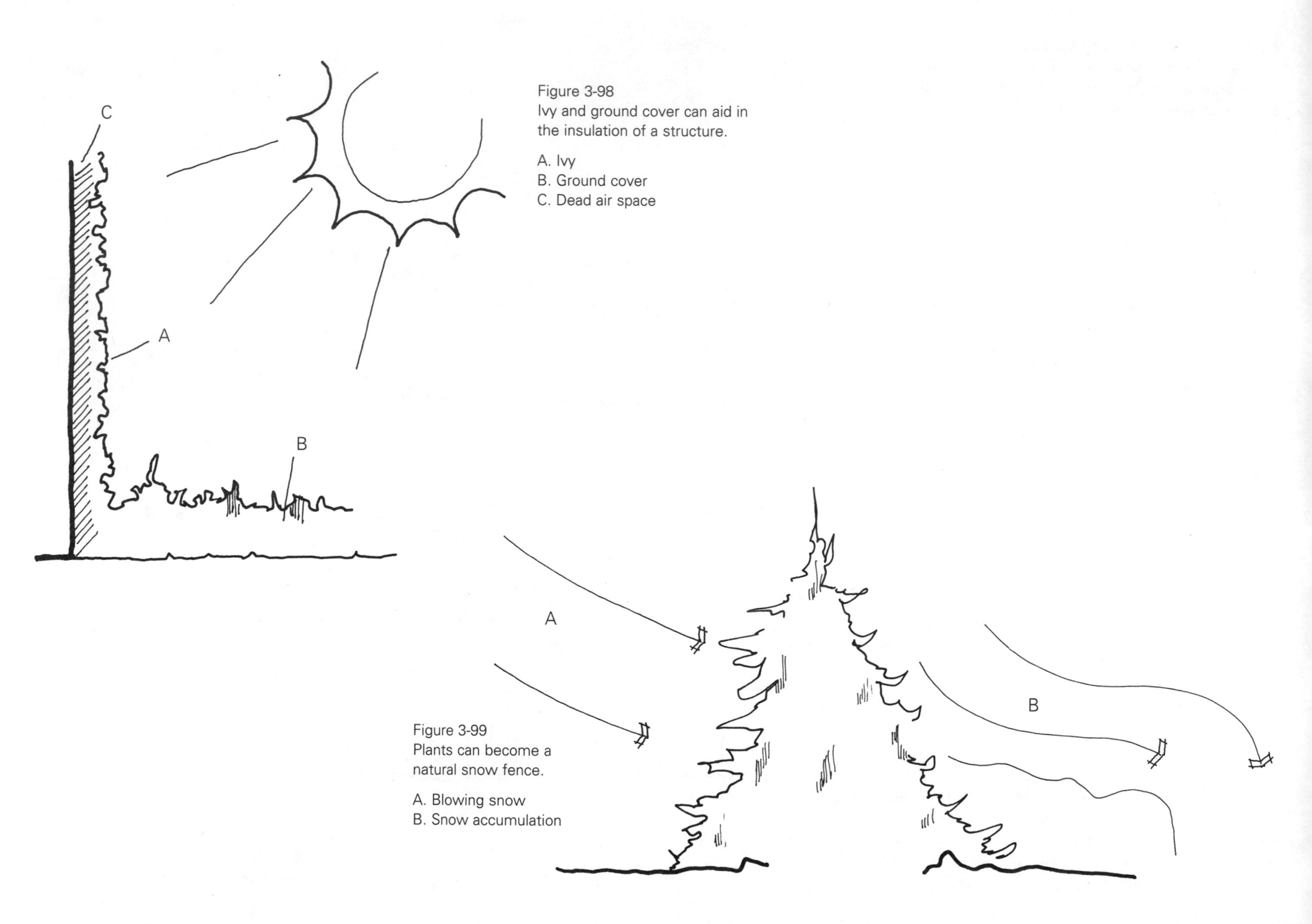

Figure 3-98
Ivy and ground cover can aid in the insulation of a structure.

A. Ivy
B. Ground cover
C. Dead air space

Figure 3-99
Plants can become a natural snow fence.

A. Blowing snow
B. Snow accumulation

Canopy elements can shade the environment, allowing for cooler air temperatures below. Shrubs and vines can diffuse and reflect solar radiation away from the space and turn it into a cooler area for human use. A groundplane can assist in absorbing solar radiation and will prevent additional heat from being reflected into the landscaped environment.

With each change in season, large volumes of air begin to move around the surface of the earth at different velocities. As this air moves, winds of different intensities and temperatures are created, which bring to us pleasant cooling breezes or undesirable, often violent, windstorms. Most of the scientific knowledge regarding plants and wind control was obtained during the 1930s from the shelterbelt programs established throughout the Great Plains. It is from this program that we have learned to use plants to help control living environments.

Landscape plant materials can assist the designer in controlling wind by obstructing its flow, guiding it in a specific direction, changing its direction, and reducing its momentum. Obstructing wind with large shrubs and trees reduces its speed and thus reduces the strain on other more conventional forms of insulation. If plants are combined with landforms or architectural elements, a very pleasing climate-controlling feature can be created.

Carefully placed shrub rows and small trees can guide a slow breeze through a porch, patio, or outdoor room. A solid mass of dense plantings can deflect a strong winter wind away from a large glass door, reducing its exposure to the cold. An open spacing of trees and shrubs can filter a strong wind, allowing a reduced-velocity breeze to reach a specific area for added comfort (Fig. 3-100 to 3-104).

Selecting the proper plant type is very important in controlling wind. Deciduous trees and shrubs are good for filtering cold winds in the winter but are relatively ineffective for obstructing, guiding, or deflecting. Evergreen trees, while useful in the cold winter, may block the more desirable air movements of the spring and summer.

Every designer understands that trees often protect individuals from rainfalls during a light or medium spring shower. As a matter of fact, plant canopies can prevent from 60 to 80 percent of the falling water from reaching the environment below. The structure of the canopy, however, is the main controlling element — not the size of the tree. The leaf arrangement and condition affects the canopy's structure. Evergreen or softwood trees have a leaf pattern that creates a greater number of sharp angles, which tend to trap water droplets. Large-leafed deciduous trees often only deflect the rain from its original direction.

Plants can also control sleet and snow by intercepting the crystals and directing the wind to alter the location of drifts. Sleet and snow usually stick to the surfaces of leaves, branches, or needles. This factor allows the designer more control of this cold element in the design. As wind velocity is slowed, ice particles are deposited near the plant and not toward other features of the space.

STREET PLANTINGS

A major factor in the improvement of urban neighborhoods and rural communities alike is the establishment of landscape development programs. Too often, however, the orientation is toward the planting of "street trees," and not toward the overall character of the planting environment.

The landscape designer needs to look beyond the use of tree canopies and consider the total relationship of the spaces to be developed. The first step in any planting program is to inventory the neighborhood or community and evaluate existing conditions. Categories should be developed according to the degree of existing vegetation:

1. Unwooded street: vegetation exists on 30 to 60 percent of the project area.
2. Semiwooded street: vegetation exists on more than 60 percent but less than 80 percent of the project area.
3. Wooded street: vegetation exists on more than 80 percent of the project area.

Plants in the right functional categories (based on growth habits) can then be applied to project needs (Fig. 3-104).

1. Overhead-zone materials are the major covering components; they have large, dense crowns of foliage and are used to provide greater visual impact into and within the project area.
2. Intermediate-zone materials are eye-level plantings of screens and baffles that define the spaces on either side of the street core. As an understory feature, they can also be used to accent large architectural site elements and to serve as specimen plantings.
3. Ground-zone materials are small shrubs and ground covers used to accent ground spaces and to identify and control pedestrian areas within the development.

WILDLIFE HABITATS

Animals, like people, may seek a landscaped environment for very special reasons. People often want the solitude of such a space to rest from the complications of the day. Animals, on the other hand, need from the space the three essentials for their survival: food, shelter, and protection from predators.

Birds and small mammals are the easiest to attract to a space because ornamental plant materials can be used for food, shelter, and protection. Food (and water) is found in the form of seeds, nuts, fruits, berries, and nectar, and even the insects that are attracted to these. Shelter from the elements and protection from predators can be provided by an individual plant, a plant mass, or a landform created to support a design.

You should use a more natural approach in designing the space if you wish the animals to stay for any length of time. Rotten trees or stumps can be left or added to enhance the overall character of the composition. Remember, however, to consider the carrying capacity of the site when attracting wildlife. Otherwise animals may overburden the designed environment.

SUPPORTING THE PLANTS IN A COMPOSITION

The general availability of landscape plants also plays a role in program developments. When ornamental vari-

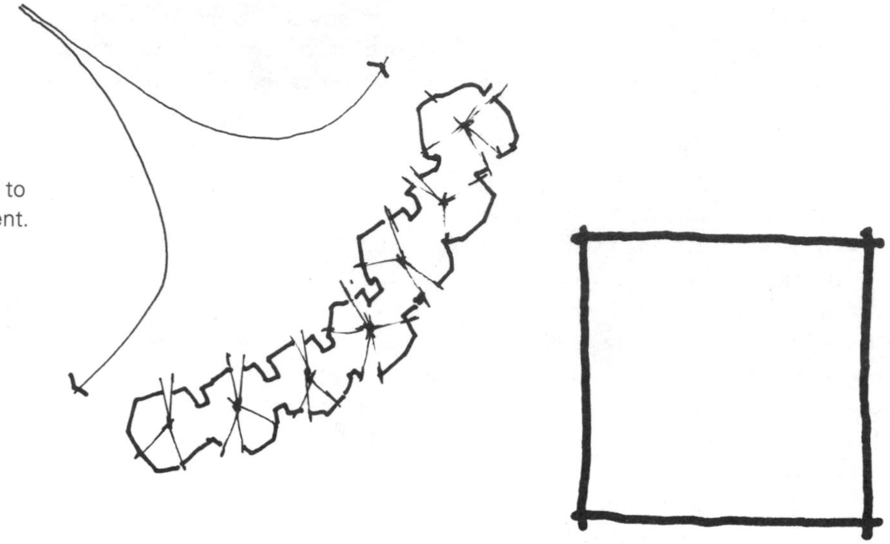

Figure 3-101
Plants can be used to deflect air movement.

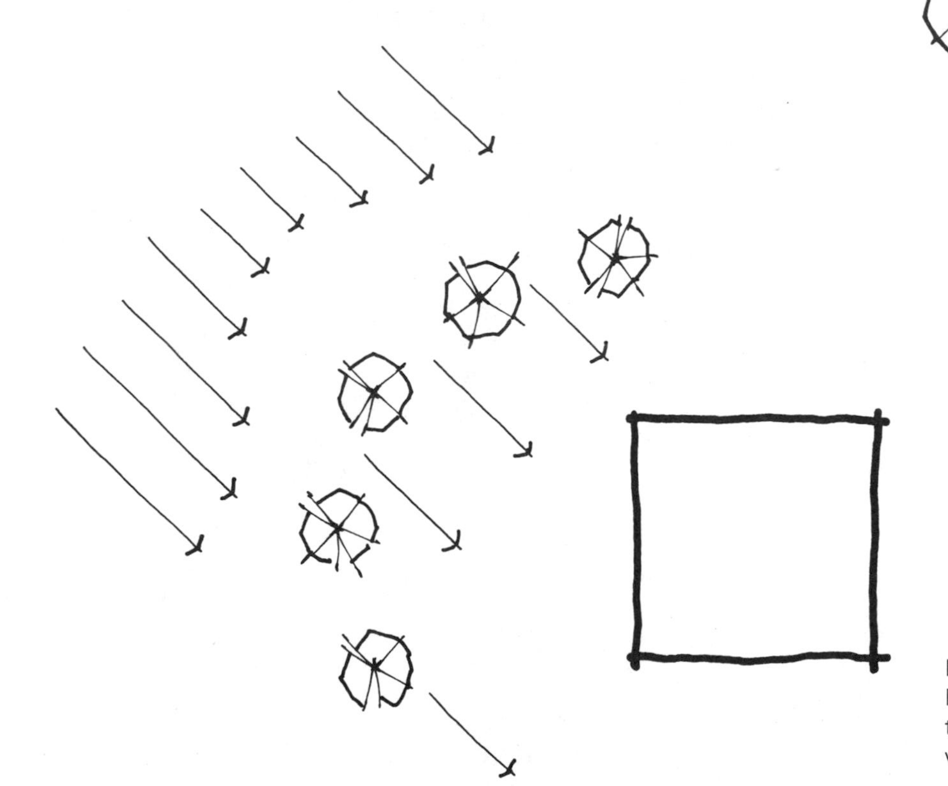

Figure 3-100
Plant screens can be used to reduce the amount of wind that reaches a space.

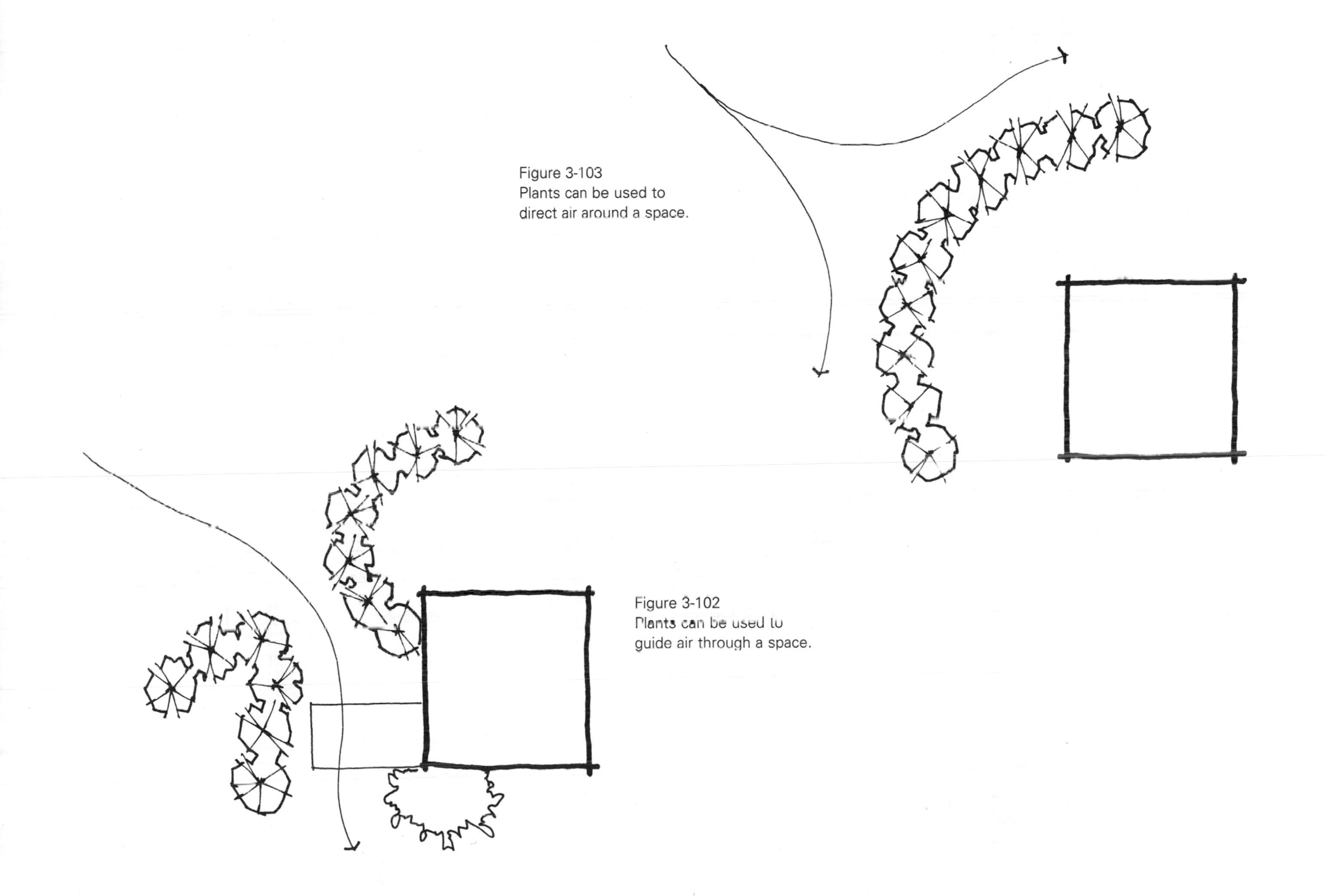

Figure 3-103
Plants can be used to direct air around a space.

Figure 3-102
Plants can be used to guide air through a space.

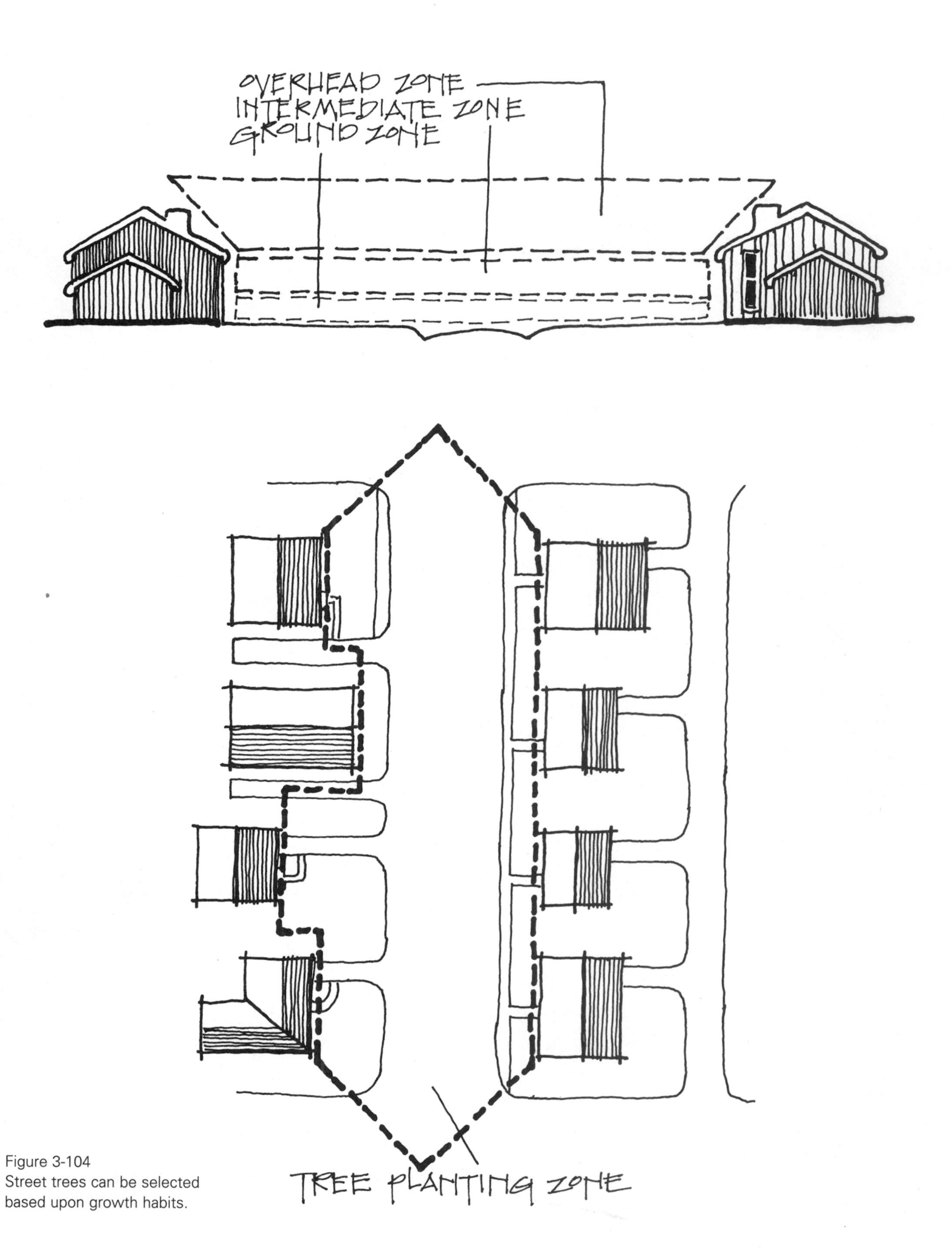

Figure 3-104
Street trees can be selected based upon growth habits.

eties are scarce because of diseases or nursery supply shortages, the planting designer may use several alternative materials to supplement the use of plants.

STONE

The most popular of these materials is stone. Appearing as either layered outcroppings or large accent boulders, this feature can add interest to a planting environment. The aesthetic qualities of stone are often quite striking, but its functional aspect is the key to successful application. Flat, rounded, or layered stones provide cool soil temperatures for the plants that need this habitat in order to survive. Other plants may not function as well with these stones. Some important factors when using stone are (Fig. 3-105 to 3-112):

1. Allow soil pockets to collect below and between the stones. This provides the shade needed to support plant growth.
2. Do not place stones perpendicular to the soil base. This does not allow the stones to protect the soil for plant growth.
3. Allow only a portion of a large stone to appear above ground; expose only the weathered part.
4. If stratified material is used, make sure that all stones follow the same random formation.
5. With a large collection of stone material, use large boulders for the central elements and support them with smaller ones around the edges of the composition.

WATER

Another popular alternative material is water. As a reflecting pool, a producer of soothing sounds, or a supplier of moisture for exotic plants, water can be an excellent support element for planting designs. It can be represented in large ponds, small pools, streams, or creeks and can be easily controlled for quality and quantity. A small pool or fountain can provide color or texture to support a transitional flow toward an accent feature. Water can also be combined with lights or moving objects.

Plants and water work well together in a design composition. Some plant varieties need only to be placed near water, while others — the aquatic plants — can be planted in water. Aquatic varieties can be classified as deep aquatics, marginal aquatics, or floating aquatics and can be used in an environment in the following manner (Fig. 3-113).

1. Deep aquatics usually require a depth of more than 10 inches to survive. The roots of these plants can be planted in the base soil or in containers resting on the bottom of the water feature. These plants are important for the production of oxygen in the water.
2. Marginal aquatics grow with their roots in shallow water and their crowns (stems, leaves, and flowers) above the waterline. They do not produce any measurable amounts of oxygen for the water.
3. Floating aquatics float on the surface with their roots exposed and free of any soil base. They reduce the amount of sunlight reaching the water below, thus reducing the amount of algae.

SCREENS AND FENCES

In an area where the need for functional space is critical, a landscape designer may choose a decorative screen or fence to support a planting composition. A screen is merely a freestanding visual barrier, while a fence functions as a physical barrier as well.

Construction materials for either feature can vary from wood to glass to brick; the choice for a given planting design should be determined by the available space. Screens and fences can be used independently from plants, in association with small shrubs or groundcovers, or as the framework for the support of vines or climbing ground covers.

BERMS

On the other hand, when space is relatively open and lacking in aesthetic character, the designer may choose to use modified landforms — or berms — to enhance the plantings. Berms are mounds of soil, used when visual niches or vistas are needed in the composition. This feature should not dominate the space but work with the plant materials to support the overall intent (Fig. 3-114 and 3-115).

PLANT CONTAINERS

Containers are a popular alternative to conventional planting techniques and can be useful for introducing annuals or exotic species into a composition. The container itself should not be the major concern of the planting designer. The plants in the container are more important, and regular design approaches should be used in working with these plants. This does not mean, however, that attractive containers should be avoided. Brick, clay, and decorative pots always add an attractive theme to any landscape setting.

DESIGNING THE NATURAL COMPOSITION

A natural composition should consist only of plant materials found in the immediate geographic region. If an alternate material is used, the final composition will fall within the ornamental classification.

The following principles may help in developing a natural landscape setting:

1. The final composition should lack formality and repetition of elements. The plants should be placed according to their environmental needs first — and then according to their design functions. No artificial or mechanical devices should be used to supplement growing conditions.
2. The design forms should follow the basic life forms as they are found naturally.
3. The composition should represent, as closely as possible, the successional stages in which the plant materials are found (Fig. 3-116).
4. If plants die, they should not be removed. They should be allowed to decompose according to natural conditions.

Figure 3-106
Boulders can blend with flowering groundcovers.

Figure 3-105
A small boulder can be used to soften a planting edge.

Figure 3-107
A boulder can blend
with a shrub planting.

Figure 3-108
Use a boulder to accent the
base of a small evergreen.

Figure 3-109
A boulder can be used on a lawn edge.

Figure 3-110
A larger boulder can be used in place of a shrub.

Figure 3-111
Small shrubs can
accent larger boulders.

Figure 3-112
Boulders can be subtle accents
in a sea of ground cover.

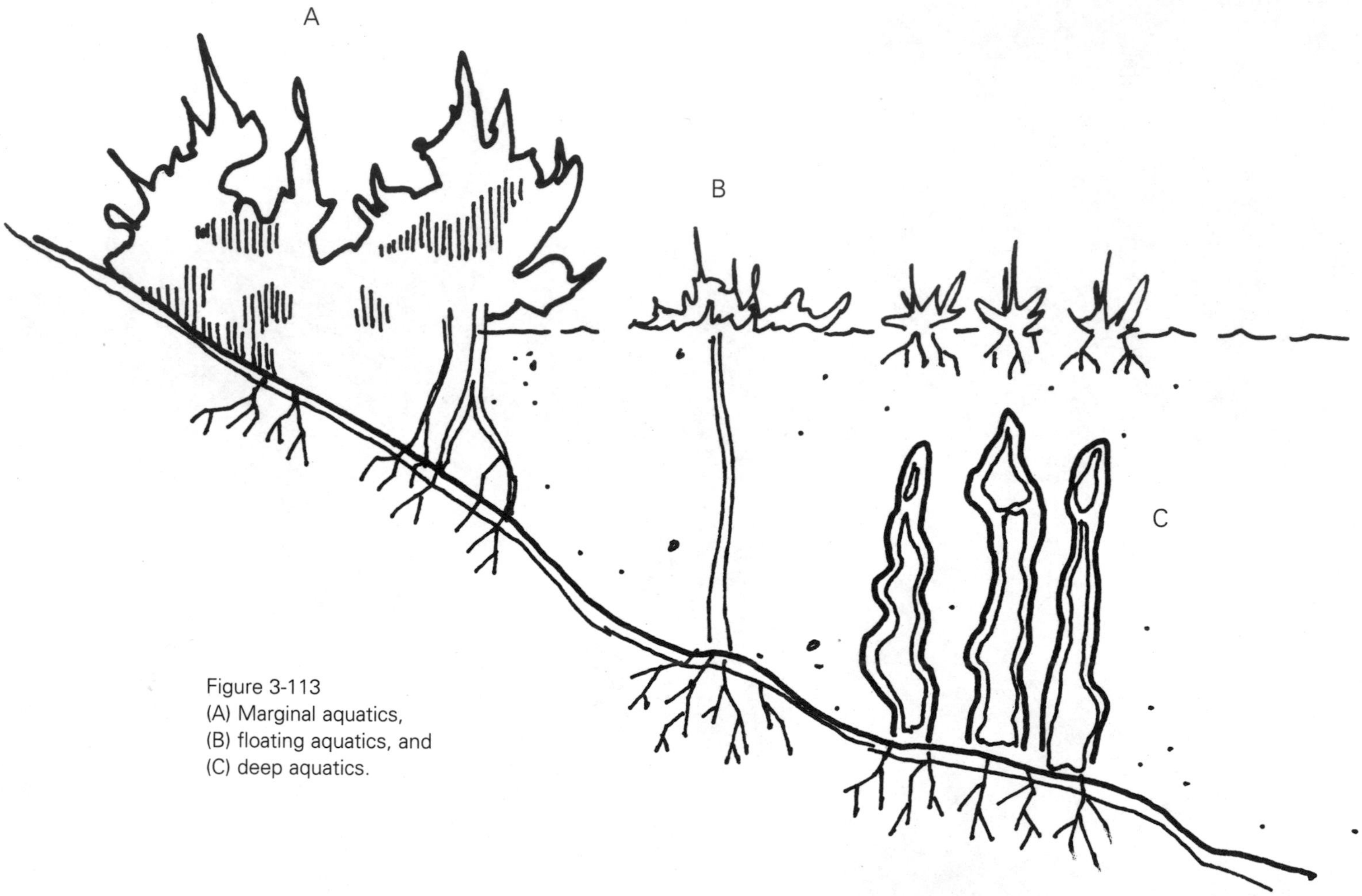

Figure 3-113
(A) Marginal aquatics,
(B) floating aquatics, and
(C) deep aquatics.

Figure 3-114
A berm with just a few trees has a minimal affect.

Figure 3-115
Adding tree masses to this large berm enhances its screening function.

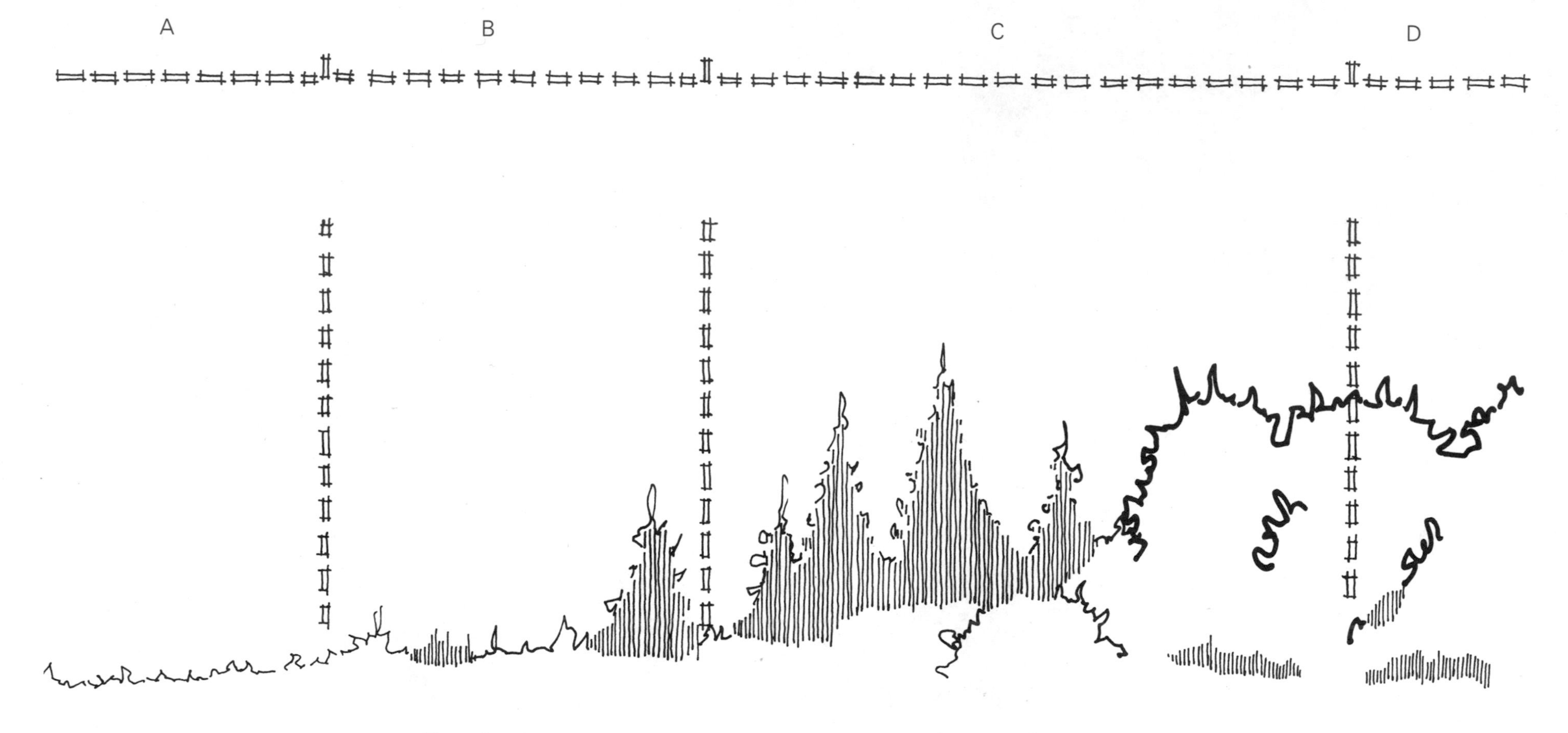

Figure 3-116
The successional stage of plant growth.

A. Annual weeds, 1–5 years for development.
B. Perennial grass, shrubs and young white pine, 3–20 years for development.
C. Old white pine with young hardwoods underneath, 75–150 years for development.
D. Self-replacing birch-beech-maple forest, 200+ years for development.

CHAPTER 4

PLANTING PLAN GRAPHICS

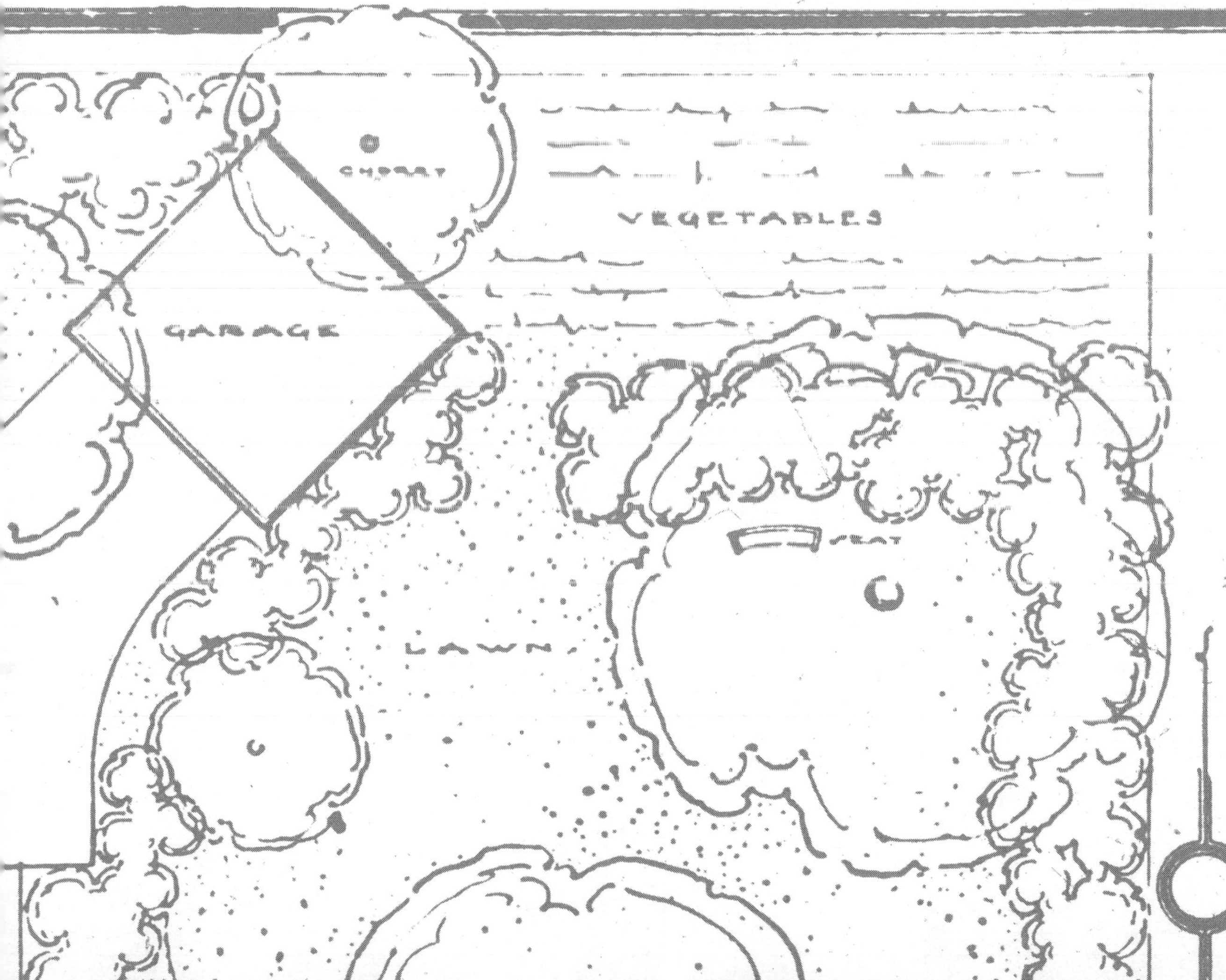

The planting plan serves as the basic communication tool for the implementation of the planting design and is the primary link between the client, the designer, and the contractor.

The client needs the plan to obtain a clear understanding of the activities that will take place on the site. The planting plan also serves as an instrument for establishing a development budget for the client and the contractor.

The landscape contractor uses the plan to install plant materials according to the designer's specification. The plan should thus include formal planting specifications and construction and planting details. All information neeeded to implement the plan in a satisfactory manner should be placed on the plan, and one should not depend on any verbal explanations to the contractor. The landscape contractor also uses a planting plan as a basis for price setting, labor determinations, tool requirements, and the acquisition of plant materials.

Planting plans may also be used to contract for plant materials from nurseries in advance of need and construction. Since many unique plant types are becoming more difficult to find, this use should be of primary importance.

THE COMPONENTS OF THE PLANTING PLAN

The sheet layout for planting plans should be well composed. The plan contains a tremendous amount of information, and the arrangement of all the plan components should be taken into careful consideration. The following outline shows the components that need to be included on the plan. It should be noted, however, that this list will vary according to the size of the project and the scale of the drawing. In order to obtain a manageable scale on large projects, more than one drawing may be necessary. However, only one plant schedule should be necessary for each project.

- A. Scale, both written and graphic (Fig. 4-1)
- B. North arrow (Fig. 4-2)
- C. Existing plant materials
- D. Plants to be removed or relocated
- E. Structures, overhangs, paving (both existing and proposed)
- F. Topography where applicable
- G. Details where needed (a separate sheet is usually required)
- H. Small orientation map
- I. Title block
  - 1. Name of project
  - 2. Address of project
  - 3. Landscape architect
    - A. Name
    - B. Address of firm
    - C. Registration seal

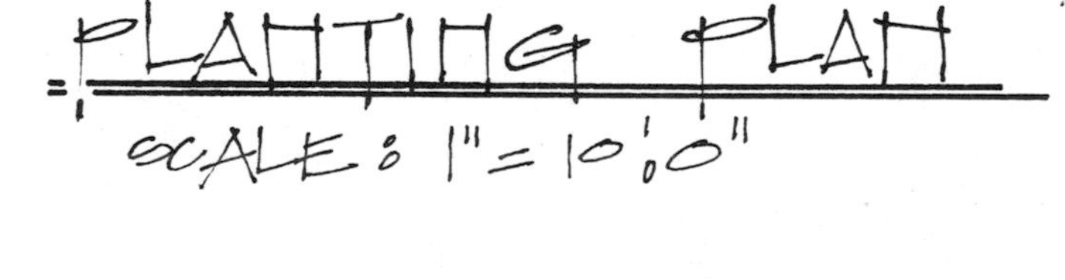

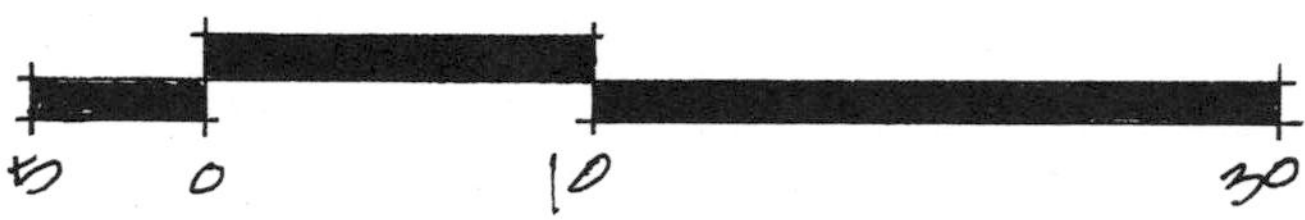

Figure 4-1
Plan Scale
All planting plans should have a designated scale in both written and graphic forms. The scale bar will help those reading the work in the event the plan is reduced or converted to an electronic format.

Figure 4-2
Graphic north arrows determine project orientation.

4. Name or initials of drafter
5. Date
6. Page number

J. Plant schedule (Fig. 4-3)

1. Item number (or symbol if used)
2. Number of plants
   - A. On location
   - B. Totals
3. Plant name
   - A. Common name
   - B. Botanical name
   - C. Variety name
4. Size and condition of plant
   - A. Size
     - (1) Container
     - (2) Height of plant
     - (3) Caliper
   - B. Condition
     - (1) Size of container
     - (2) Balled and burlapped (B&B)
     - (3) Bare root (B.R.)
5. Spacing for shrubs and ground covers
6. Notes when required, such as "multitrunk" or "espalier"
7. Plant divisions (by trees, shrubs, and ground covers)
8. Cost estimate (or space for contractor/ bidder to supply cost figures)

K. Turf areas (on both plan and plant schedule; if turf is existing, it should appear only on the plan as existing)

Figure 4-3
A plant schedule indicates the quantity, name, size, and condition of each plant at the time of installation.

QUANT.	NAME	SIZE/COND.
TREES		
4	LIVE OAK / QUERCUS VIRGINIANA	2" CAL./BB
2	RED BUD / CERCIS CANADENSIS	1" CAL./BB
6	WHITE PINE / PINUS STROBUS	2" CAL./BB
SHRUBS & GROUNDCOVERS		
140	VINCA / VINCA MINOR	2¼" PP
14	ROCK COTONEASTER / COTONEASTER MICROPHYLLA	2 GAL.
22	BARBERRY / BERBERIS THUNBERGII	5 GAL.

BASIC GRAPHIC TECHNIQUES

The planting plan is essentially a construction document. It communicates specific planting requirements for the materials chosen for a landscaped environment. With this in mind, the planting designer should prepare the final plan to direct the installation of the materials—possibly by someone other than a member of the design team.

The following graphic techniques are the most commonly used for the preparation of a planting plan:

I. Symbolic (Fig. 4-4)

A. Characteristics

1. Plants are keyed
2. A graphic key is linked to a symbol on the plant list
3. Symbols are placed upon a general site plan with no rendering

B. Advantages

1. Easy to place on drawing
2. Gives accurate location of plants
3. Used primarily by general contractors and engineers
4. Can be used in highly complicated plans
5. Takes very little time to produce

C. Disadvantages

1. Does not represent plant masses
2. Does not give the client a clear picture of actual plantings
3. Difficult to find symbols for all plants (for example, four sizes of one plant type)
4. Does not represent plant size on sheet

Figure 4-4
The Symbolic Graphic Technique

II. Semisymbolic (Fig. 4-5)

D. Characteristics

1. Shows size relationship of plants
2. Plants are keyed
3. Key is linked to a plant list
4. No rendering

E. Advantages

1. Easy to place on drawings
2. Gives exact location of plants
3. Used primarily by landscape contractors
4. More easily understood by client
5. Takes very little time to produce

F. Disadvantages

1. Inconvenient to link symbols to plant list
2. Difficult to find symbols for all plants
3. Finished product is not always clear

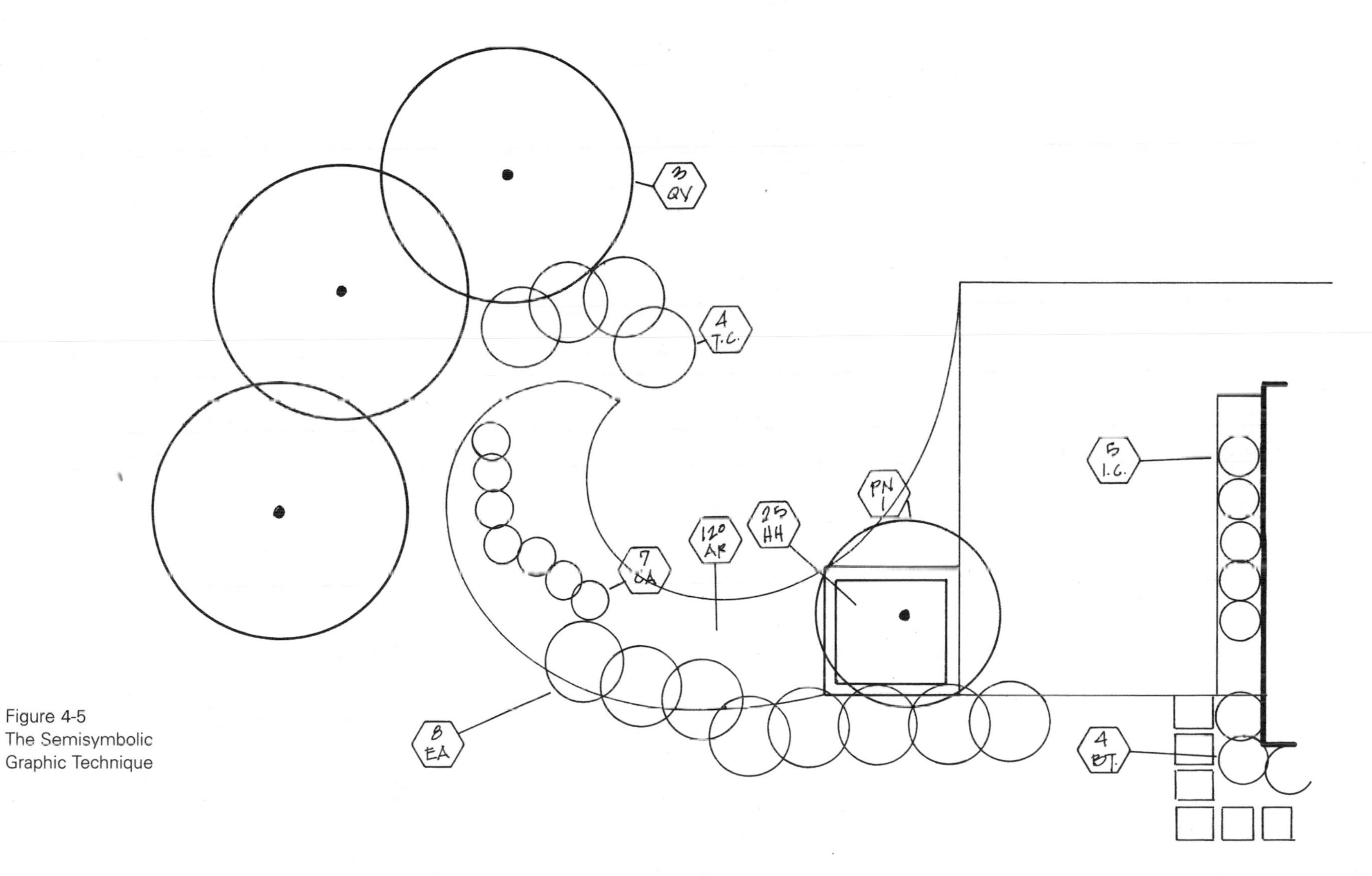

Figure 4-5
The Semisymbolic
Graphic Technique

III. Symbolic representational (Fig. 4-6)

G. Characteristics

1. Plants have representational form
2. Rendering is common
3. Name of plant is used
4. Plants are not keyed

H. Advantages

1. Plants' forms and shapes are more easily understood by client
2. Gives fairly accurate location of plants
3. Good for client presentations
4. Takes moderate amount of time for completion

I. Disadvantages

1. Plan can get too busy for complicated arrangements

To illustrate specific planting requirements, a designer may need concept sketches to support the communication effort. Examples of sketches used primarily to support the planting plan are show in figures 4-7 to 4-65.

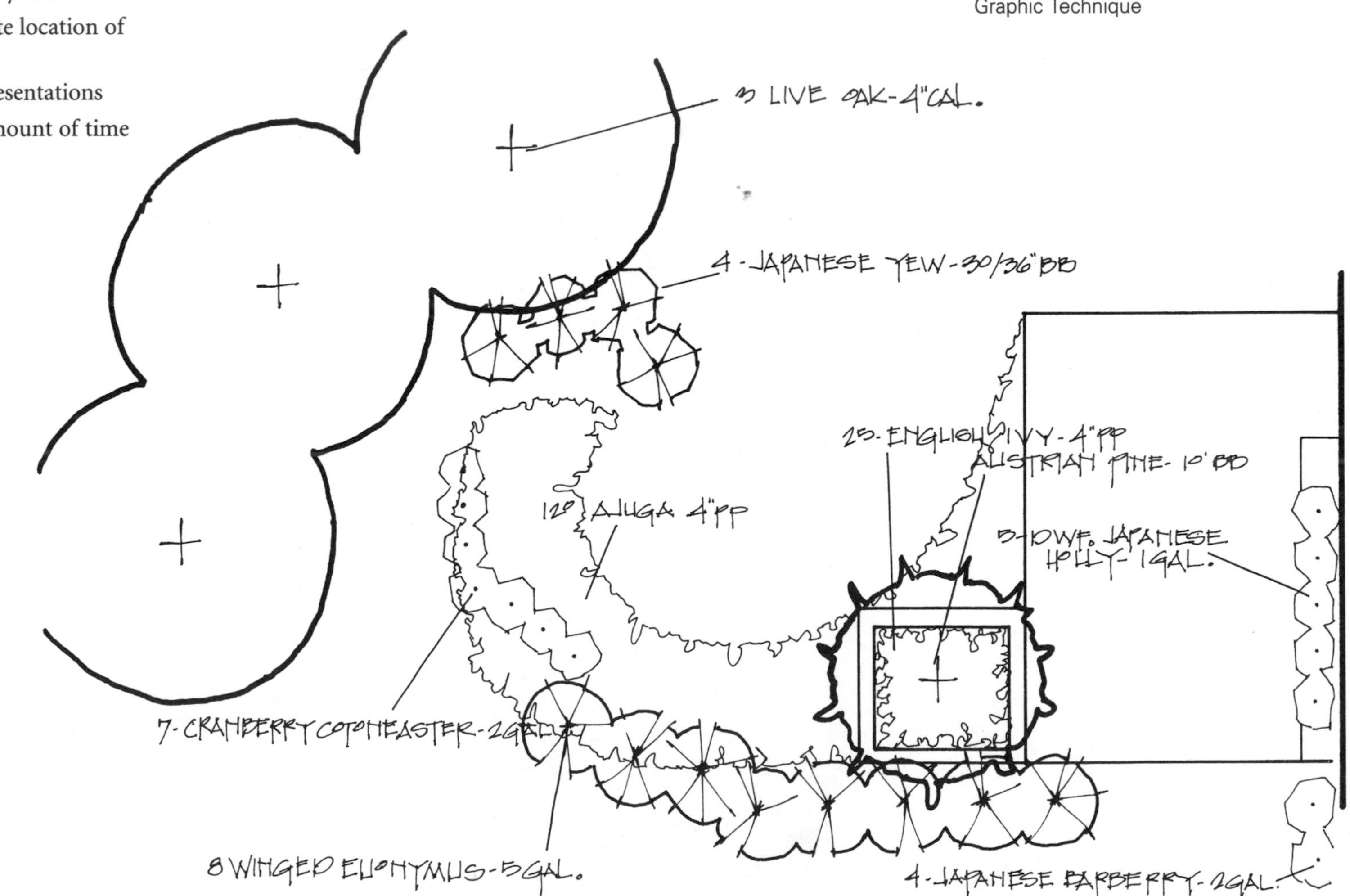

Figure 4-6
The Symbolic-Representational Graphic Technique

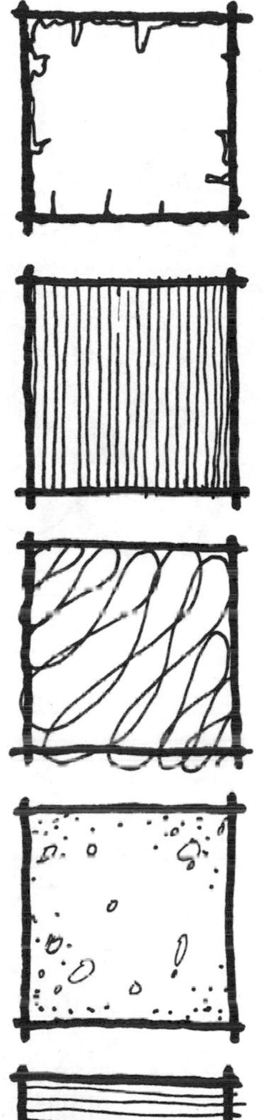

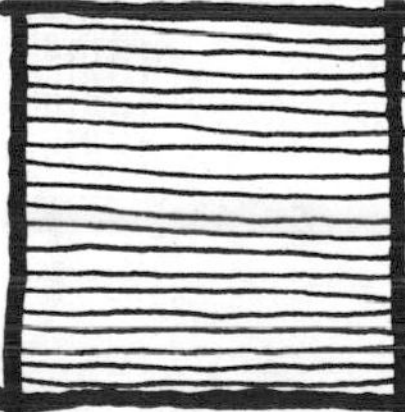

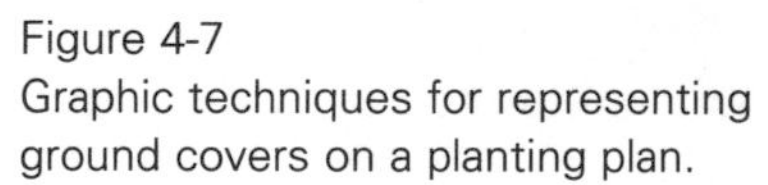

Figure 4-7
Graphic techniques for representing ground covers on a planting plan.

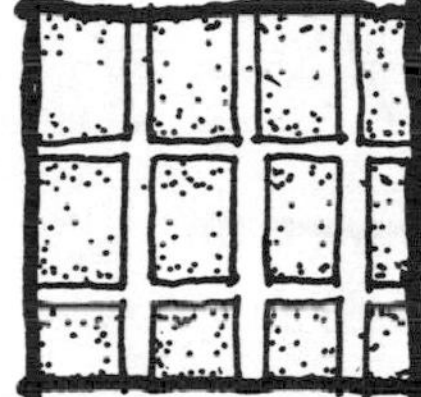

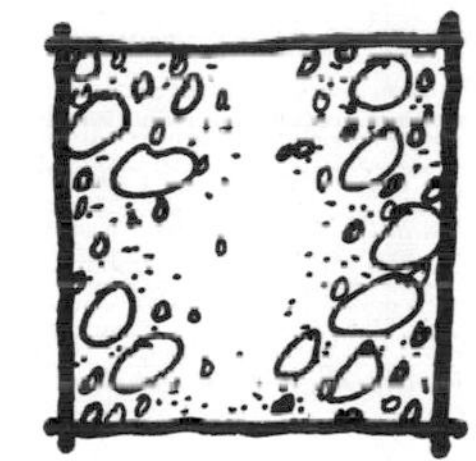

Figure 4-8
Graphic techniques for representing stones and rocks on a planting plan.

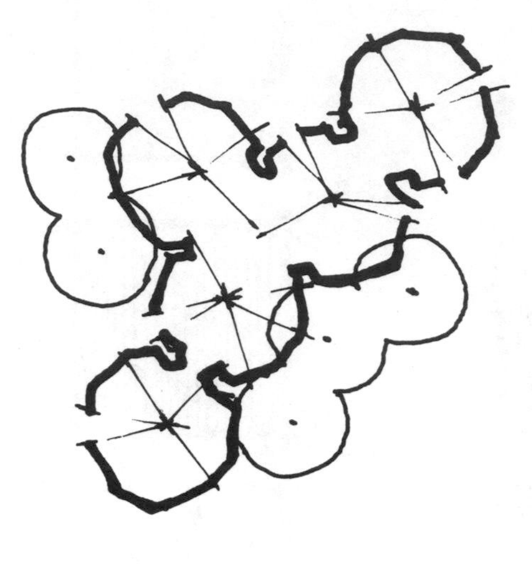

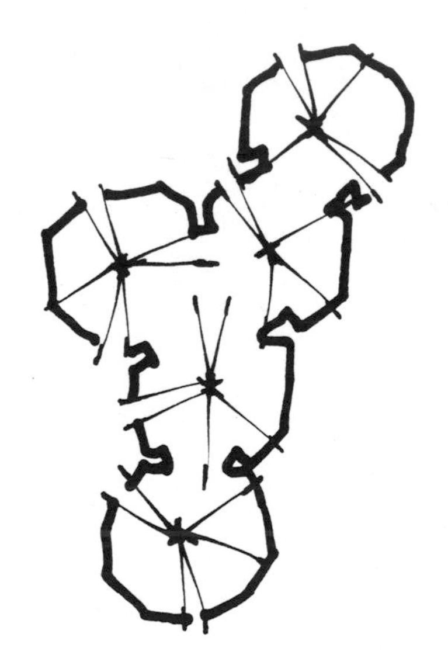

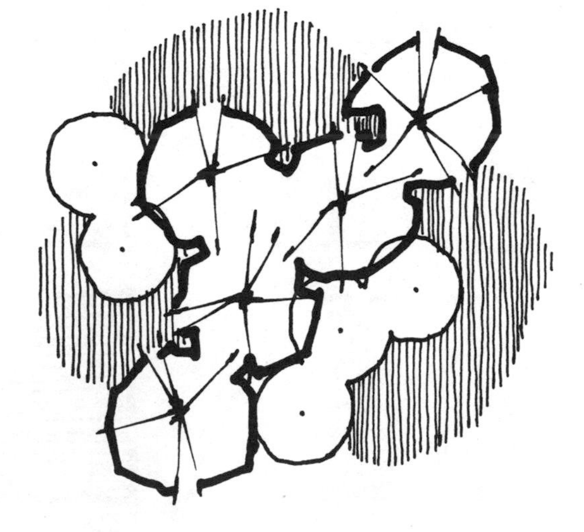

Figures 4-9 to 4-16
Graphic techniques for representing trees and shrubs on a planting plan.

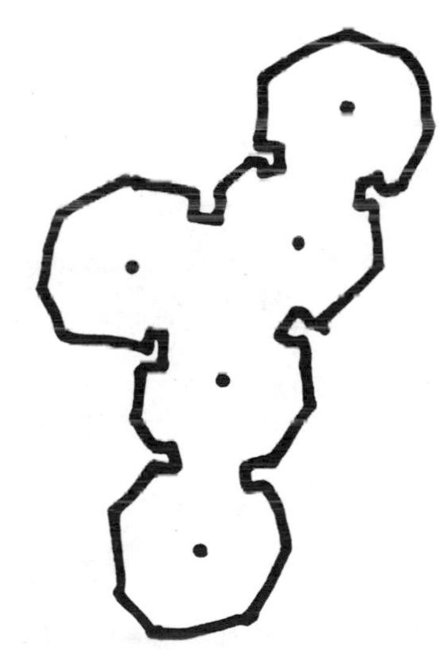

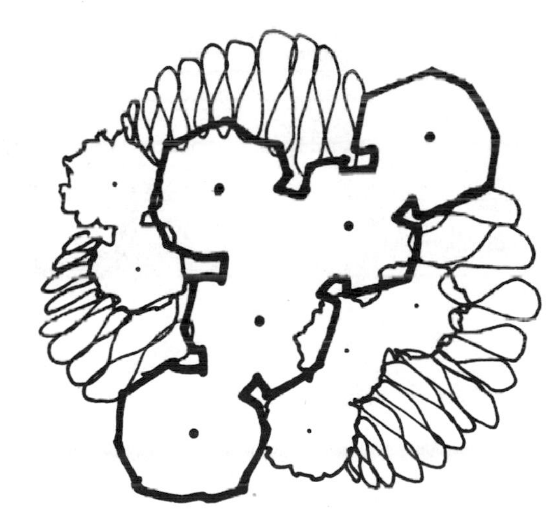

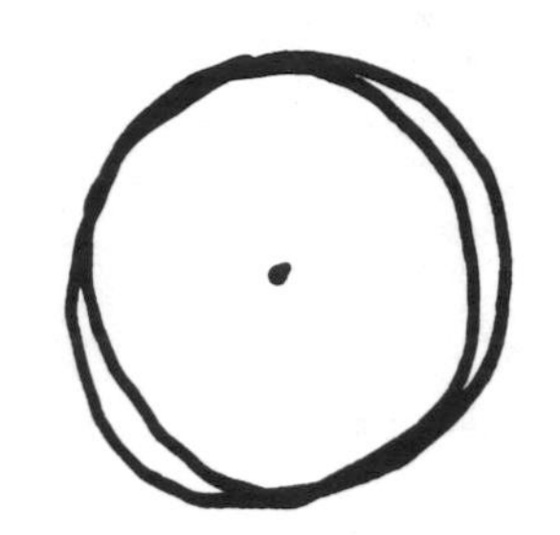

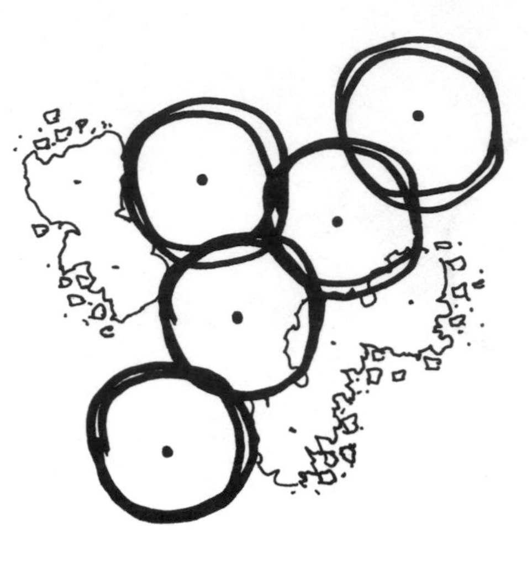

Figures 4-17 to 4-24
Graphic techniques for representing trees and shrubs on a planting plan.

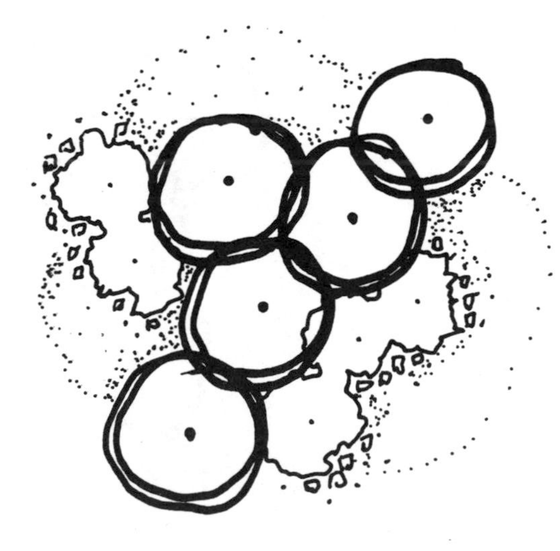

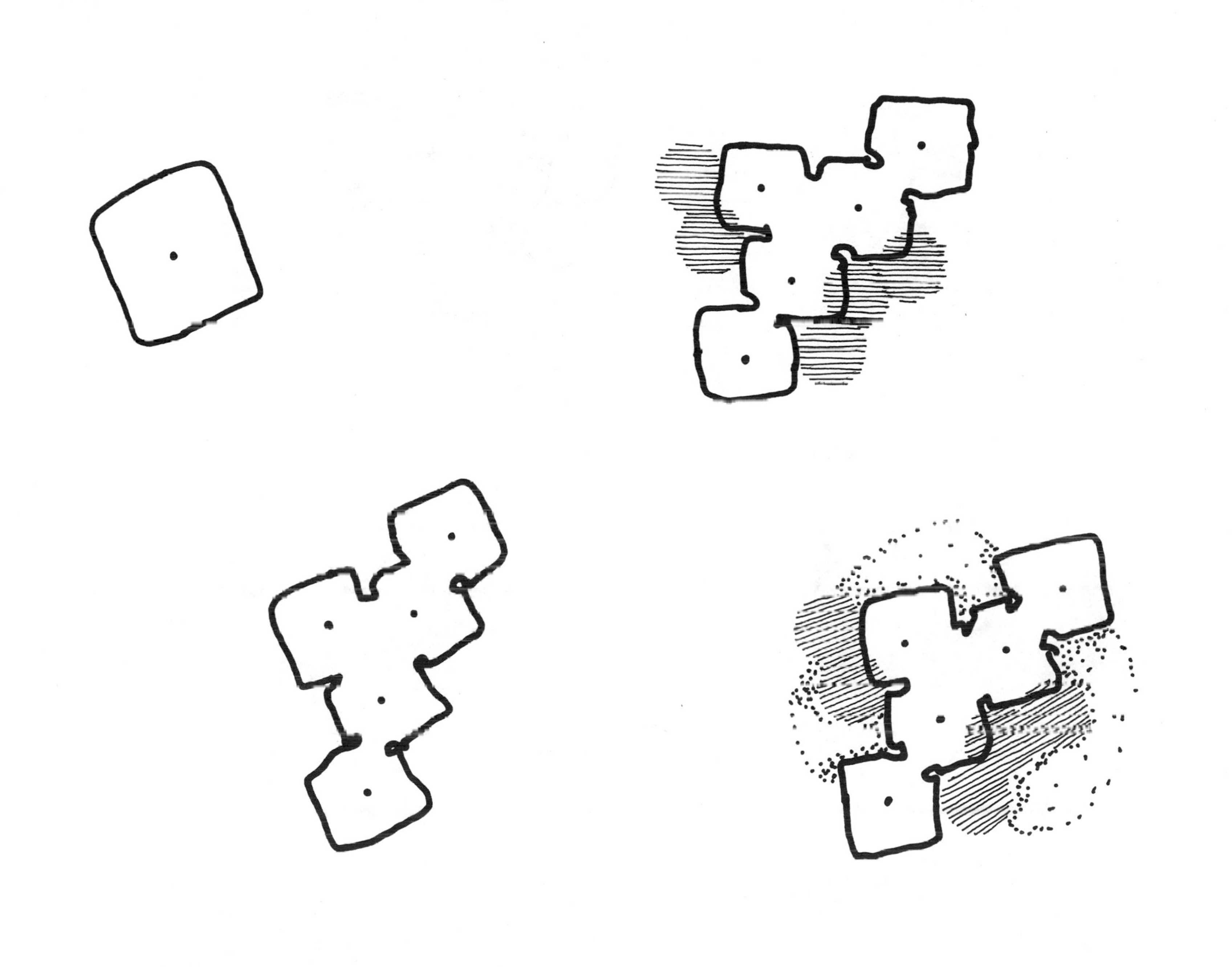

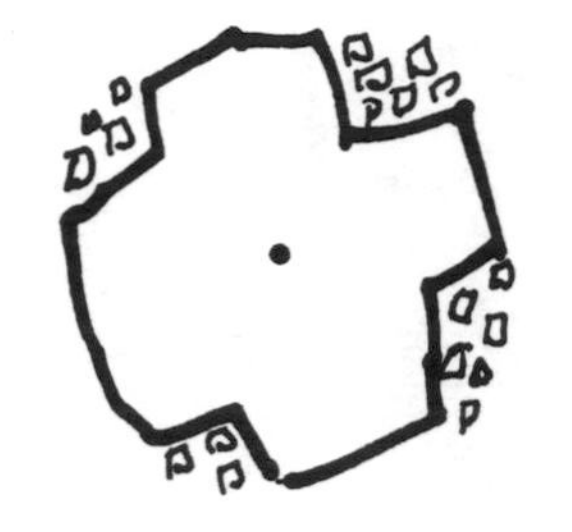

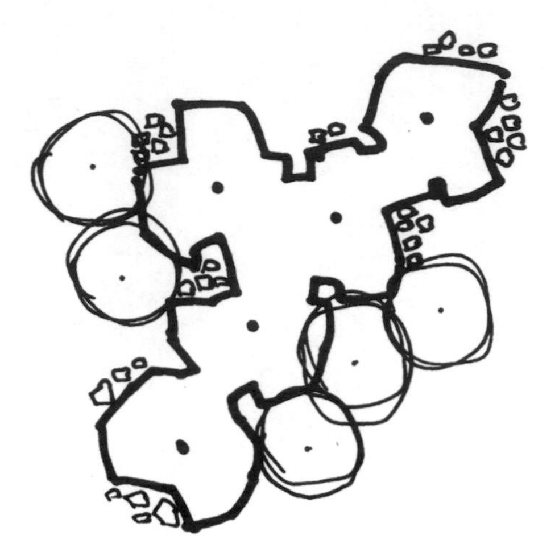

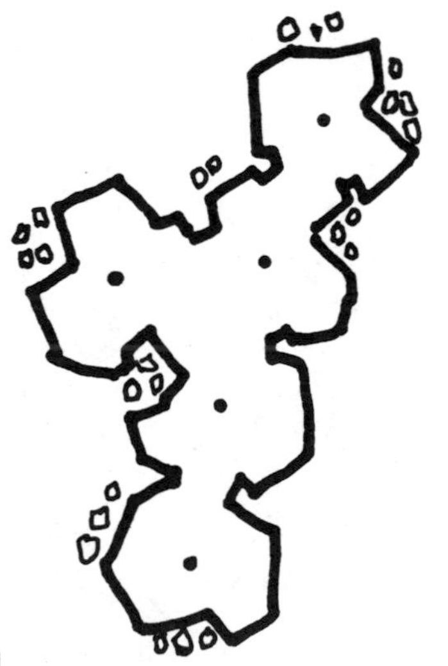

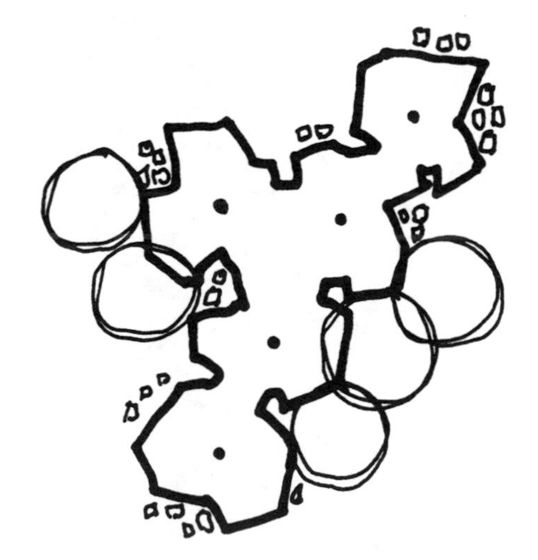

Figures 4-25 to 4-32
Graphic techniques for representing trees and shrubs on a planting plan.

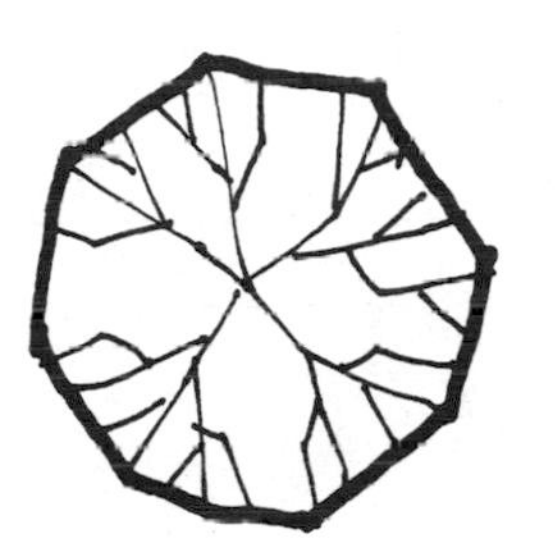

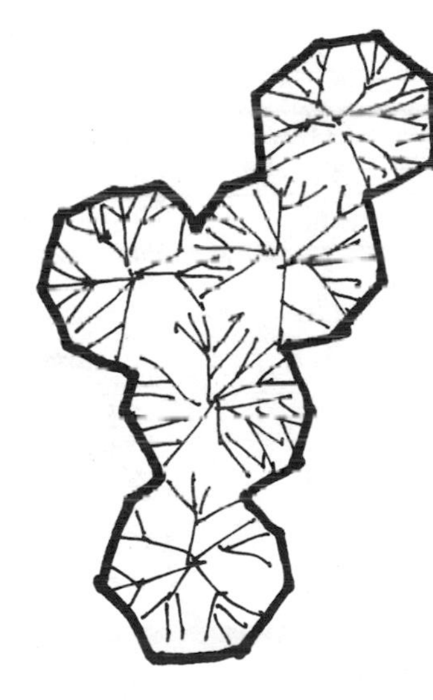

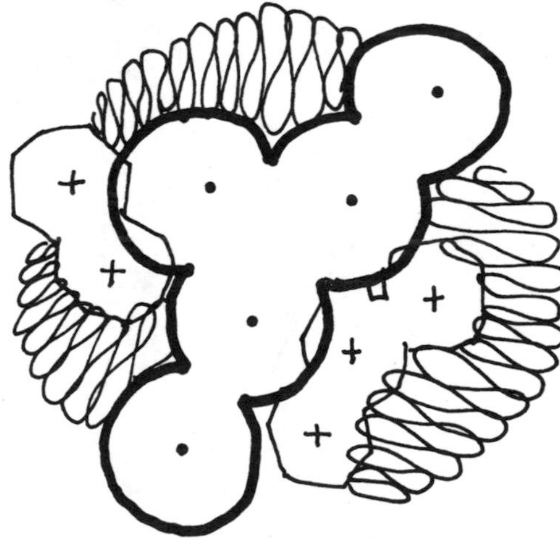

Figures 4-33 to 4-40
Graphic techniques for representing trees and shrubs on a planting plan.

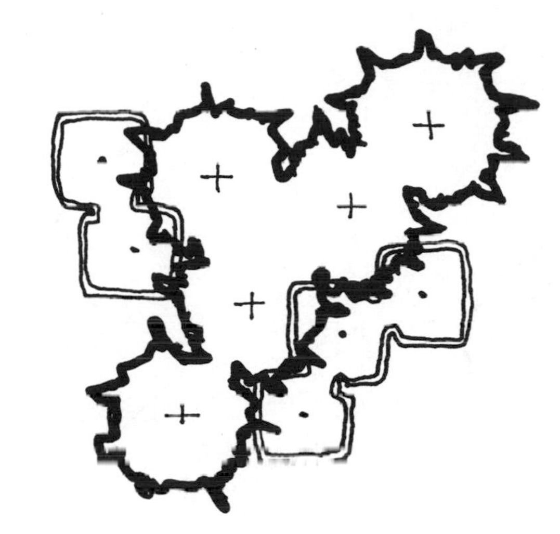

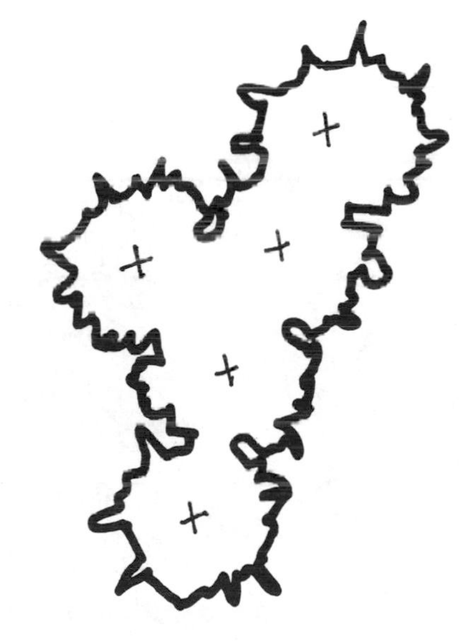

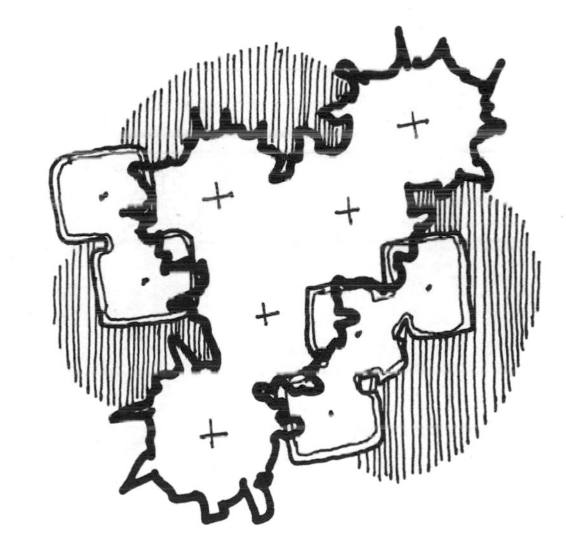

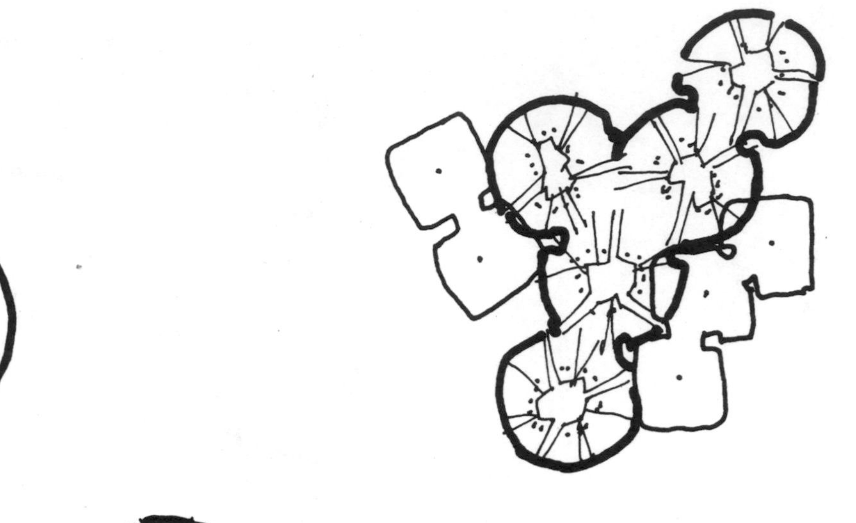

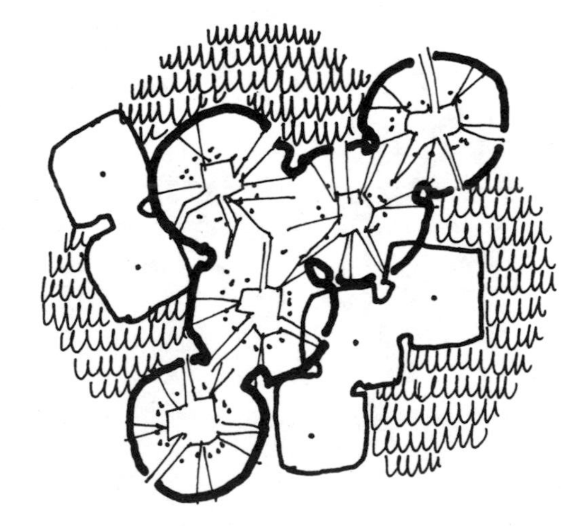

Figures 4-41 to 4-48
Graphic techniques for representing trees and shrubs on a planting plan.

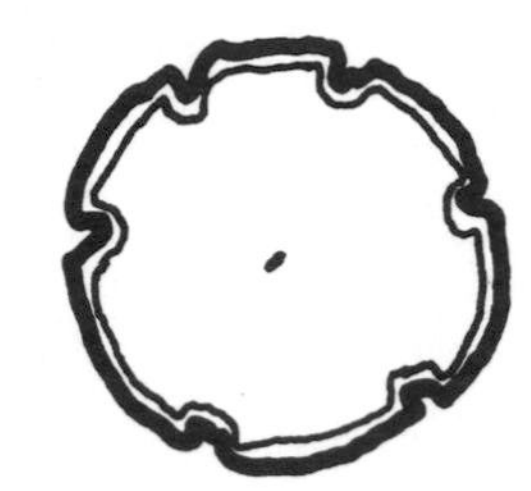

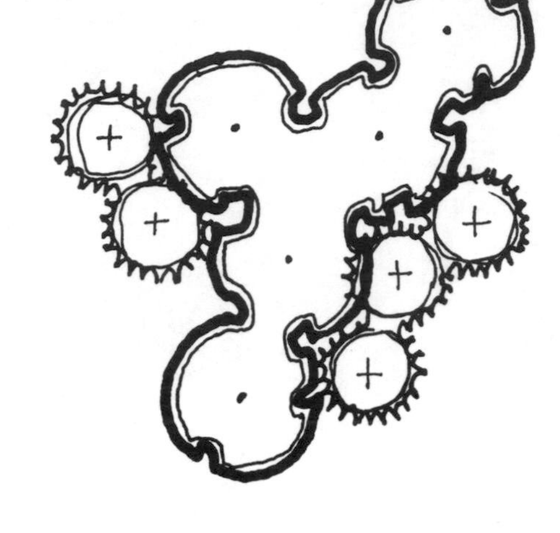

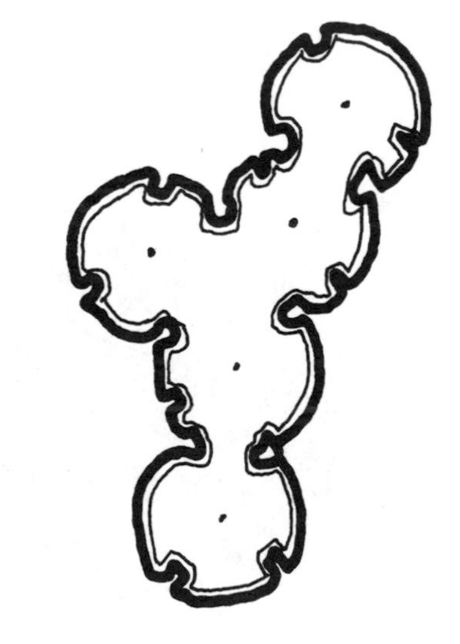

Figures 4-49 to 4-52
Graphic techniques for representing trees and shrubs on a planting plan.

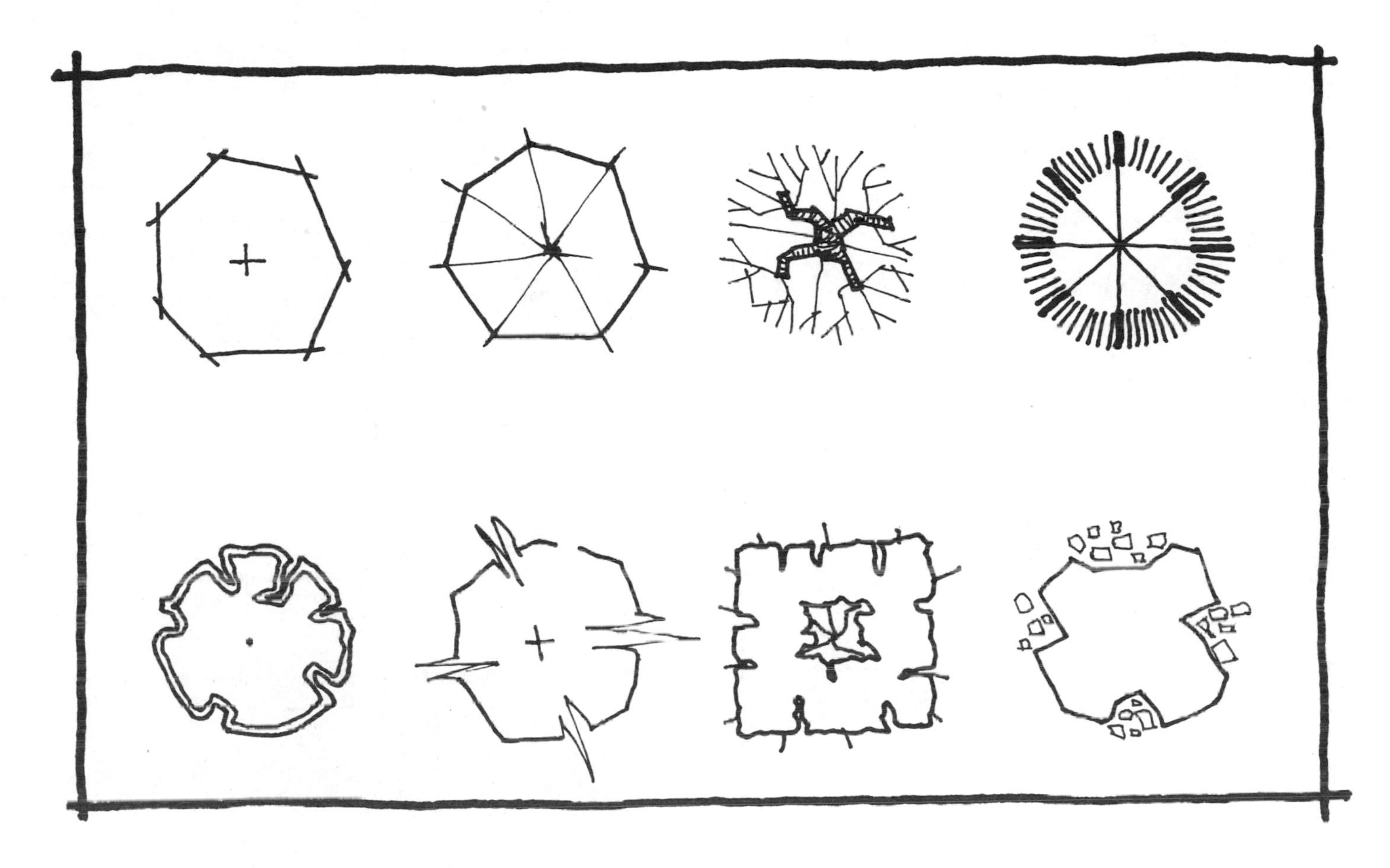

Figure 4-53
For special presentations, these graphic techniques may be effective.

Figure 4-54
An overhead canopy representation
for a public park.

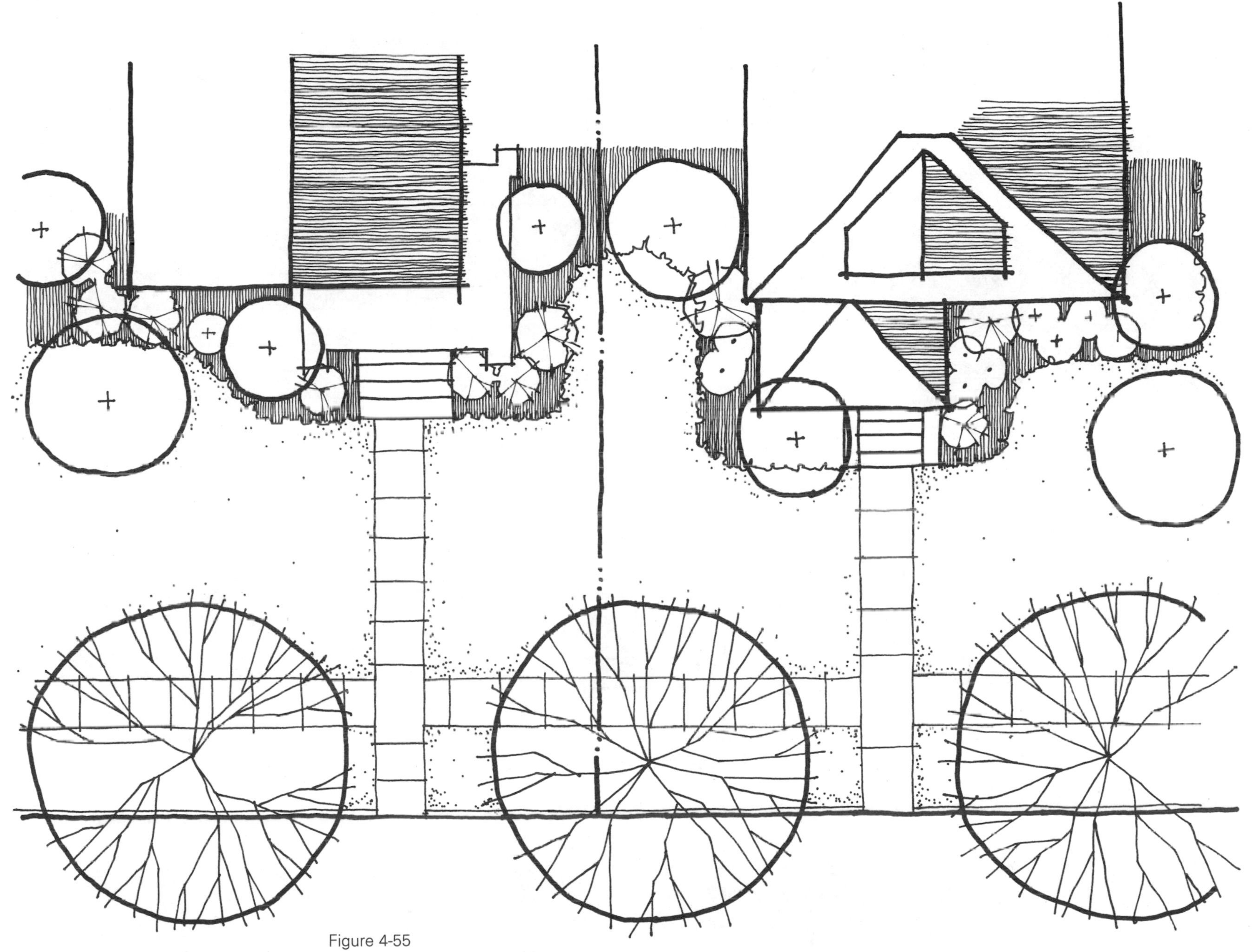

Figure 4-55
A street tree planting graphic.

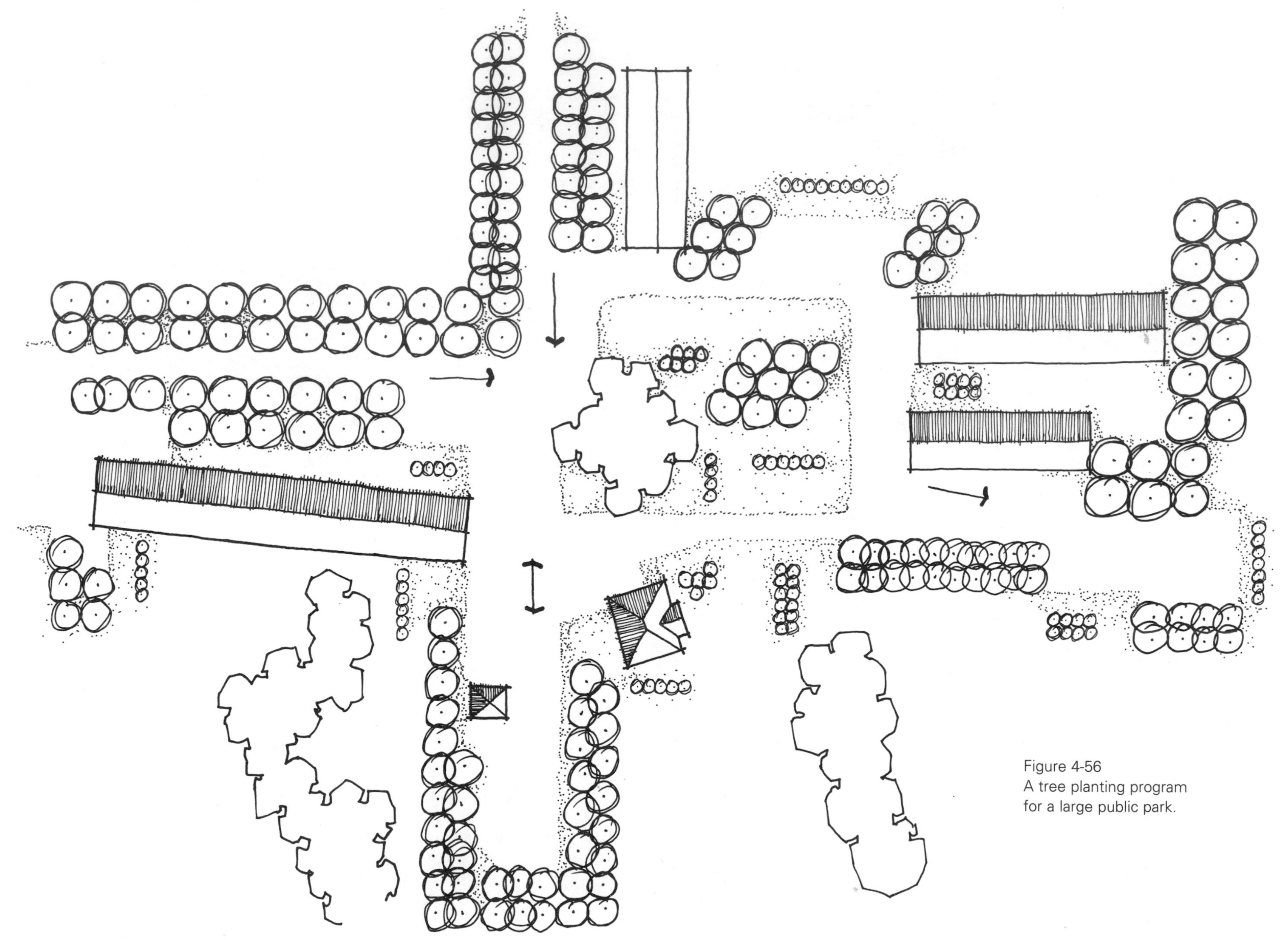

Figure 4-56
A tree planting program for a large public park.

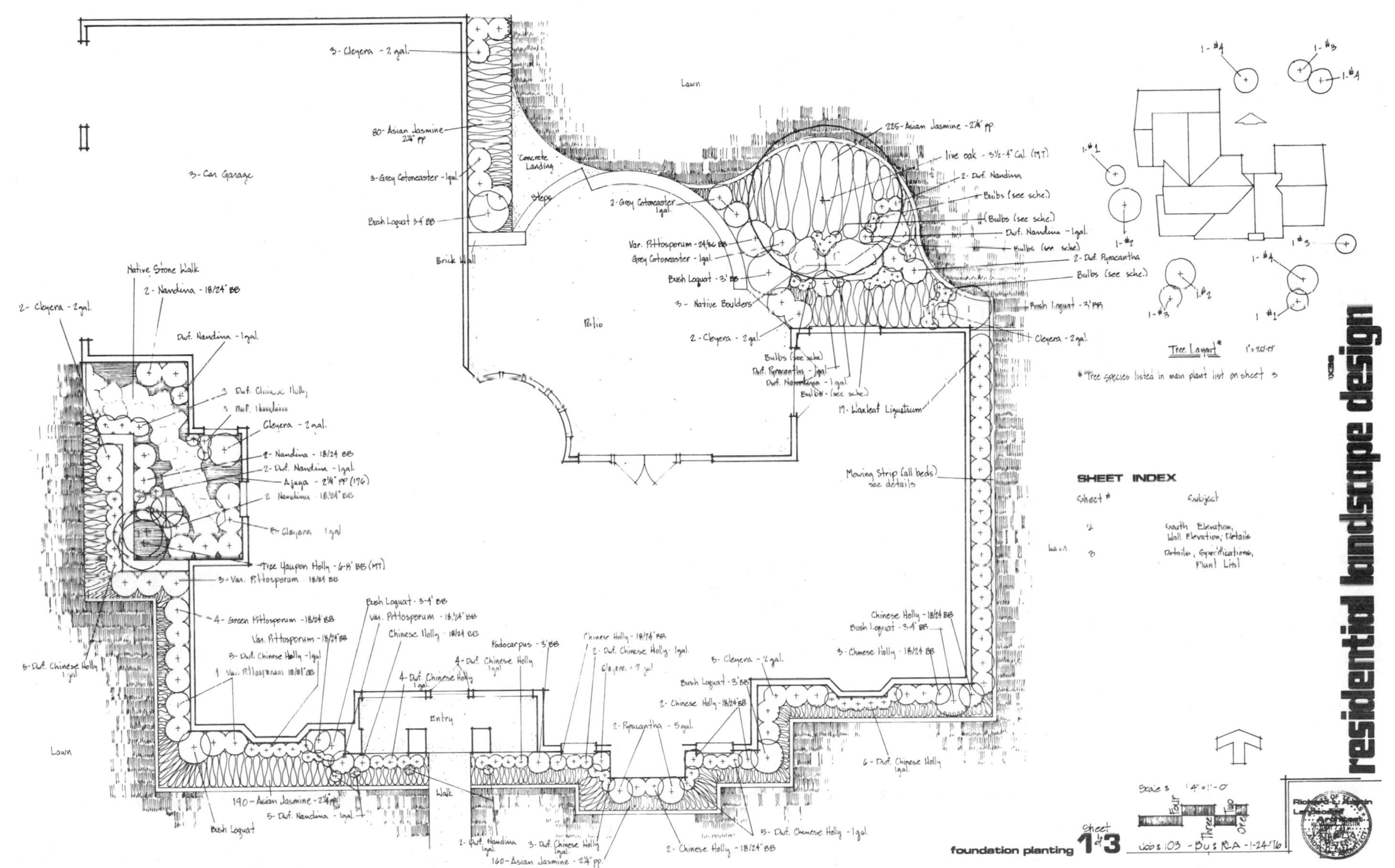

Figure 4-57
A residential planting plan.

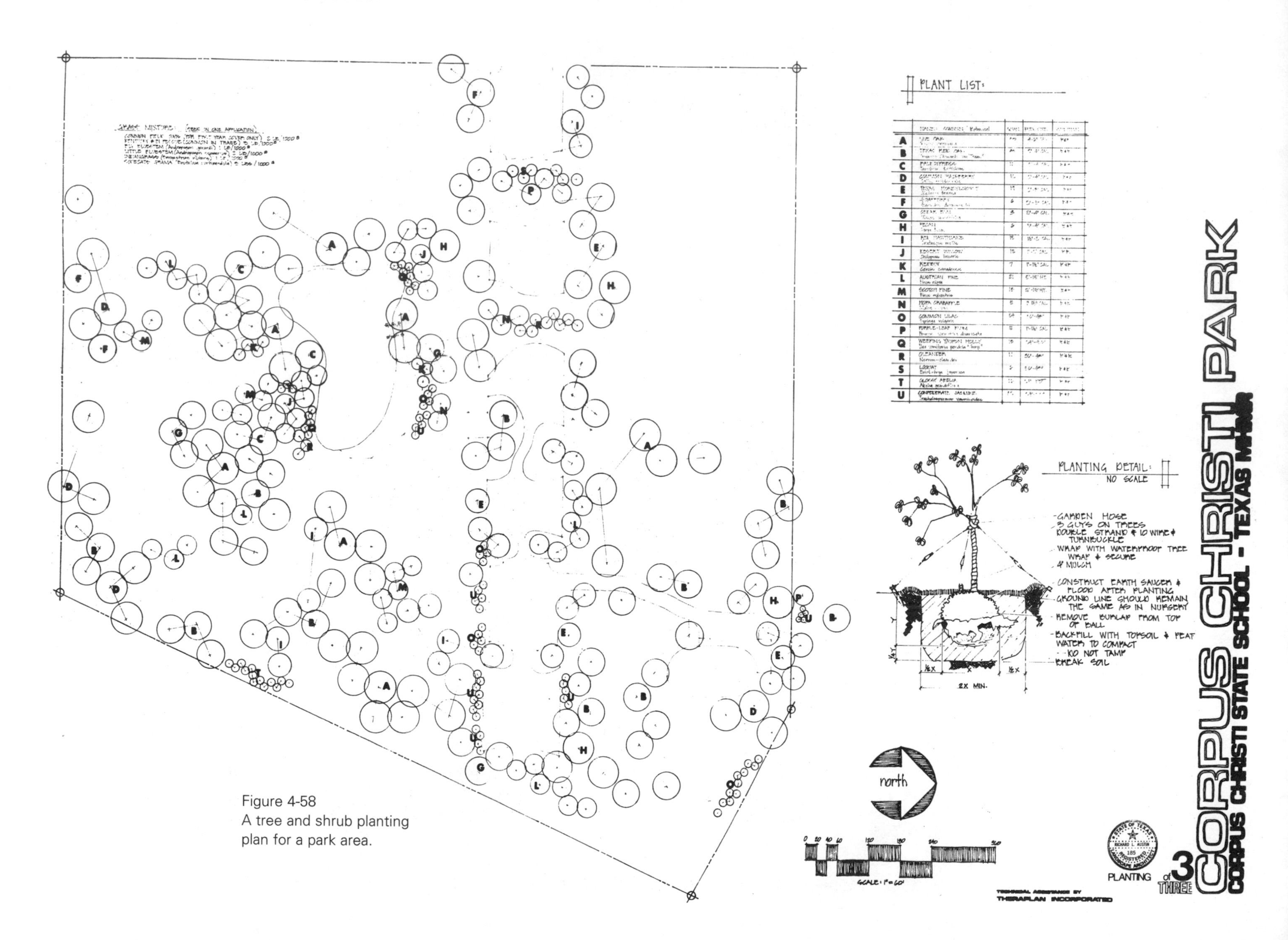

Figure 4-58
A tree and shrub planting plan for a park area.

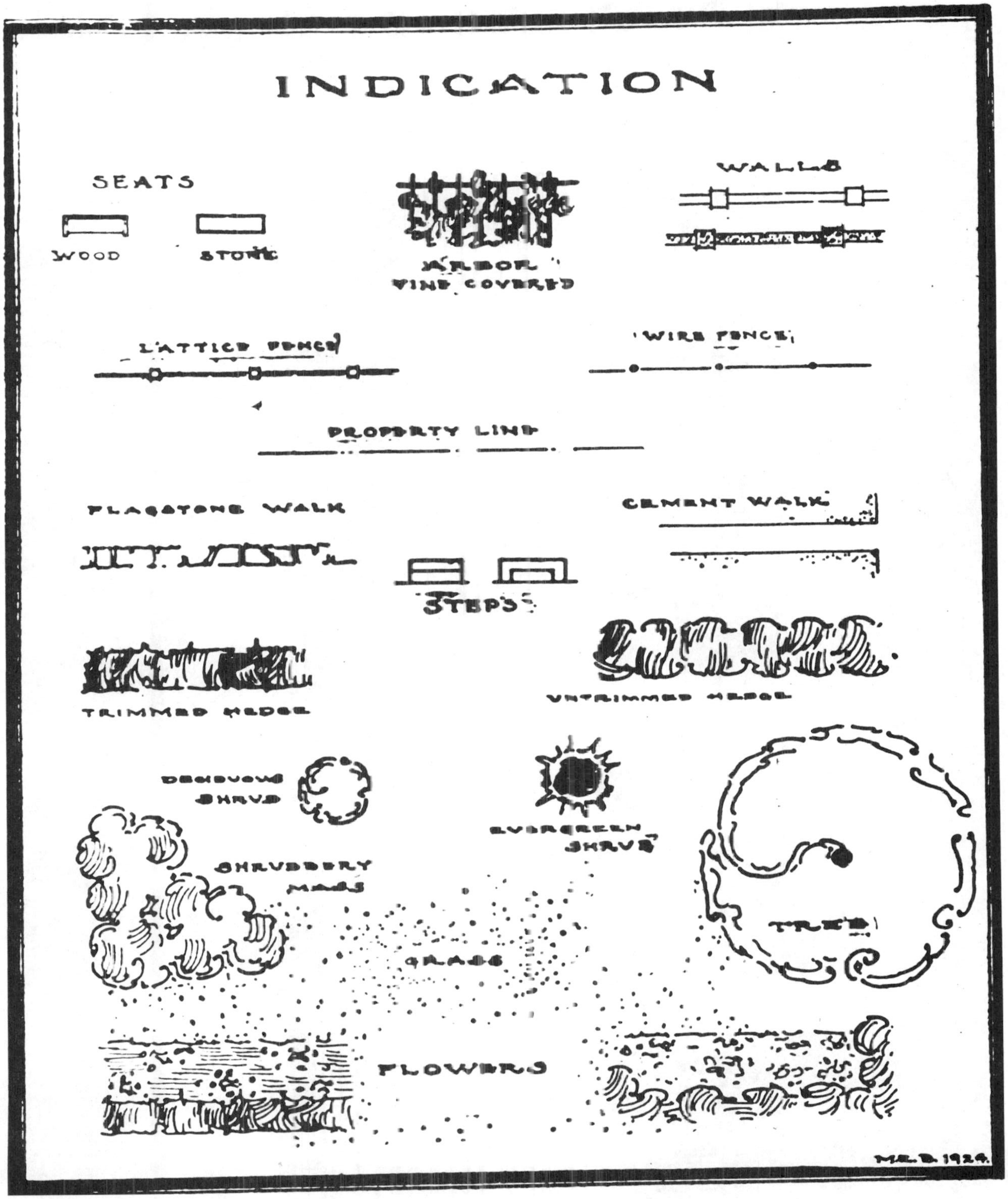

Figure 4-59

The graphic identification of plan elements, called "indications." The graphic expression of planting design has changed very little since landscape architecture began. This and the following illustrations represent various types of planting compositions since the 1920s.

Figure 4-60
Sketches of entry plantings.

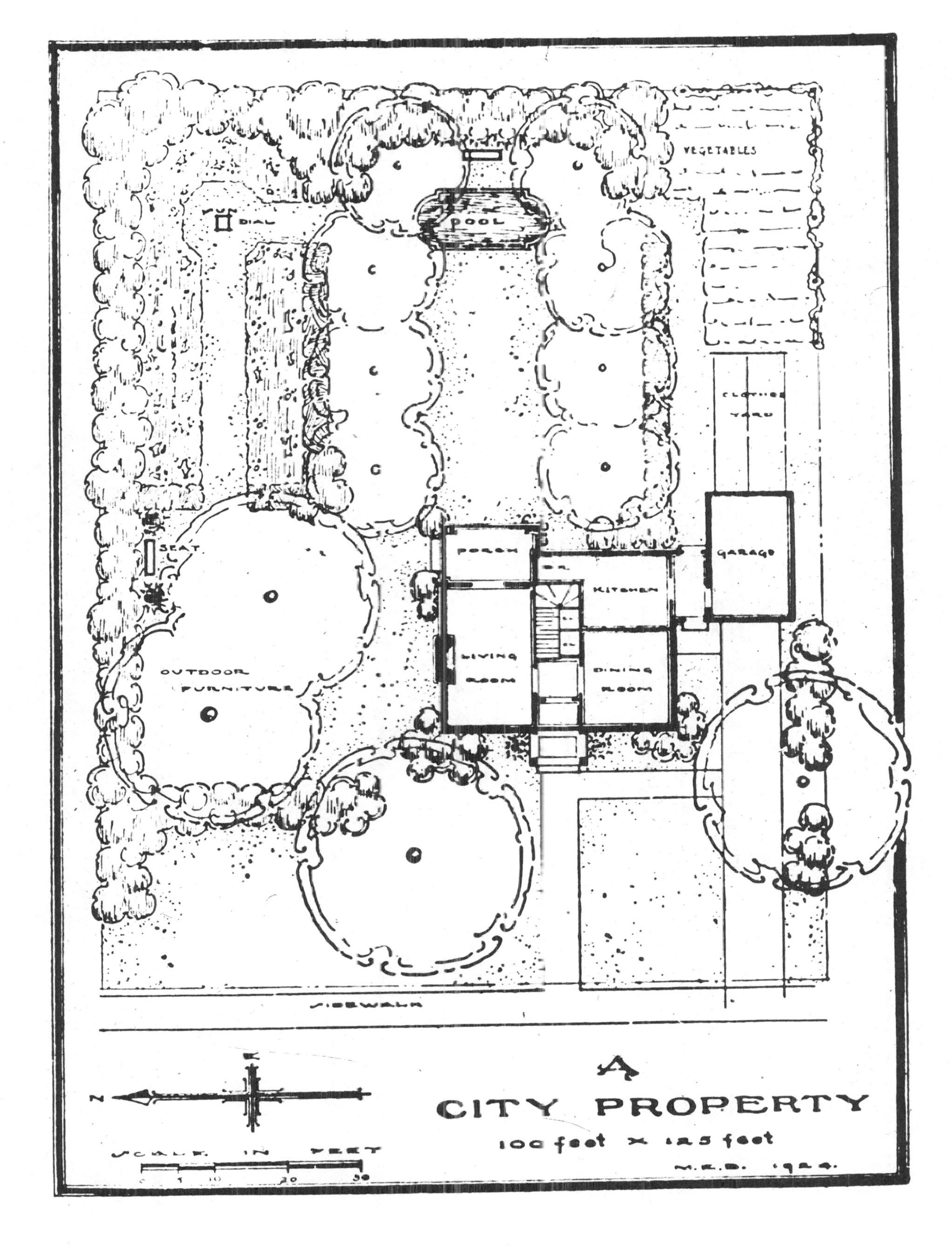

Figure 4-61
A planting plan of a city property.

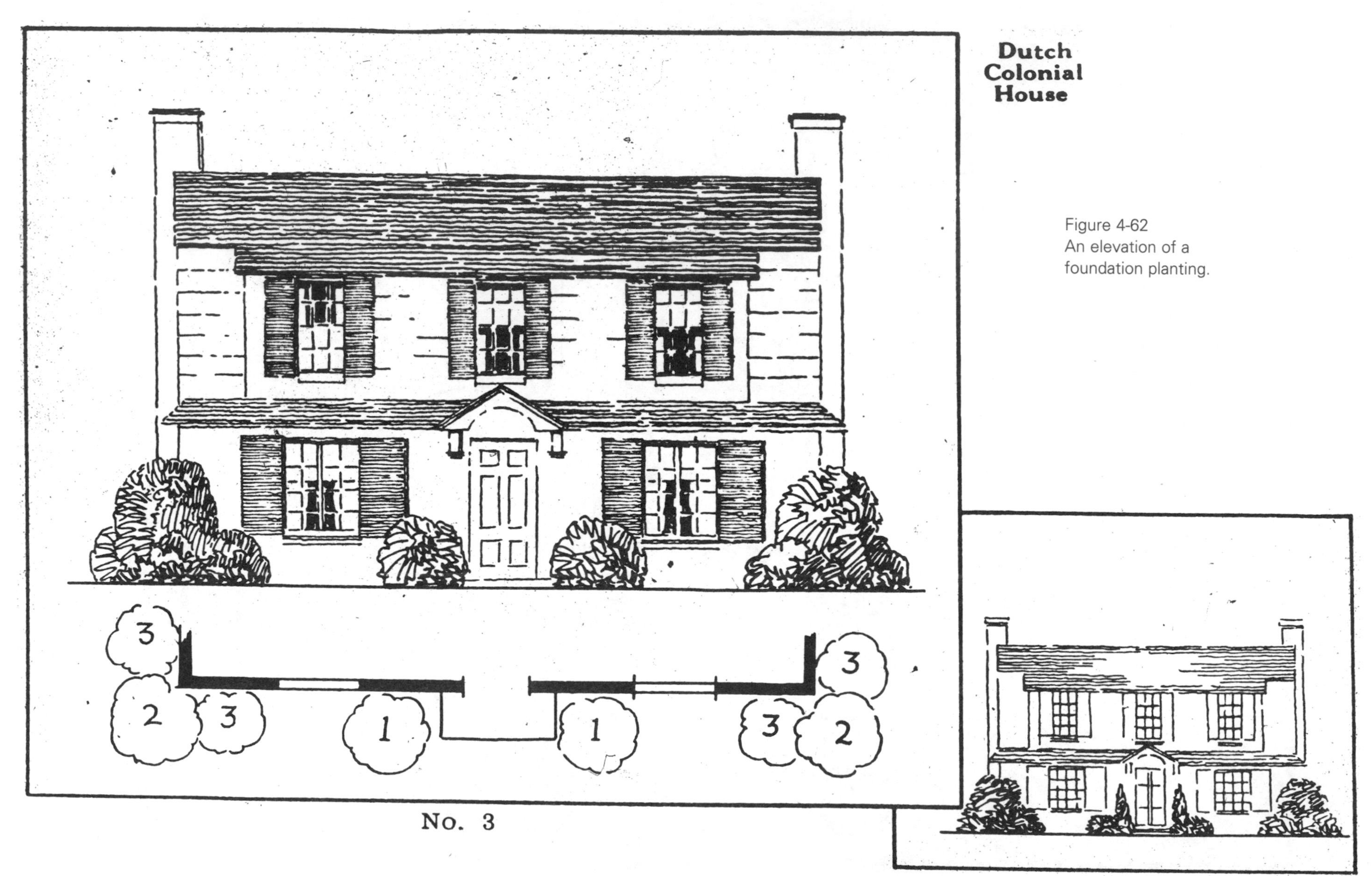

Figure 4-62
An elevation of a foundation planting.

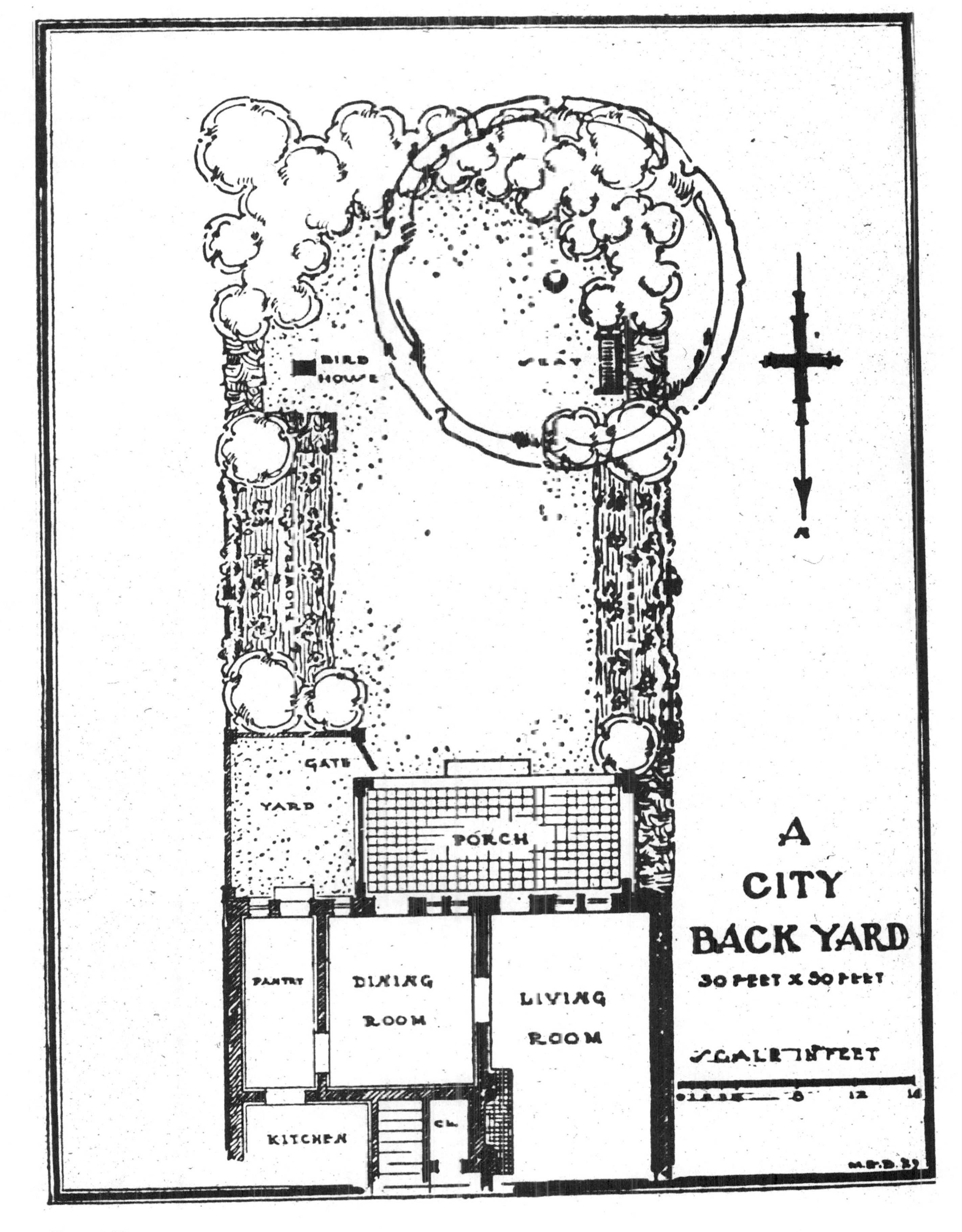

Figure 4-63
A planting plan of a city backyard.

Figure 4-64
A perspective of a backyard planting.

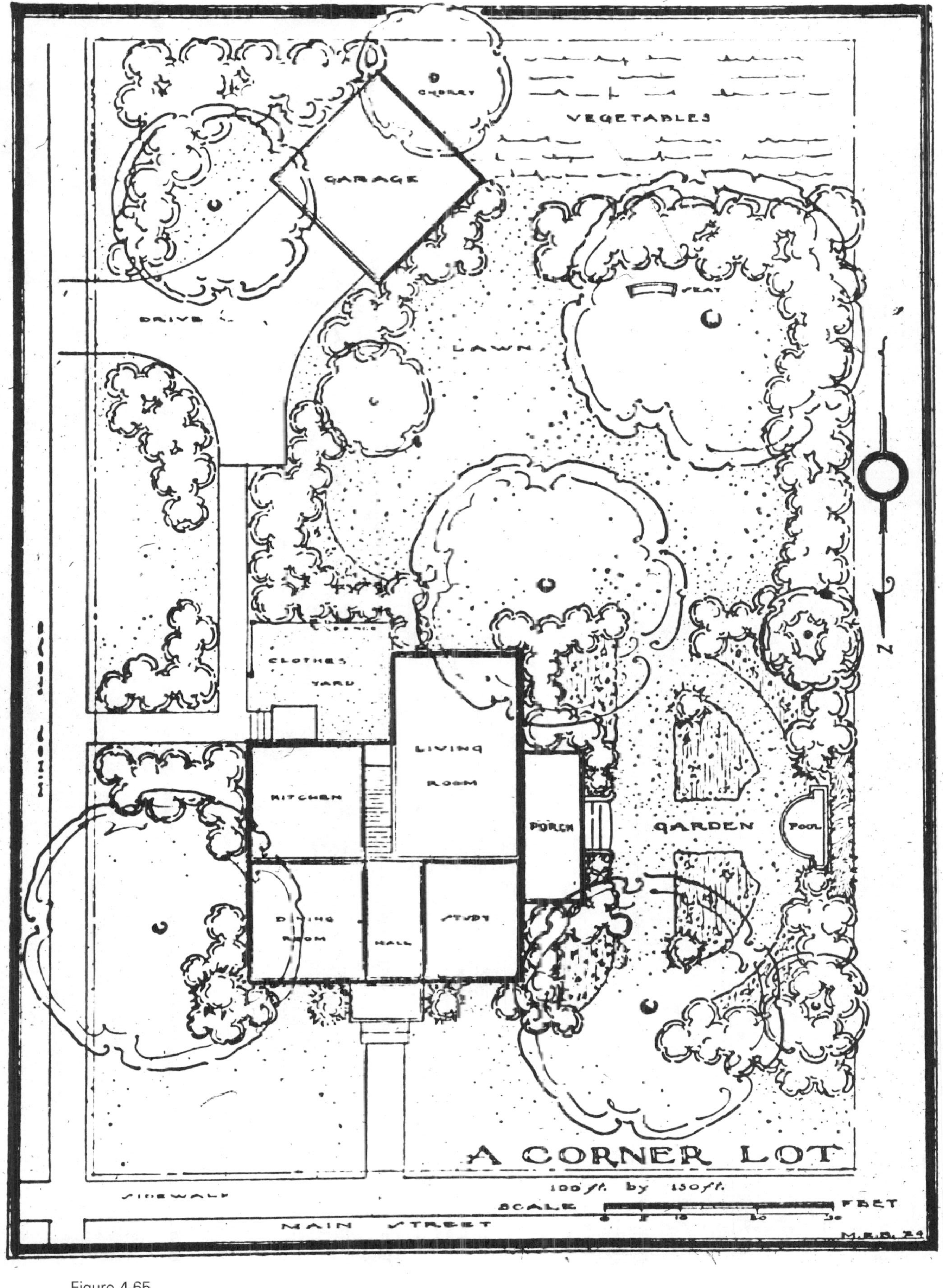

Figure 4-65
A planting plan of a corner lot.

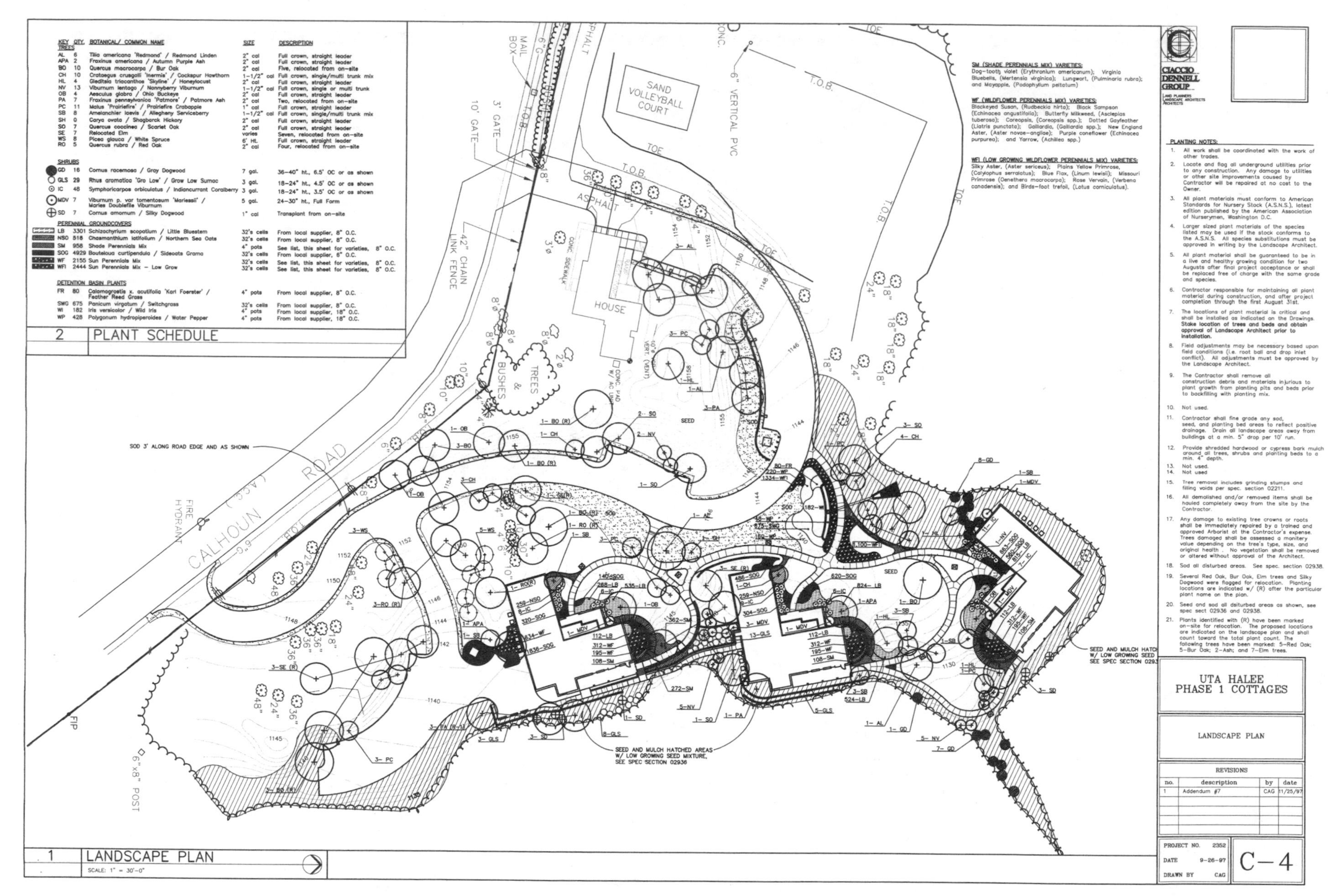

Figure 4-66
A commercial landscape plan specifying the name and location of plant materials. Courtesy of David J. Ciaccio, Ciaccio Dennell Group, Omaha, Nebraska.

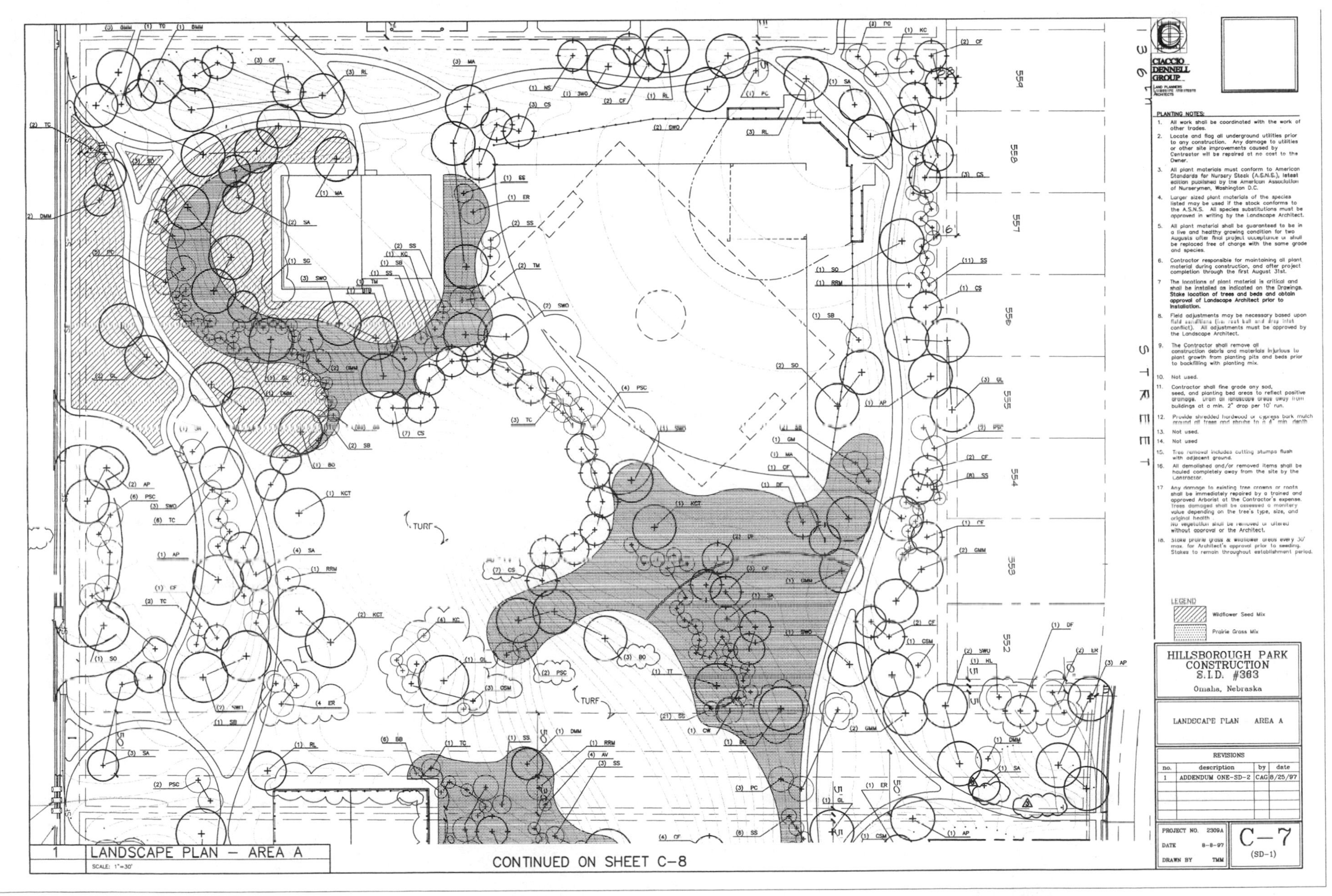

Figure 4-67
"Area A" of a large-scale, multiple-sheet planting plan for a city park. Courtesy of David J. Ciaccio, Ciaccio Dennell Group, Omaha, Nebraska.

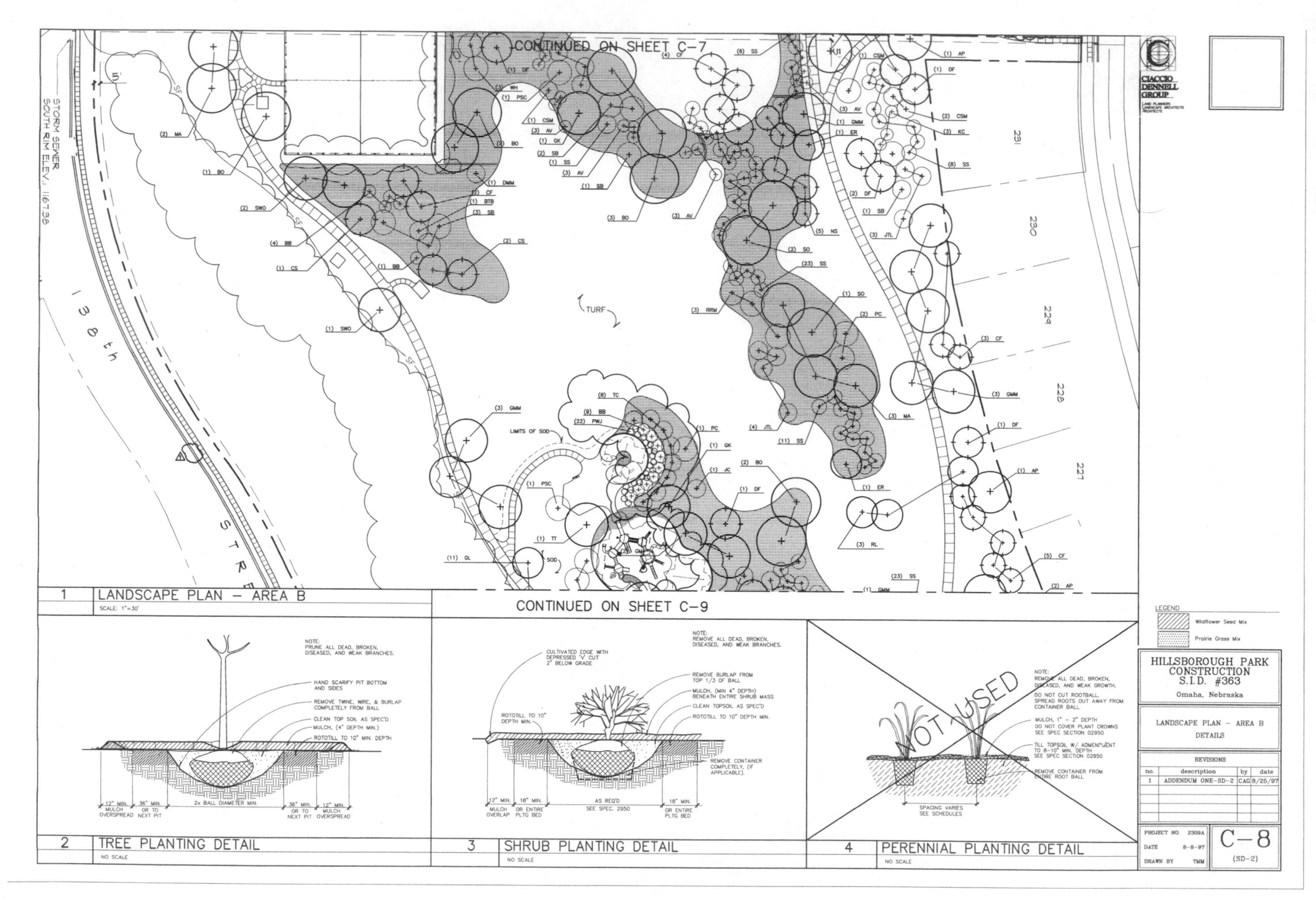

Figure 4-68
"Area B" of a large-scale, multiple-sheet planting plan for a city park Courtesy of David J. Ciaccio, Ciaccio Dennell Group, Omaha, Nebraska.

Figure 4-69
"Area C" of a large-scale, multiple-sheet planting plan for a city park. Courtesy of David J. Ciaccio, Ciaccio Dennell Group, Omaha, Nebraska.

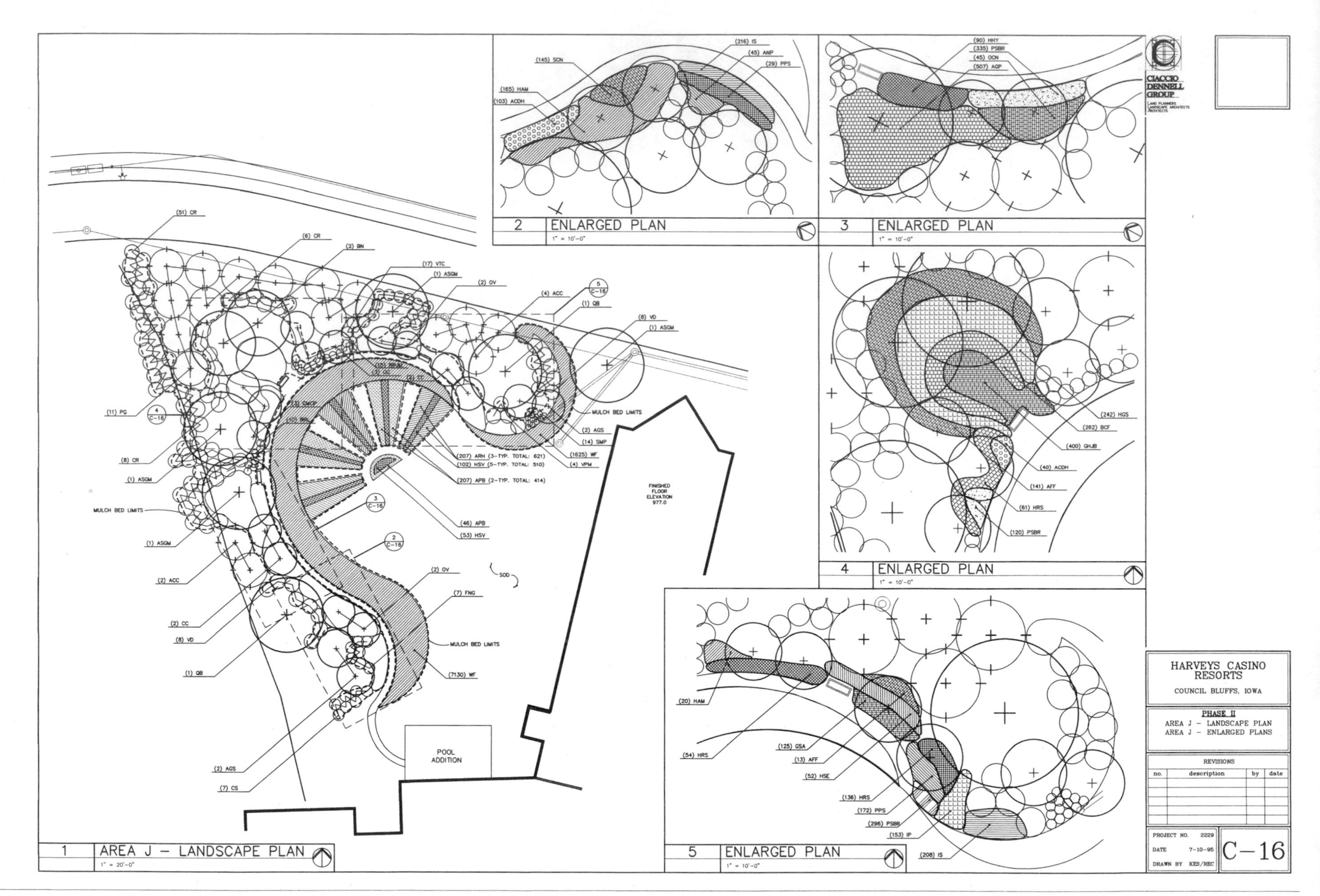

Figure 4-70
Detail of planting plans for annual/perennial areas for a large casino project. Courtesy of David J. Ciaccio, Ciaccio Dennell Group, Omaha, Nebraska.

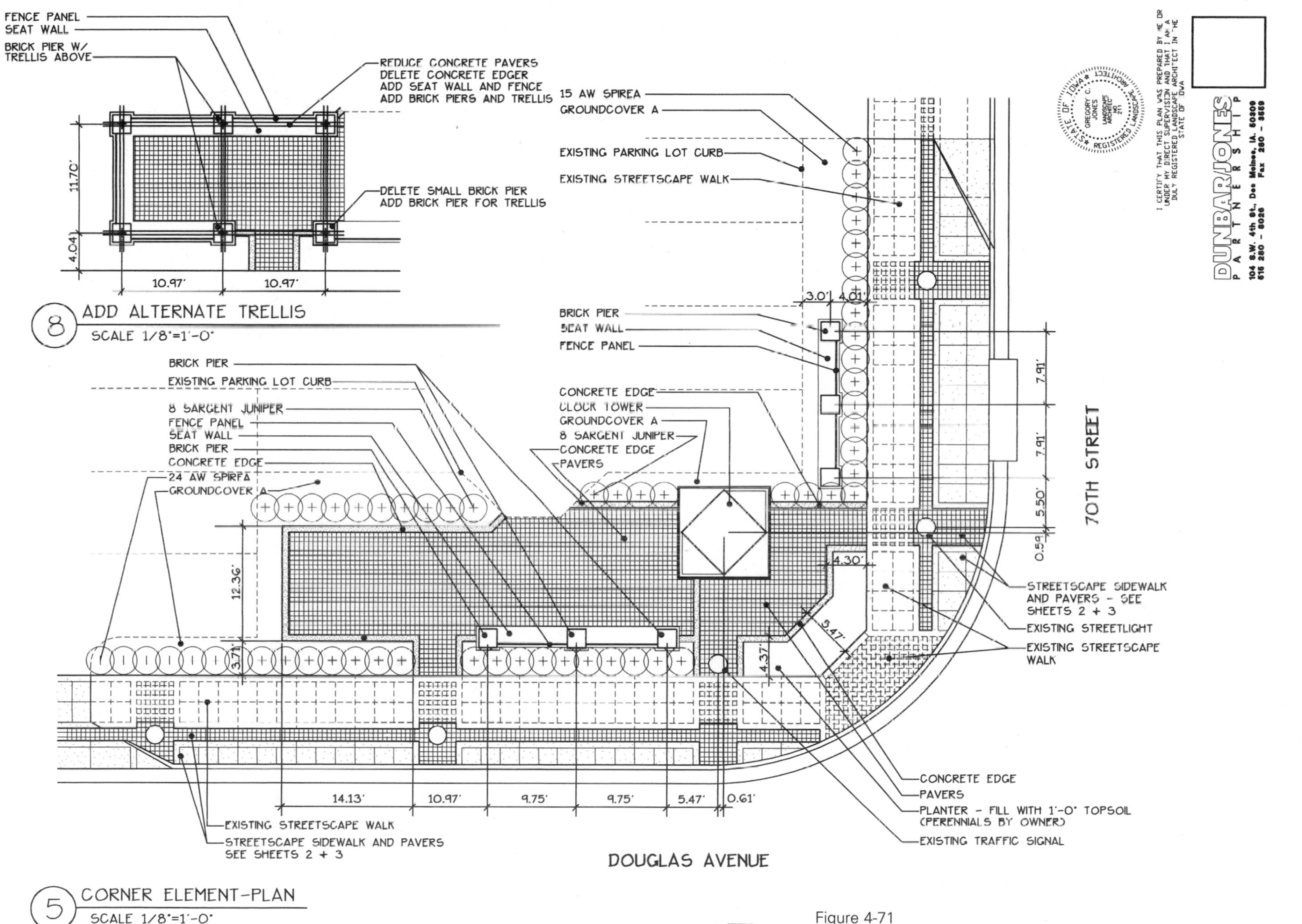

Figure 4-71
A tree planting plan for a downtown development. Courtesy of Thomas R. Dunbar, Dunbar/Jones Partnership, Des Moines, Iowa.

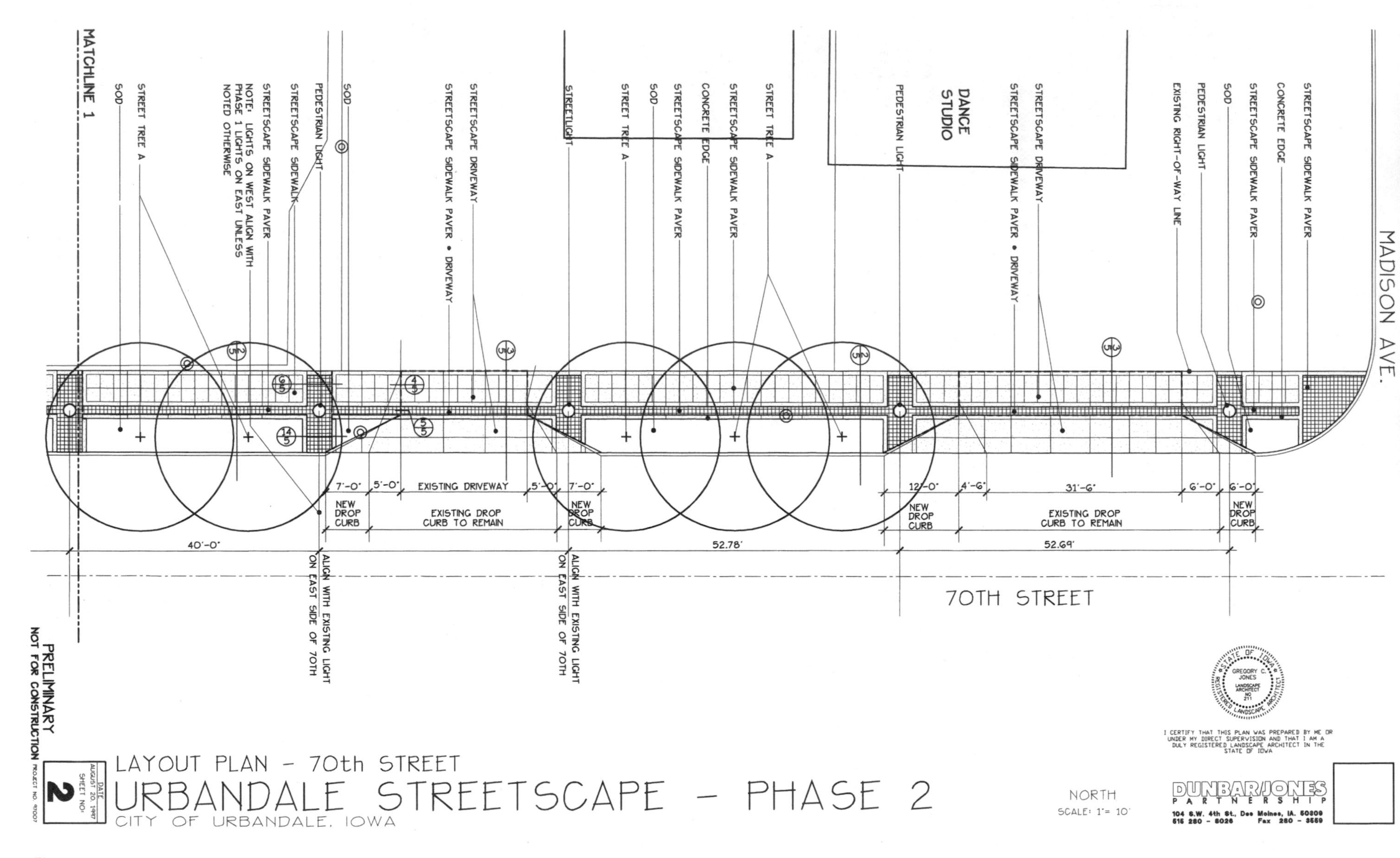

Figure 4-72
A streetscape layout. Courtesy of Thomas R. Dunbar, Dunbar/Jones Partnership, Des Moines, Iowa.

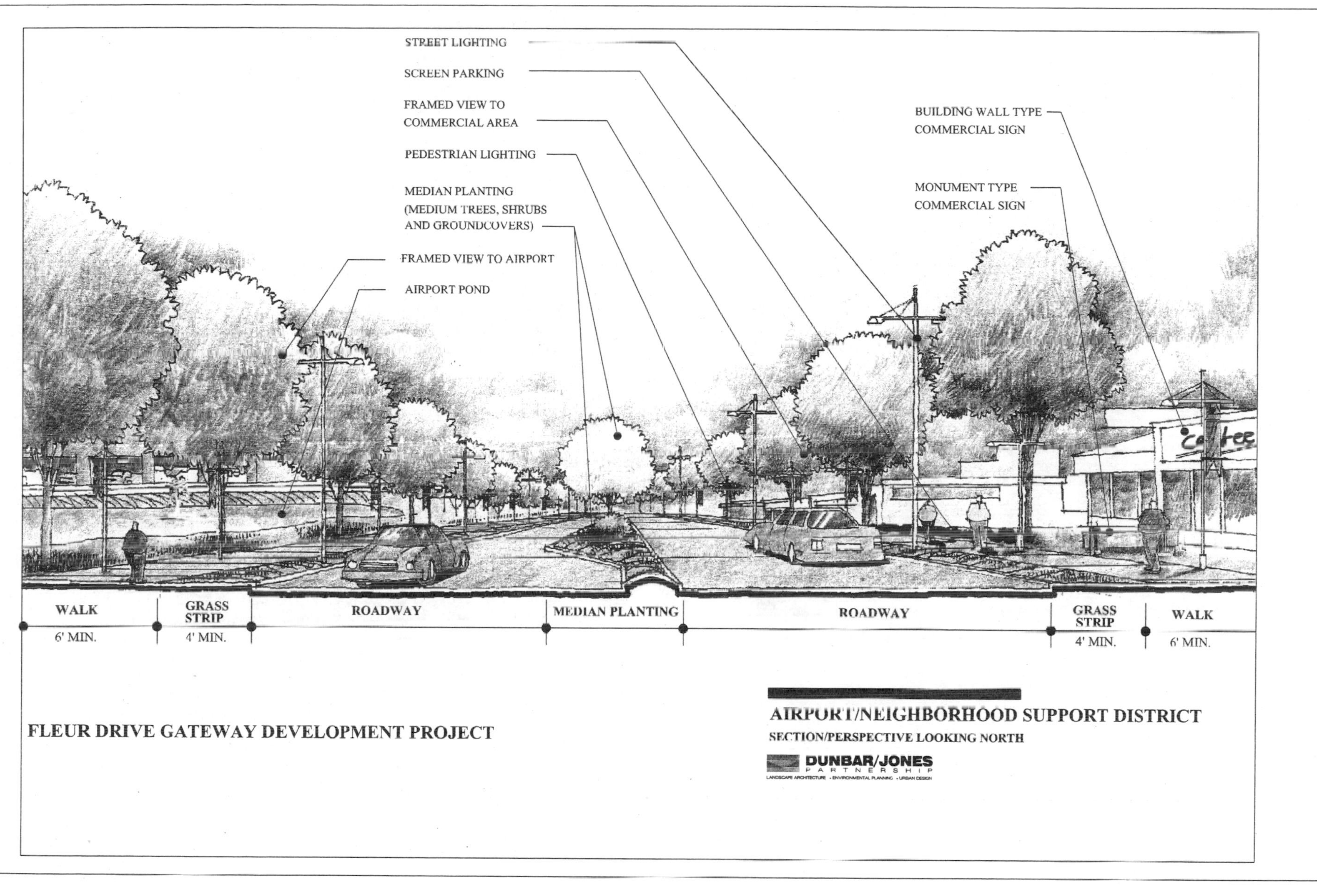

Figure 4-73
A conceptual plan for a streetscape project. Courtesy of Thomas R. Dunbar, Dunbar/Jones Partnership, Des Moines, Iowa.

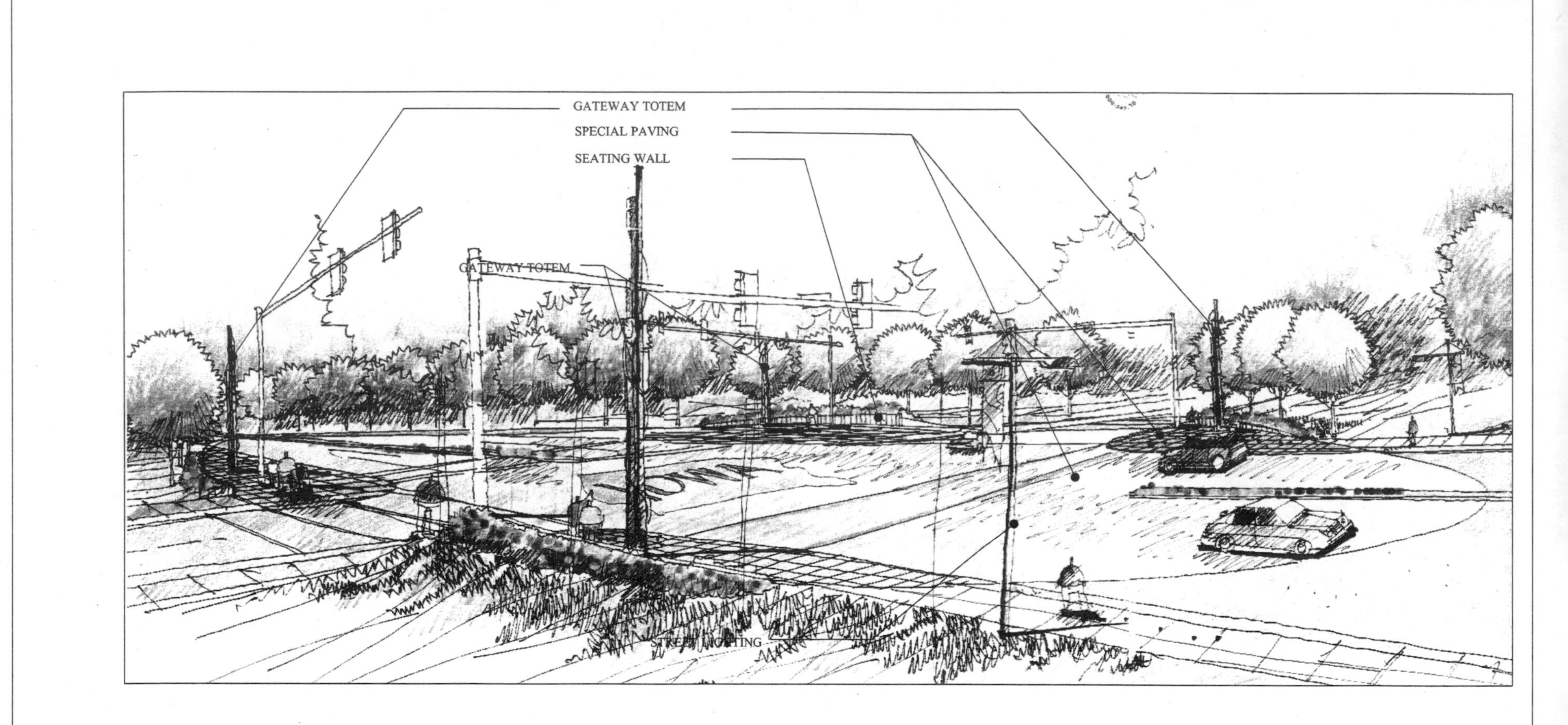

Figure 4-74 An intersection-planting concept. Courtesy of Thomas R. Dunbar, Dunbar/Jones Partnership, Des Moines, Iowa.

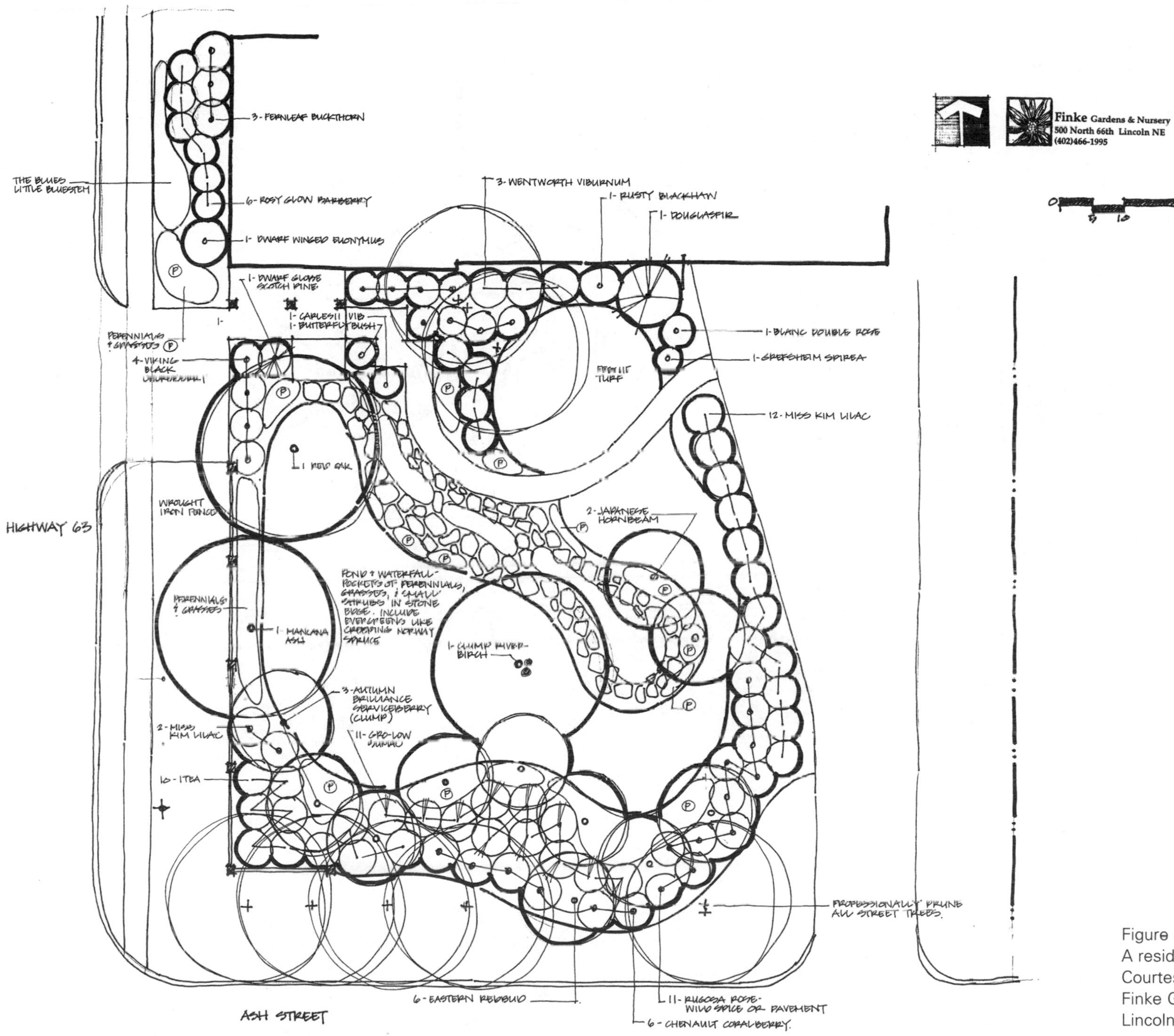

Figure 4-75
A residential planting plan.
Courtesy of Kim W. Todd,
Finke Gardens and Nursery,
Lincoln, Nebraska.

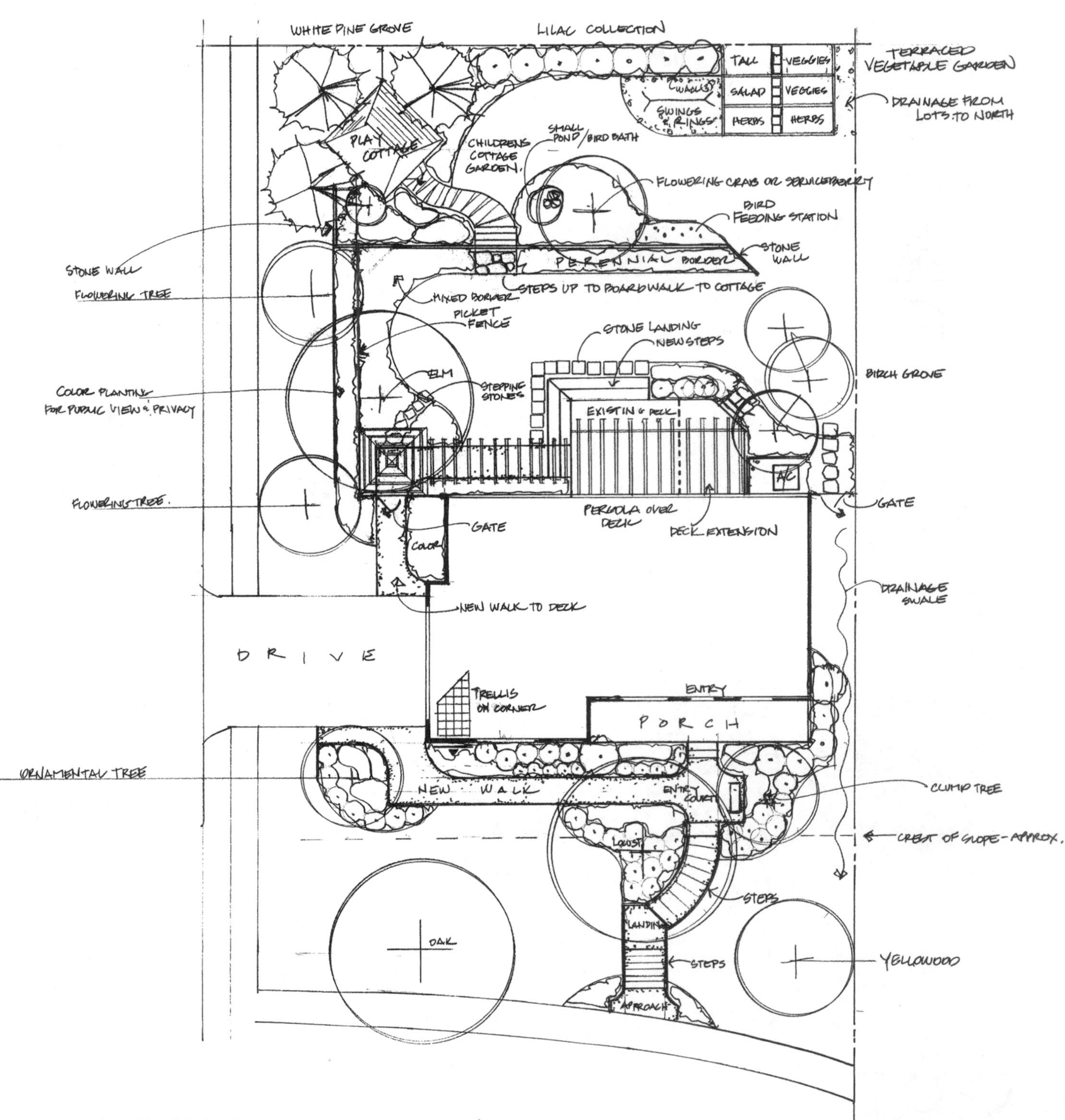

Figure 4-76 A residential planting plan. Courtesy of Brian Kinghorn, Kinghorn Horticultural Services, Omaha, Nebraska.

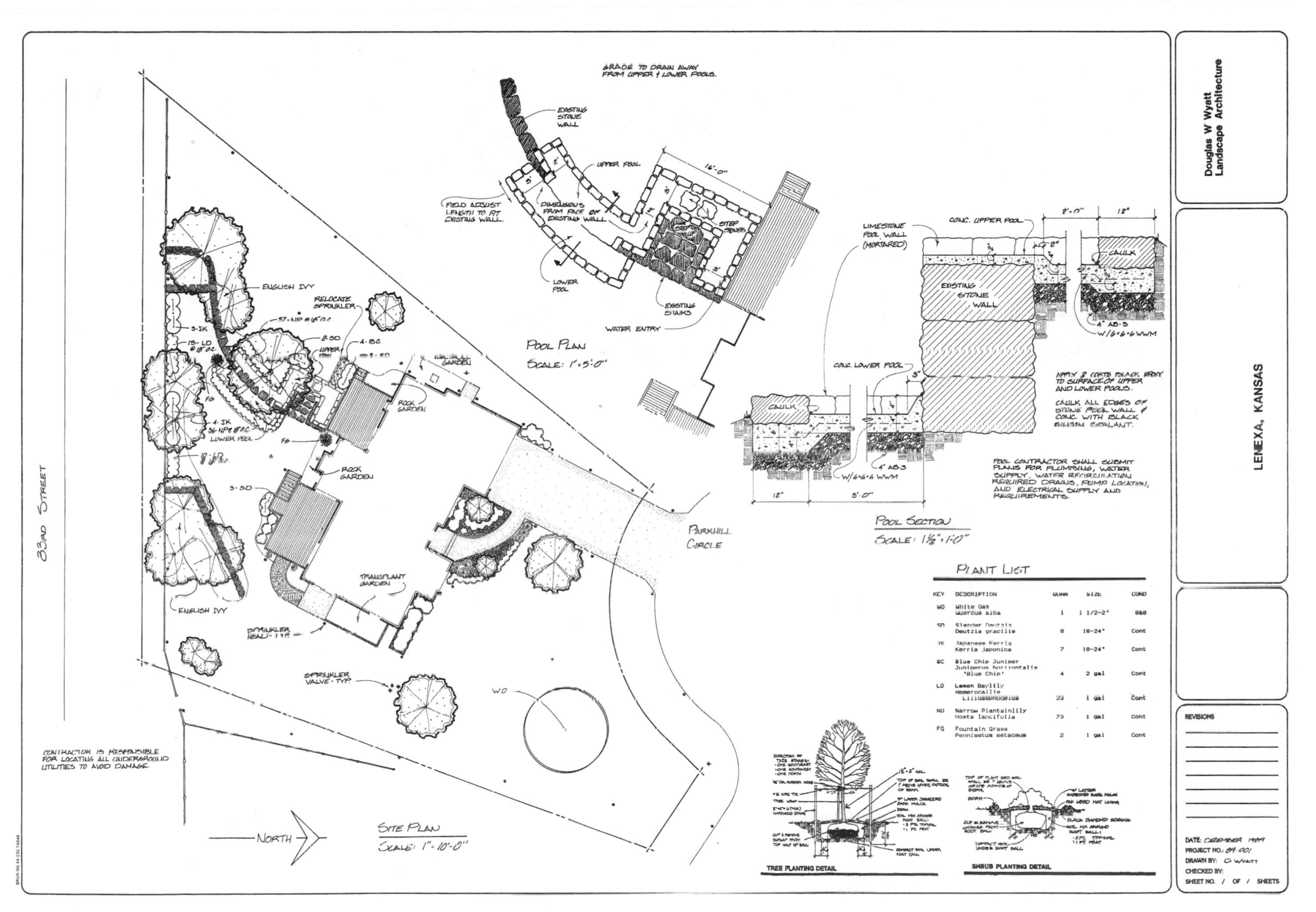

Figure 4-77
A site-planting concept for an acerage. Courtesy of Douglas W. Wyatt, landscape architect, Prairie Village, Kansas.

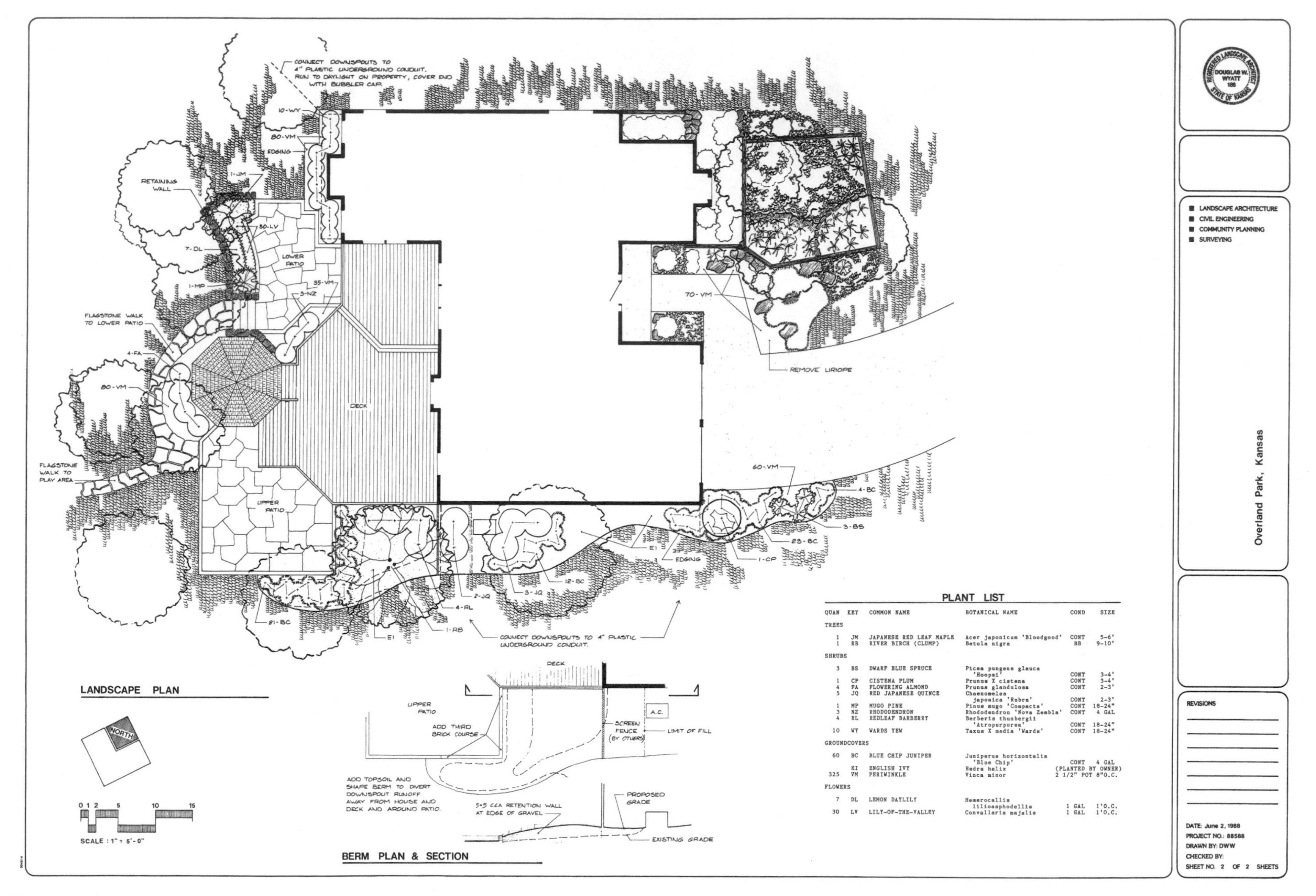

QUAN	KEY	COMMON NAME	BOTANICAL NAME	COND	SIZE
TREES					
1	JM	JAPANESE RED LEAF MAPLE	Acer japonicum 'Bloodgood'	CONT	5-6'
1	RB	RIVER BIRCH (CLUMP)	Betula nigra	BB	9-10'
SHRUBS					
3	BS	DWARF BLUE SPRUCE	Picea pungens glauca 'Hoopsi'	CONT	3-4'
1	CP	CISTENA PLUM	Prunus X cistena	CONT	3-4'
4	FA	FLOWERING ALMOND	Prunus glandulosa	CONT	2-3'
5	JQ	RED JAPANESE QUINCE	Chaenomeles japonica 'Rubra'	CONT	2-3'
1	MP	MUGO PINE	Pinus mugo 'Compacta'	CONT	18-24"
3	NZ	RHODODENDRON	Rhododendron 'Nova Zembla'	CONT	4 GAL
4	RL	REDLEAF BARBERRY	Berberis thunbergii 'Atropurpurea'	CONT	18-24"
10	WY	WARDS YEW	Taxus X media 'Wards'	CONT	18-24"
GROUNDCOVERS					
60	BC	BLUE CHIP JUNIPER	Juniperus horizontalis 'Blue Chip'	CONT	4 GAL
	EI	ENGLISH IVY	Hedra helix	(PLANTED BY OWNER)	
325	VM	PERIWINKLE	Vinca minor	2 1/2" POT	8"O.C.
FLOWERS					
7	DL	LEMON DAYLILY	Hemerocallis lilioasphodellis	1 GAL	1'O.C.
30	LV	LILY-OF-THE-VALLEY	Convallaria majalis	1 GAL	1'O.C.

Figure 4-78
A residential planting plan. Courtesy of Douglas W. Wyatt, landscape architect, Prairie Village, Kansas.

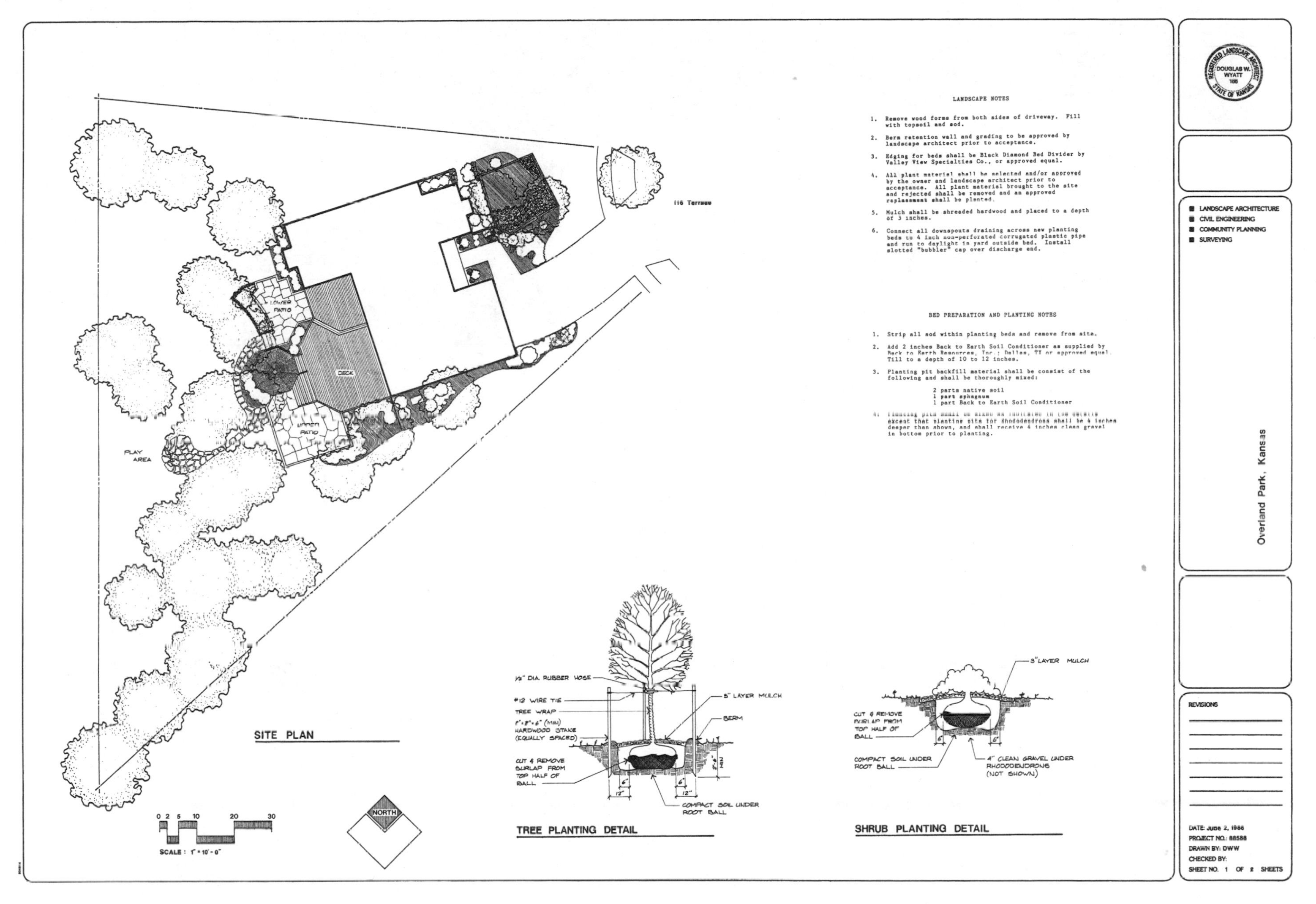

Figure 4-79
A planting-plan concept and planting-plan details. Courtesy of Douglas W. Wyatt, landscape architect, Prairie Village, Kansas.

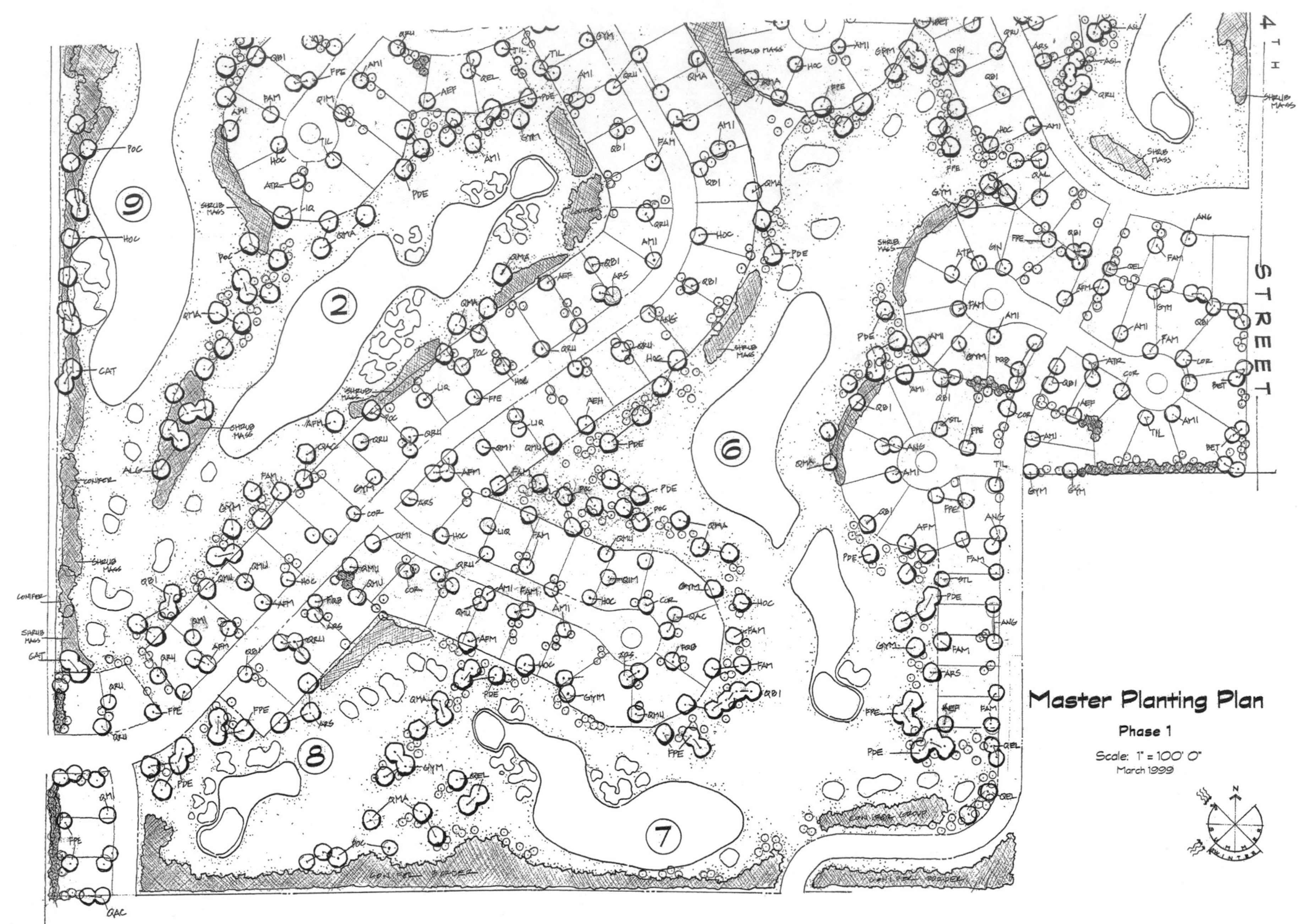

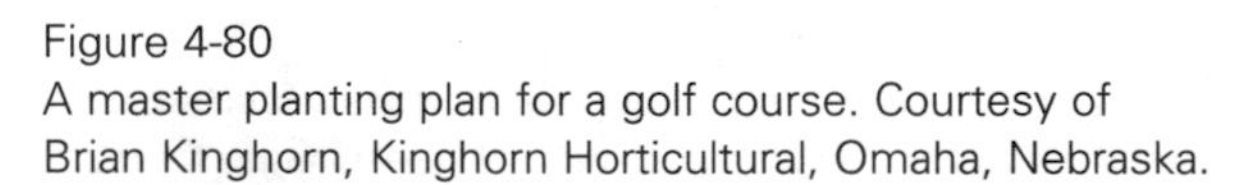
Figure 4-80
A master planting plan for a golf course. Courtesy of Brian Kinghorn, Kinghorn Horticultural, Omaha, Nebraska.

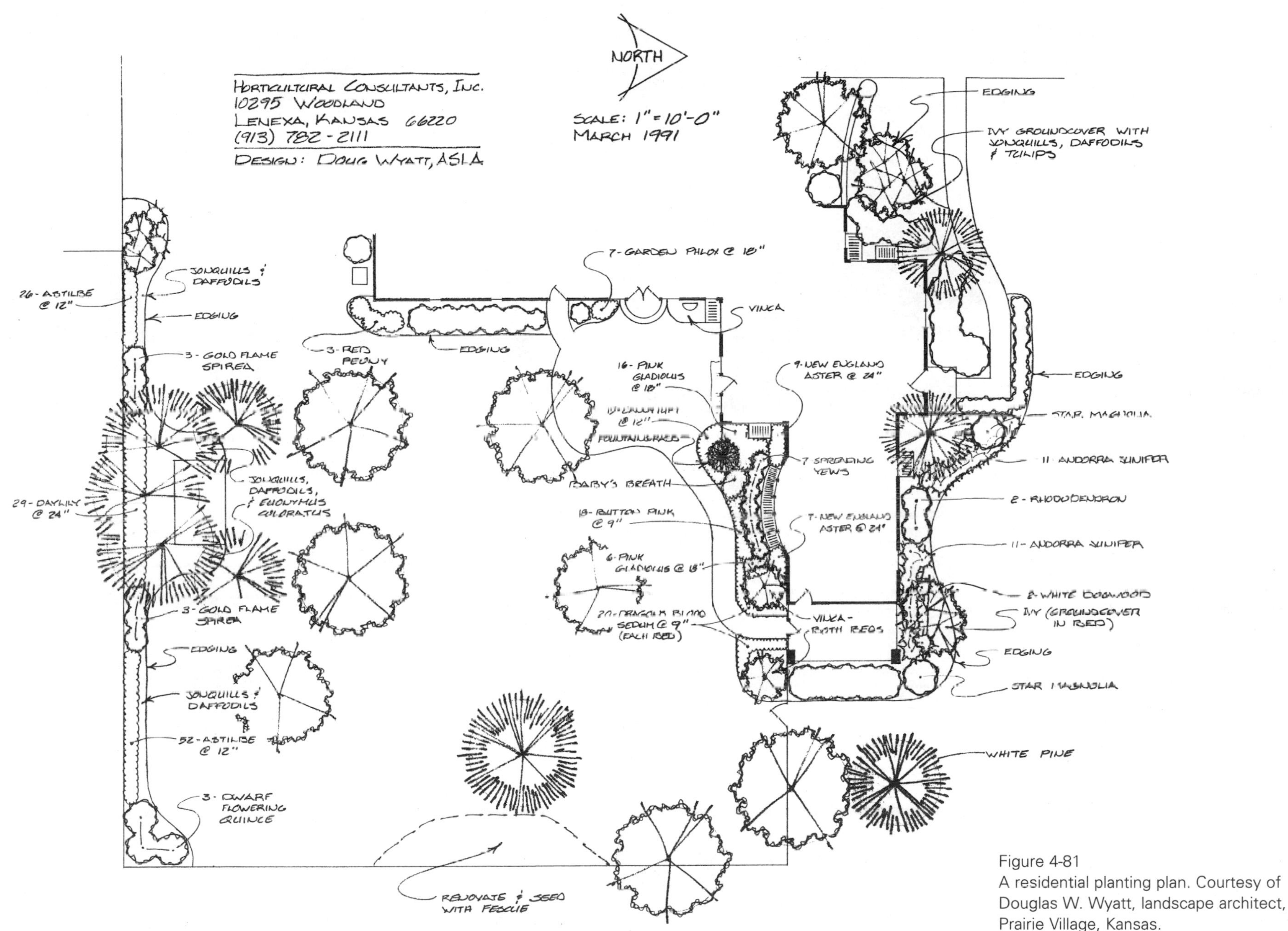

Figure 4-81
A residential planting plan. Courtesy of Douglas W. Wyatt, landscape architect, Prairie Village, Kansas.

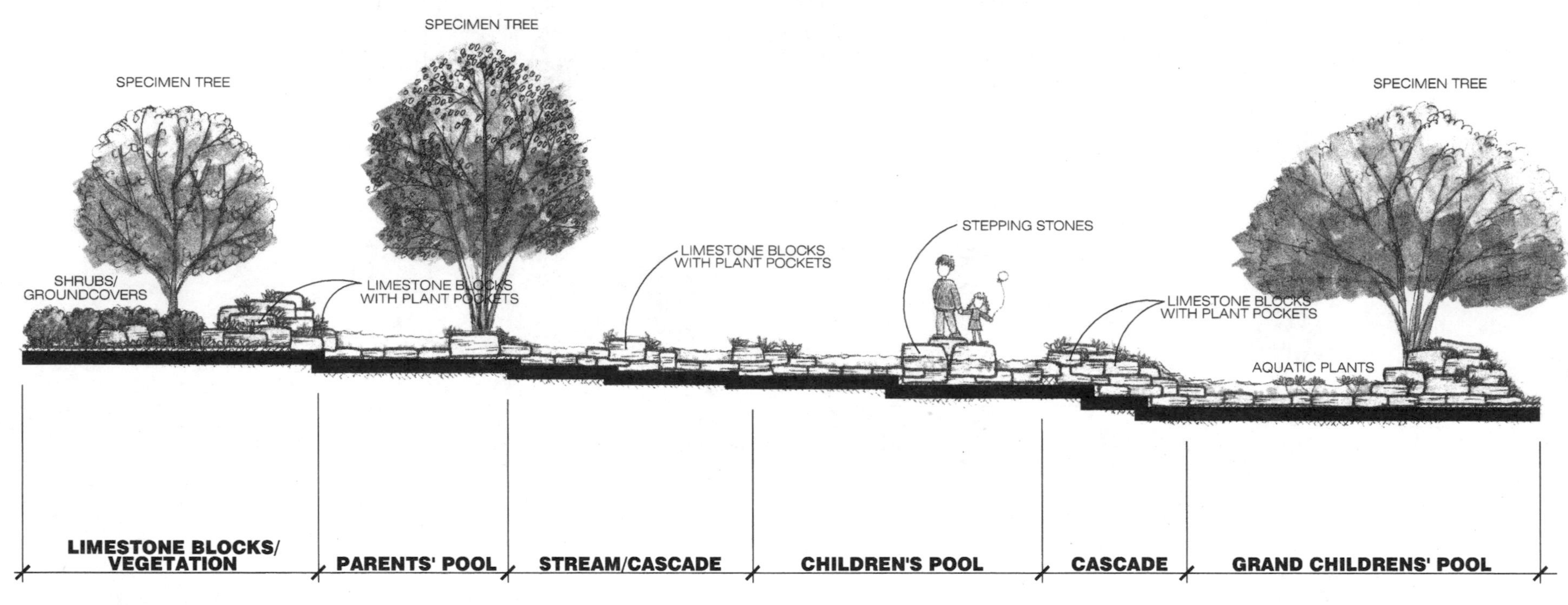

Figure 4-82
A section of a planting area for a botanical garden. Courtesy of Thomas R. Dunbar, Dunbar/Jones Partnership, Des Moines, Iowa.

CHAPTER 5

RESOURCES

Resource A
Client Interview Questionnaire

The following questions should be directed to a nonresidential client to identify the essential characteristics of the proposed design:

- How many persons will be using the space/site?
- What is the average age of these individuals?
- What type of pedestrian access is needed to the space/site?
- Are there to be walks, ramps, or steps?
- What type of vehicular access is needed to the site?
- Is there a need for off-street parking, delivery lanes, or emergency access?
- How will the space/site be used?
- Is there a need to specify public areas, private areas, or service needs?
- Is the space/site to be used in a passive or an active manner?

You may wish to add these questions:

1. What type of utility lighting is required? Will structures, plants, or open spaces need to be illuminated?
2. Is permanent seating/outdoor furniture required? If so, where, how much, and what type?
3. What type of overhead structures (if any) are needed over seating areas, walks, entrances, or exits?
4. What type of paved surface materials are needed?
5. What type of structural enclosures are needed?
6. What type of accommodations are needed for service/maintenance equipment and supplies?
7. What type of container planting areas are desired/required for the space?
8. How much miscellaneous outdoor storage is needed/required?

Family Inventory

Family members: Names ____________ Age ____________

Sex Hobbies

Public Area

Driveway ____________ Number of cars in family ____________

Off-street parking needed? ____________ For guests? ____________

Privacy from the street ____________ Entry walk ____________

Entry garden or walk ____________

Utility lighting ____________ Landscape lighting ____________

Outdoor Living Area

Maintenance, how much is desired (hours) ____________

Family allergy considerations ____________

Hobby garden? ____________

Flower borders: Annuals ____________ Perennials ____________ Mixed ____________

Favorite plants

Number of hours spent in yard/week ____________

Entertaining: Large groups ____________ Small groups ____________

Formal ____________ Informal ____________

Paved terrace or patio: Number of people ____________

Material ____________

Number of chairs ____________ Style ____________

Number of tables ____________

Permanent seating: Benches ____________ Seat-height (walls or planters) ____________

Shade required? ____________ Where ____________

Table umbrella ____________ Overhead structure ____________

Area lighted? ____________

Games: ____________ What types ____________

Outdoor cooking: Permanent grill ____________ Size ____________

Gas ____________ Charcoal ____________ Portable grill ____________ Size ____________

Sink ____________ Water ____________ Electrical outlets ____________

Storage ____________

Swimming pool: Permanent ____________ Semipermanent ____________

Other ______ Legal requirements

Liability insurance considered ______

Materials ______ Size ______ Lighting ______

Shape ______

Diving area ______ Paved decks ______

Enclosure for pool ______ Architectural fence or wall ______

Lighting ______ Dressing facility ______

Equipment storage ______

Service Area

Vegetable garden ______ Size ______

Flower garden ______ Size ______

Compost bin ______ Cold frames ______

Greenhouse ______ Size ______

Doghouse ______

Are clotheslines necessary? Yes ______ No ______ Size ______

Recreation vehicle storage ______

Lawn and garden storage ______

Patio furniture ______

Trash containers ______

Children's Play Area

Sandbox ______ Slide ______ Swings ______ Ropes ______

Playground ______ Playhouse ______

Is shade desired? ______

Structures ______

Should a fence be installed? Yes ______ No ______

Height ______ Type ______

What type of surfacing material is desired? Sand ______ Grass ______

Woodchips ______ Small gravel ______

Paved area ______

Special Features

Sculpture ______ Landscape lighting ______

Water features: Fountain ______ Reflecting pool ______

Fish ______ Plants ______

Interest in birds? Bird feeder ______ Bird-attracting plants ______

Bird bath ______ Birdhouses ______

Site Placement

Schools:

High school: Miles ______ Min. ______

Elementary: Miles ______ Min. ______

Kindergarten: Miles ______ Min. ______

Nursery: Miles ______ Min. ______

Shopping Facilities:

Major center: Yes ______ No ______

Neighborhood store: Yes ______ No ______

Recreation (location): Playgrounds ______ Park ______

Swimming ______ Golf ______ Other ______

Adjacent Structures

Note the location, size, shape, condition, and possible influence of site and off-site structures upon the design.

Utility Data

Public water supply connections: Yes ______ No ______

Location ______

Distance and size of the nearest main ______

Will this project require a private system? Yes ______ No ______

Subdivision plant ______

Septic tank ______

Individual system ______

Private wells ______

Public sewage disposal: Yes ______ No ______

Snow removal and sanding: Yes ______ No ______

Police protection: Yes ____________ No ______________________

Fire protection: Yes ____________ No ______________________

Storm sewers ____

Electric service ____________ Company ______________________

Gas ____________ Company ______________________

Telephone ____________ Policy on installations ______________________

Street lighting ____

Trash collection ____

Resource B
Sample Planting Design Agreements

The implementation of a planting design requires a variety of contracts, special forms, and planting specifications. Successful management of a planting plan in a competitive, changing economy requires the ability to adapt information and procedures from several sources. Forms should be developed to save processing time in the office and to ensure the protection of both the designer and the client.

The Planting Design Service Agreement

This legal document establishes the scope of the work to be performed by the planting designer. All parties involved in the program should be fully aware of each clause, and a thorough definition of the project goals should be outlined. Legal assistance should be obtained to establish the initial contract form because of variations in state laws. The following sample contracts outline the basic elements needed for a project document.

Sample Contract A

Date

(Name)

(Address)

(City)

This AGREEMENT entered into this _________ day of ______, 20_____, by and between ____________________________ (hereinafter called the "Owner") and ____________________________ (hereinafter called the "Landscape Designer / Landscape Architect").

The Owner does hereby request that the Landscape Designer/Landscape Architect provide professional services to the landscape improvement of the property at (Address)

The professional services of the Landscape Designer/Landscape Architect shall be as follows:

A. Prepare preliminary studies of the (REAR, FRONT, ENTIRE PROPERTIES) ______________________________ to include:

____________________ TERRACE AND PATIO ADDITIONS

____________________ WALLS, RETAINING WALLS, FENCES, and/or SCREENS

____________________ PLANTING AREAS

____________________ SWIMMING POOL

____________________ CABANA

____________________ OVERHEAD STRUCTURES

____________________ GRADING and DRAINAGE PLANS

B. From preliminary studies and conferences with the Owner, a set of working drawings will be prepared to include:

POOL DESIGN and LAYOUT

PAVING AREAS

QUANTITIES, TYPE, and LOCATION OF PLANT MATERIALS

WALLS, SCREENS, and FENCES

LIGHTING SUGGESTIONS

BASIC PLANTING SPECIFICATIONS

The Owner agrees to pay the Landscape Designer/Landscape Architect a fee of ____________________ DOLLARS upon completion of the plans and their presentation to the Owner.

The Owner shall furnish to the Landscape Designer/Landscape Architect at the Owner's expense all necessary property lines, house plans, site elevations, and topographic maps applicable to the designated area to be improved. A fee of ____________________ DOLLARS (separate and in addition to the basic fee for design services) will be required if the Landscape Designer/Landscape Architect is requested to provide property and structure measurements plus site elevations.

The Landscape Designer/Landscape Architect shall furnish two sets of FINAL PRINTS upon completion to the Owner. All other prints shall be furnished at a cost of_________.

Upon acceptance of the FINAL PLANS by the Owner, the Landscape Designer/Landscape Architect, at the Owner's request, may provide FULL SUPERVISION SERVICES (as opposed to DESIGN SERVICES) of all Contractors hired by the Owner to execute the LANDSCAPE PLANS for a fee of _________________ per hour or a lump sum of ____ DOLLARS.

This AGREEMENT may be terminated at any time by the Owner or the Landscape Designer/Landscape Architect upon giving a thirty (30) day written notice. Upon termination at the Owner's request, payment to the Landscape Designer/Landscape Architect shall be determined by the percentage of work completed in accordance with this AGREEMENT. This AGREEMENT, unless terminated by written notice, shall be terminated by the final payment for the finished work.

The parties hereto have executed this AGREEMENT as of the day and year first written above.

OWNER:

____

____

____

LANDSCAPE DESIGNER/LANDSCAPE ARCHITECT

____

____

____

Sample Contract B

(Date)

RE: Landscape Designer Services (Project)

The following scope of SERVICES and AGREEMENT are presented for your authorization. It is necessary that the proper representatives of the OWNER, (Owner's Name) sign and date this document and return one copy to our office. PROCEDURE: THE LANDSCAPE DESIGNER / LANDSCAPE ARCHITECT, (Name) , hereby agrees to perform the following landscape design services for (Project Name) , located , in consideration of the fees as stated in Section C-2.

A. COLLECTION OF DATA AND ON-SITE STUDY

Purpose: To acquaint the Landscape Designer/Landscape Architect with the proposed site and examine additional planning data pertinent to the site.

Scope:

TOPOGRAPHIC MAPS

SOIL TESTS AND REPORTS

WATER AVAILABILITY AND QUALITY

ACCESS POINTS

EXISTING PLANT MATERIALS

AVAILABLE UTILITIES

PROGRAM REQUIREMENTS

Results: All reviewed data will become an integral and complementary part of the site plan. From preliminary studies, a set of working drawings will be prepared to include:

QUANTITIES, TYPE, AND LOCATION OF PLANT MATERIAL

BASIC PLANTING SPECIFICATIONS

B. OWNER'S RESPONSIBILITY

The Owner shall provide or make available all existing data related to the work as outlined in Section A, and additional information or data which may develop during the term of the Agreement, which may possibly have a bearing on the decision or recommendations made by the Landscape Designer/Landscape Architect. If the Owner cannot conveniently procure this information or data, then the Landscape Designer/Landscape Architect will obtain it at the Owner's expense.

Items the Owner will provide:

1. Topographic maps of the site and affected adjacent areas.
2. Architectural drawings of the site and building structures showing all areas to be affected by landscape planting.

C. FEES FOR PROFESSIONAL SERVICES

1. The fee is payable in proportion to the work completed and due upon completion of the plans and their presentation to the Owner.
2. The Owner agrees to pay the Landscape Designer/Landscape Architect a fee of (Fee) as outlined in Section A.

D. TIME OF COMPLETION

The services contracted for in Section A of this Agreement shall be completed within thirty (30) working days from the date of acceptance.

IN WITNESS WHEREOF the parties have made and executed this Agreement.

(Owner)

By ______________________________ Date ______________________

(Landscape Designer / Landscape Architect)

By ______________________________ Date ______________________

Resource C
Bid Proposal Form

Bid Proposals

In a design/build operation, the service contract will often be followed by a proposal to complete the features developed in the planting plan. The bid proposal form should also be thorough and specific for the protection of the client and designer. The one that follows is for unit pricing of a planting plan installation.

BID PROPOSAL FORM

(Date)

Proposal of (Company Name)

To: (Owner)

The Undersigned having carefully examined the Instruction to Bidders and Contract Documents comprising the Drawings and Specifications and all Documents bound therein, as prepared by and under the direction of (Landscape Architect's Name), and having examined the physical site of the project and being familiar with the various conditions affecting the work, the Undersigned agrees to furnish all services, labor, equipment, and materials required for the performance and completion of all landscaping work as called for on the Drawings and in the Specifications for the Base Bid Lump Sum and/or sums listed below:

Base Bid for Landscaping Work (Amount in Dollars and Cents)

Base Bid includes all Sales Taxes, Excise Taxes, and any other taxes for all materials, appliances, and/or service subject to and upon which taxes are levied.

UNIT PRICES:

Unit prices include the cost of work and materials in place, including all materials, equipment, labor, bed preparation, fertilization, taxes, overhead, profit, maintenance, and guarantee required to render the same complete. In the event a greater or lesser amount of work is done, the following unit prices will apply:

(Each plant or plant type should be listed and priced where a single tree, shrub or ground cover can be added or deducted from the project without a formal rewrite of the bid. The cost of guying and bracing should also be unit-priced for each large tree and each small tree.)

ITEM	DESCRIPTION	ADD	DEDUCT
Equipment Rental		Costs Per Hour	
Truck		______	______
Tractor		______	______
Tool		______	______

Labor Charges		Costs Per Hour
Foreman		_______ _______
Common Labor		_______ _______
Tractor Operator		_______ _______
Truck Operator		_______ _______
Soil	(Per Yd.)	_______ _______
Tree Wrapping	(Per Tree)	_______ _______
Erosion Control Netting (if required)	(Per Sq. Yd.)	_______ _______

STARTING WORK:
The undersigned agrees that the Work to be performed under contract shall be commenced not later than _______________ calendar days after the date of written notice from the Landscape Designer/Landscape Architect authorizing the Landscape Contractor to proceed with the Work.

COMPLETION DATE:
The undersigned agrees to complete the work covered by the proposal in _________ calendar days, commencing on the date construction starts. Work shall start immediately upon awarding of a contract.

BID BOND:
The undersigned's Bid Security, payable to the Owner, in the form of (Cashier's Check), (Certified Check), (Bid Bond) for _______ percent of Total Sum of Bid, which 10 percent shall equal _________________________ Dollars ($). The Bid Security shall be left with the Owner in Escrow and is the measure of liquidating damages which the Owner will sustain by the failure of the undersigned to execute and deliver an Agreement and Bonds, and if undersigned defaults in executing an Agreement within ________ days of written notification of the Award of the Contract to him or in furnishing any required Bonds within _______ days thereafter then the Bid Security shall become the property of the Owner, but if this proposal is not accepted within ______ days of the date set for the submission of bids, or if the undersigned executes and delivers said Contract and required Bonds, the Bid Security shall be returned to him on receipt thereof.

PERFORMANCE BOND AND LABOR AND MATERIAL BOND
The undersigned agrees, if awarded the Contract, to execute and deliver to the Owner, within ________ days after signing the Contract, a Performance Bond and Labor and Material Payment bond, signed by himself as principal and by an established reputable bonding or insurance company (satisfactory to the Owner) or surety on the forms as specified in the penal sum of 100% of the Contract Price, on each Performance and Payment Bond. Such bonds shall remain in full force and effect from the date of signing the Contract until the acceptance of the Work by the Owner. The Contractor shall promptly file a signed copy of the Contract and the Performance Bond and Labor and Material Payment Bond with the County Clerk's office in full compliance with the law.

The undersigned agrees to purchase and furnish Performance and Payment Bonds for the Total Sum of _________________________________ Dollars ($).

INSURANCE:
The undersigned agrees, if awarded the Contract, to deliver to the Owner, within ______ days after the date of written notice to proceed with the Work and before proceeding with any Work, the Certificates of Insurance as specified.

Name of the Insurance Company used by this Bidder:

TAXES:
The above prices include all applicable taxes, insurance, benefits, overhead, and profit.

Bidder understands that the Owner reserves the right to reject any or all bids and to waive any informalities in the bidding.

The bidder agrees that this bid shall be good and may not be withdrawn within _______ days after the actual date of the opening thereof.

Respectfully submitted,
(Company Name)
By
Title
Address
Telephone

RESOURCE D
PLANTING DESIGN SPECIFICATIONS

The specifications a designer uses can determine the success or failure of a planting project, for it is the specifications document that sets forth the protective measures and communication elements that allow a third party to execute the design. Whether the document is used in-house for a design/build operation or in a competitive bid for a public installation, the following sample illustrates its most important components.

SAMPLE INSTRUCTIONS TO BIDDERS

A. Preparation and Submission of Bid

1. Bids shall be submitted to ______________________________ (Owner) and shall be signed in ink. Erasures or other changes in a bid must be explained or noted over the signature of the Bidder. Bids shall not contain any conditions, omissions, unexplained erasures, or items not called for in the proposal, or irregularities of any kind.
2. Each bid must give the full business address of the bidder and be signed by an authorized representative. Bids by partnerships must furnish the full name of all partners and must be signed in the partnership name by one of the members of the partnership, or by an authorized representative, followed by the signature and designation of the person signing. Bids by corporations must be signed with the legal name of the corporation, followed by the signature and designation of the President, Secretary, or other persons authorized to bind it in the matter. The name of each person signing shall also be typed or printed below the signature. A bid by a person who affixed to his signature "President," "Secretary," "Agent," or other designation, without disclosing the principal, may be held to be the bid of the individual signing
3. Bids shall be enclosed in sealed envelopes which shall have marked on the outside the following: (State how addressed and how coded) . If forwarded by mail, the sealed envelope containing the bid must be enclosed in another envelope addressed as specified above.

B. Modification and Withdrawal of Bids

1. Telegraph bids will not be considered, but modifications by telegraph or letter of bids already submitted will be considered, if received prior to the hour set for opening.
2. Bids may be withdrawn by written or telegraphic request, sent in a sealed envelope immediately to the office to which the written bid was submitted.
3. Two signed copies of the telegram should be forwarded in a sealed envelope immediately to the office to which the written bid was submitted.

C. Examination of Plans and Sites

1. The Bidders shall carefully examine the plans and specifications to fully understand the location, extent, nature and amount of work to be performed.
2. Each Bidder shall visit the site of the proposed work and thoroughly acquaint himself with conditions relating to the work.

D. Rejection of Bids

1. The competency and responsibility of Bidders will be considered in making the award.
2. The Owner or duly appointed representative reserves the right to reject any or all bids, and to waive any informality in bids received.

E. Specifications and Drawings

1. Specifications are intended to be complementary, and anything mentioned in the specifications and not shown on the plans, or shown on the plans and not mentioned in the specifications, shall be of like effect as if shown or mentioned in both. In the event of conflict between the drawings and specifications, it shall be brought to the attention of the Landscape Architect of Landscape Designer immediately for clarification.
2. Omissions from the plans or specifications, or the misdescription of details or work that are necessary to carry out the intent of the plans and specifications, shall not relieve the Bidder/Contractor from performing such details or work, but they shall be performed as if fully and correctly set forth and described in the plans and specifications.
3. The Bidder/Contractor shall check all plans and specifications furnished to same, immediately upon their receipt, and shall promptly notify the Landscape Architect or Landscape Designer of any discrepancies therein.
4. If any discrepancies are brought to the attention of the Landscape Architect or Landscape Designer, he/she will notify and send written instructions to all Bidders.
5. The Bidders/Contractor's authorized representative shall have a set of plans (with a list of omissions, ambiguities, or discrepancies in the plans) with him/her on the site. During the course of the work, should any errors, omissions, ambiguities, or discrepancies be found on the plans or in the specifications, or should there be found any discrepancies between the plans and specifications to which the Contractor has failed to call attention before submitting the bid, then the Owner will interpret the intent of the plans and specifications, and the Bidder/Contractor shall abide by the Owner's interpretation and shall carry out the work in accordance with the decisions of the Owner. The Owner may interpret or construe the plans and specifications as so to secure, in all cases, the most substantial and complete performance of the work as consistent with the needs and requirements of the work.
6. Laws and regulations. The Bidder's attention is directed to the fact that applicable state laws, municipal ordinances, and the rules and regulations of all authorities having jurisdiction over construction of the project shall apply to the contract throughout, and they will be deemed to be included in the contract the same as though herein written out in full.
7. Insurance. The Contractor, before starting work on the project, must furnish to the Owner a "Certificate of Insurance" or other acceptable evidences from a reputable insurance company or companies licensed to write insurance in the State of ______________________________, showing that the Contractor is covered by insurance as follows:
   (a) Workmen's Compensation Insurance
   (b) Contractor's and Subcontractor's Public Liability and Property Damage Insurance

Insurance as above stipulated must be maintained throughout the period of time required for construction and until the work is accepted. The certificates or evidence of insurance shall be set forth so that the Insurance Carrier will notify the Owner in the event such insurance is canceled or terminated prior to acceptance of the work.

8. Contractor's cooperation. Bidder's attention is called to the fact that there may be other Prime Contractors working on the project and it is expected that the Bidder/Contractor will cooperate to expedite all phases of construction.
9. The Contractor will be furnished two copies of the plans and one copy of the specifications. If necessary, extra copies of the plans and/or specifications will be furnished at Owner's expense.

SAMPLE SPECIFICATIONS

Specifications for (Name of Job, Job Number)

Job Locations (Street Number, City or Town)

I. Scope of Work

Extent: In general the item of work to be performed under the section shall include, but not be limited to:

All materials, equipment, tools, transportation, services, and labor required for the complete installation:

1. Lawn construction
2. Planting of trees
3. Protection, maintenance, and replacement of lawns and trees and all related items necessary to complete the work indicated on the drawings and/or specified herein.

II. Plant Materials

A. The Contractor shall furnish and plant all plants shown on the drawings, as specified, and in quantities listed on the plant materials list. A list of plants is shown on the planting plan and at the end of these specifications.

B. Quality and size: Plants shall have a habit of growth that is normal for the species and shall be sound, healthy, vigorous, and free from insect pests. They shall be equal to or exceed the measurements specified in the Plant List, which are minimum acceptable sizes. They shall be measured before pruning, with branches in normal position. Any necessary pruning shall be done at time of planting. Requirements for measurements, branching, and grading quality of plants in the Plant List generally follow the code of standards currently recommended by the American Association of Nurserymen, Inc., in the American Standard for Nursery Stock. The Owner shall have the option to select and tag any or all plants at the Nursery prior to delivery to the job site. When plants of a specified kind or size are not available within a reasonable distance, substitutions may be made upon request by the Contractor, if approved by the Owner or his representative. All plants shall conform to the measurements specified in the Plant List. Exceptions are as follows:

1. Plants larger than specified in the Plant List may be used if approved by the Owner or his representative, but use of such plants shall not increase the contract price. If the use of larger plants is approved, the spread of root or ball of earth shall be increased in proportion to the size of the plants.
2. Up to 10% of undersized plants in any one variety of grade may be used provided that there are sufficient plants above size to make the average equal to or above specified grade and provided that undersized plants are larger than the average size of the next smaller grade.

C. Type of protection to roots:

1. Balled and burlapped plants: Plants designated B&B in the Plant List shall be balled and burlapped. They shall be dug with firm, natural balls of earth of sufficient diameter and depth to encompass the fibrous and feeding root system necessary to full recovery of the plant. Balls should be firmly wrapped with burlap or similar materials and bound with twine or wire mesh.
2. Container-grown plants: Plants grown in containers will be accepted as B&B, provided that the plant had been growing in the container for one full growing season prior to delivery.
3. Protection after delivery: The balls of B&B plants that cannot be planted immediately on delivery shall be covered with moist soil or mulch, or other protection from drying winds and sun. All plants shall be watered as necessary until planted.

III. Materials (Other than Plants)

A. Topsoil to be furnished: If the quantity of excavated topsoil is inadequate (as determined by the Landscape Architect or Landscape Designer) for planting purposes, the sufficient additional topsoil shall be furnished on the site by the (Bidder or Owner).

B. Commercial fertilizer: Commercial fertilizer shall be an organic fertilizer containing the following minimum percentage of available plant food by weight: N ____________ P ____________ K____________. Mixed nitrogen — not less than (Percent) from organic source. Inorganic chemical nitrogen shall not be derived from the sodium form of nitrate or from ammonia nitrate. It shall be delivered to the site in unopened original containers, each bearing the manufacturer's guaranteed analysis. Any fertilizer that becomes caked or otherwise damaged, making it unsuitable for use, will not be accepted.

C. Water: Water shall be suitable for irrigation and free from ingredients harmful to plant life. The Contractor will furnish hoses and watering equipment required for work. Water for work will be furnished by Owner.

D. Sod: Sod shall contain a good cover of living or growing grass. At least _____% of the plants in the sod shall be composed of (Name) . The sod shall be freshly dug, well rooted, and relatively free from weeds or undesirable plants, and it shall be entirely free of nut grass, large stones, roots, and other material that might be detrimental to the development of the sod. It shall be of uniform thickness with a minimum ________ inch thickness of soil and roots.

E. Grass seed: Grass seed shall be of kind named, harvested within one year prior to planting, and free of weeds, to the limits allowable under applicable State seed laws. The seed shall be hulled and have a germination and purity that will produce a pure live-seed content of not less than 75%.

F. Antidesiccant (optional): Antidesiccant shall be "Wilt Pruf" or equal, delivered in manufacturer's containers and used according to the manufacturer's instructions.

G. Mulch: Mulch shall be wood chips, ground bark, bark peelings, peat, hay or straw, salt marsh hay, sugar cane, ground corn cobs, or peanut hulls.

IV. Protection of Existing Trees

A. Before beginning any clearing work and before beginning any excavation or stripping work the Contractor shall consult with the designer on the selection and protection of all existing trees designated on the drawings and/or marked to remain on the site.

B. Tree protection shall consist of a fence of a minimum 5-foot height, of sturdy and approved construction, utilizing cedar or wood fence posts with 2" x 4" stringers at the top and bottom, and 1" x 6" vertical boards spaced 9 inches from centers. The fence shall be constructed a minimum distance of 5 feet from the out trunks.

C. All such fencing shall be maintained throughout the work under this Contract until such time as the area is ready for lawns and planting work, at which time it shall be removed and disposed of by the Contractor.

D. The fenced areas shall not be used for storage of materials of any kind or for any purpose likely to damage tree roots or branches. Repair injuries to bark, trunk, and branches of fenced trees (if required) by dressing, cutting and painting as directed by the Landscape Architect/Landscape Designer.

E. For any tree designated to remain that is removed or damaged to the extent that it will not live, or damaged to the extent it cannot be used in the landscape development, as determined by the Landscape Architect/Landscape Designer, the Contractor shall replace the tree with another of equivalent size, as selected by the Landscape Architect/Landscape Designer and at no cost to the Owner.

V. Removal of Trees

Trees designated to be removed on plans shall be grubbed out ______ feet below natural ground to include all main roots and the cutting of the tap root, and said trees shall be removed from the site.

VI. Installation (General)

A. Seasons for planting: Planting may be done whenever the weather and soil conditions are favorable or as otherwise authorized by the Owner or his representative and with the consent of the Contractor.

B. Planting tree pit size: Minimum diameter (width) and depth of planting pits for balled and burlapped, bare-root, and container-grown plants shall be as follows:

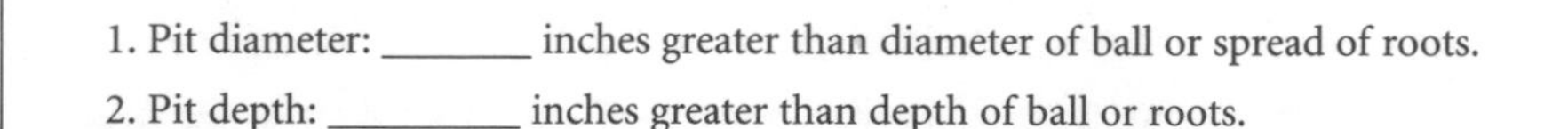

1. Pit diameter: ________ inches greater than diameter of ball or spread of roots.
2. Pit depth: __________ inches greater than depth of ball or roots.

C. Preparation of planting areas: Before excavations are made, the surrounding turf shall be covered in a manner that will satisfactorily protect all turf areas that are to be trucked over, and upon which soil is to be temporarily stacked pending its removal or reuse as specified herein. Existing trees, shrubbery, and beds that are to be preserved shall be barricaded in a manner that will effectively protect them during the planting operations.

D. Setting plants: Unless otherwise specified, all plants soil in pits, centered, and set on prepared soil to such depth that the finished grade level at the plant after settlement will be the same as that at which the plant was grown. They shall be planted upright and faced to give the best appearance or relationship to adjacent structures. No burlap shall be pulled from under the balls. Platform wire and surplus binding from top and sides of the balls shall be removed. All broken or frayed roots shall be cut off cleanly. Prepared soil shall be placed and compacted carefully to avoid injury to roots and to fill all voids. When the hole is nearly filled, add water as necessary and allow it to soak away. Fill the hole to finished grade, allowing for 2 inches of mulch, and form a shallow saucer around each plant by placing a ridge of topsoil around the edge of each pit. Remove containers after planting.

E. Staking, wrapping, guying and anchoring of trees:

1. Space trees uniformly as indicated and set trees plumb, straight, at such a level that, after settlement, normal or natural relationship of plant crown with ground surface will be established. To accomplish this remove platforms, wire, and binding from top and sides of balls, but do not remove burlap under balls; and fill pits around trees to finish grade, thoroughly soak and repeat filling until all settlement has taken place, allowing 2 inches for mulch at grade and forming a circular dam of top soil around edge of each pit.
2. All trees shall be properly staked, wrapped with burlap from base to first branches, and guyed.

F. Mulching: Trees shall be mulched within 2 days after planting by covering beds or pits with a 2-inch-deep layer of a material specified by the Landscape Architect/Landscape Designer; mulch shall be thoroughly saturated with water after placing to prevent displacement by wind and water.

G. Excess excavated soil (optional): Excess excavated soil shall be disposed of on or off the site as directed by the Owner.

H. Grass areas: Plant grass in all areas within limits of entire project site, except areas indicated or specified to be developed otherwise, as follows:

1. (Name) Grass: This shall be planted within a project boundary between curbs, walks, and buildings.
2. Grades: The areas to be spot-sodded or seeded, as established by others, shall be maintained in a true, even, and properly compacted condition so as to prevent the formation of depressions where water will stand. All areas with the grade equal to or greater than 2 to 1 shall receive solid sodding.
3. Tilling: Before any sod is planted, the areas to be planted with grass shall be thoroughly tilled to a minimum depth of 3 inches by plowing, disking, harrowing, rototilling, or other approved operations until the condition of the soil is friable and of uniform texture. The work shall be performed only during the period when beneficial results are likely to be obtained. Any irregularities in the surface of finish grades, resulting from tillage or other operations, shall be leveled out before sodding operations are begun. All stones, bricks, roots, or similar substances of 11/2 inches or more in diameter resulting from tillage shall be removed and disposed of off the site.
4. Laying of sod: Before any sod is laid, all soft spots and inequalities in grade shall be corrected. Grass sod blocks for spot sodding shall be _______ inches square. The blocks shall be planted uniformly _______ inches apart (from the center of the block). After excavation for the block but before setting the block in place, a small amount of fertilizer shall be placed under each block of sod. Then blocks are to be planted, foliage side up, to a depth of the finished-lawn grade and soil firmly placed around them. Then they shall be evenly fertilized with a mechanical spreader at the rate of ______ pounds per 1,000 square feet of area. Fertilizer shall be commercial fertilizer as specified. On completion of the fertilizing, the areas shall be rolled with a ______ pound roller and the completed, sodded surface shall be even and true to finish grade.
5. Sowing of the grass seed:
   a. Fertilizing: prior to tilling areas to be planted with grass seed, supply (Number of Pounds) commercial fertilizer at the rate of _____ pounds per acre of lawn area being prepared for seeding.
   b. Scarifying: Within 24 hours following fertilizer application and before any seed is sown, scarify the ground to be seeded as necessary, until surface is smooth, friable, and of uniformly fine texture.
   c. Seeding: Seed lawn areas evenly with mechanical spreader at rate of _____ pounds per acre. Sow half of the seeds with a sower, moving at right angles to first sowing. Do Not broadcast seeding in windy weather. The Contractor must assume full responsibility for establishing smooth, uniformly covered grass lawn.
6. Watering: Water shall be applied to sodded areas in quantities and at intervals to provide optimum growing conditions for the establishment of a healthy, uniform stand and cover of grass. Apply water by use of hose and attached sprinklers, soaker hose, or other watering equipment that will apply water at such rate as to avoid damage to finished surfaces.

I. Obstructions below ground: In the event that rock or underground construction work or obstructions are encountered in any plant pit excavation work to be done under this contract, alternate locations shall be selected by the Owner and the Landscape Contractor. The Landscape Contractor shall be paid for the removal of such rock or underground obstructions encountered at a rate per cubic yard to be agreed upon by the Owner's representative and the Landscape Contractor.

J. Planting Operations:

1. Time of planting: The Contractor shall be notified by the Owner, when other divisions of the work have progressed sufficiently, to commence work on lawns and planting. Thereafter, planting operations during the next season or seasons that are normal for such work as determined by accepted practice in the locality of the project shall be performed. At the option and on the full responsibility of the General Contractor, planting operations may be conducted under unseasonable conditions without additional compensation.
2. Layout: The locations for plants and outlines of areas to be planted, as indicated on the plan, shall be marked on the ground by the General Contractor before any excavation is made. All such locations shall be approved by the Owner and the Landscape Architect/Landscape Designer or Contractor. Where construction or utilities, below ground or overhead, are encountered or where changes have been made in the construction, necessary adjustments will be approved by the Owner. Plants shall be a minimum of (Distance) from buildings.
3. Pruning and repair: Upon completion of the work under this Contract, all existing trees and shrubs shall have been pruned and any injuries repaired. The amount of pruning shall be limited to the minimum necessary to remove dead or injured twigs or branches that interfere with new construction (buildings, roof, overhang, fences, etc.) Pruning shall be done in such a manner as not to change the natural habit or shape of the plant. All cuts shall be made flush, leaving no stubs. On all cuts over 3/4 inches in diameter, bruises, or scars on the bark, the injured cambium shall be traced back to living tissue and removed; wood shall be smoothed and

shaped so as not to retain water; and the treated areas shall be coated with a tree paint, as approved by the Landscape Architect/Landscape Designer.

VII. Maintenance

A. Grass lawn areas: Grass spot sodding and sodded lawn areas shall be protected and maintained by watering, mowing, and replanting as necessary for at least _____ days after completion of all spot sodding and acceptance. Scattered bare spots, none of which shall be larger than 4 square feet, will be allowed to a maximum of 3% of any lawn area. Correct all depressions where water will stand.

Grass-seeded lawn areas shall be protected and maintained as necessary for at least _______ days after completion of all seeding. Maintenance shall include watering, repairing any damage that has occurred in the seeded areas from erosion, mowing of weeds (when height of weeds interferes with seedlings), and reseeding as originally specified in any areas where a good stand of grass has not been obtained.

B. Other planting protection and maintenance: All trees are to be protected and maintained until the end of the maintenance period. Maintenance shall include watering, weeding, cultivating, removing dead material, resetting plants to proper grades or upright position, restoring the planting saucer, and other necessary operations. If planting is done after lawn preparation, properly protect lawn areas and repair any damage resulting from planting operations promptly.

VIII. Guarantee Periods

Plants shall be guaranteed by the Landscape Contractor from one planting season to the beginning of the following planting season.

IX. Inspection and Provisional Acceptance

A. The Owner or his/her representative shall inspect all work for provisional acceptance upon the written request of the Contractor. The request shall be received at least 10 days before the anticipated date of provisional inspection.

B. Upon completion of all repairs or replacements that may appear at the time of the inspection to be necessary (in the judgment of the Owner and the Landscape Contractor), the Owner shall certify in writing to the Landscape Contractor as to the provisional acceptance of the planting items.

C. The Owner shall pay, or cause to be paid, to the said Landscape Contractor a sum of money to be not less than 90% of the total cost of planting due the said Landscape Contractor.

X. Final Inspection and Final Acceptance

A. At the end of the guarantee period, inspection of plants will be made by the Owner or his representative upon written notice requesting such inspection, submitted by the Landscape Contractor at least 10 days before the anticipated date of inspection.

B. Any plant, as required under this contract, that is dead, not true to name or size as specified, or not in satisfactory growth, as determined by the Owner and the Landscape Contractor, shall be removed from the site.

XI. Application for Payments

A. Performance under this contract will be subject to approval or disapproval by (Landscape Architect/Landscape Designer).

B. No later than the first and fifteenth day of each calendar month, if a certified estimate has been received 10 days prior to date of payment, the Owner will make partial payment to the Contractor on the basis of a duly certified approved estimate of the work performed during the preceding semimonthly period by the Contractor. The Owner will retain 10% of the amount of each such estimate until no later than 30 working days after final completion and final acceptance of all work covered by the contract.

XII. Clean Up

Any solid, peat, or similar material that has been brought on to paved areas by hauling or other operations shall be removed promptly by the Landscape Contractor, keeping these areas clean at all times. Upon completion of planting, all excess soil, stones, and debris that have not previously been cleaned up shall be removed from the site or disposed of as directed by the Owner. All lawns and planting areas shall be prepared for final inspection.

Factors Influencing Costs

Some requirements written into specifications will cause the final project cost to vary, based upon local conditions at the time of planting. The designer should be aware of these requirements and be prepared to adjust the plan accordingly.

1. The Retail Cost of Plant Materials: Often the retail cost will act as a guide for determining a base price for installation. Some construction firms use their wholesale price and multiply this cost by a factor of 2.5, 3.3, or 4.0. Other firms use the wholesale cost of materials, add their labor costs, and then multiply with an overhead percentage. Be careful specifying which technique is allowable. It may be best to leave it to the discretion of the bidding firm to insure a competitive submission.
2. Mulching: If more than the required peat mulch is used, costs could expand proportionally to the cost and availability of the desired material.
3. Tree Staking, Wrapping, and Guying: Make sure these procedures are really needed before commencing. Staking, wrapping, and supporting trees under 2" in caliper with wires may be a waste of time and materials.
4. Material Guarantee: In some geographic areas, a guarantee of more than 60 to 90 days may add as much as 10 to 15 percent to the base price. Most plants will wilt and die during the first 90 days if they are of inferior quality.
5. Maintenance: A reasonable maintenance time of 30 days will increase the base price only slightly. It is always good to have a well maintained project for a long period after construction, but the installation contractor will add the costs of maintenance to the base price.
6. Length of Project: Make sure a reasonable amount of time is allowed to complete the installation. The designer should take into consideration the factors of material availability, labor, and transportation to the site before committing to a specific time.
7. Special Size and Conditions Materials: A unique plant or material specimen is always an attractive addition to landscape, but remember, it will be more expensive and should be budgeted accordingly — usually three to four times as much as a typical specimen.
8. Special Planting Seasons: Careful attention should be paid to the time of year of the planting operation. Depending on the season, additional expenditures for special planting techniques and material protection may be required. These costs, with overhead percentages, will be passed along to your client.

Field Considerations for Planting Developments

After the planting plan has been completed and the specifications written, the designer's attention should be directed to the inspection phases of the project. There are essentially three phases of an operation that may require the inspection services of the designer: before formal planting begins; during the planting operation; and upon completion of the project.

Preplanting Inspection

Part IX of the Planting Specifications sets forth the conditions of the plant materials to be used in a project. Some designers conduct an inspection before writing the specs to determine existing conditions and availability of desired material. Other designers prefer to inspect the materials after writing the specs. In both cases, inspections are usually completed at a nursery or garden center and offer a reasonable amount of quality control.

A good designer, however, maintains an ongoing inspection program of local nurseries and growing operations to keep up to date with trade conditions and consumer trends. It is best to know what is available and where to get it before entering a planting design program. The most comprehensive and creative plans sometimes have to be shelved because the designer used "nonexistent" plant material.

In a preplanting inspection, you should study the general condition of the plants and look specifically at the following:

1. Foliage Color: Discoloration of foliage can indicate several problems, from poor drainage to disease.
2. Growth Uniformity: If a specific plant size is needed, make sure all species in the needed size are uniform in growth quality.
3. Condition: Inspect the plants to make sure they are disease- and pest free as well as void of any damage from pruning or ice storms.

Planting Inspection

This phase will ensure the proper use of techniques suitable to the climate and trade conditions. The first step in this phase occurs when the plants arrive at the site. If the material has not been tagged (for representative samples) prior to delivery, the designer should check for discoloration of foliage, uniformity of plant growth, and general condition of each plant.

Additional inspection steps for this phase should include:

1. Bed Preparation: Check for uniformity of depth, soil mix, and tillage.
2. Pit or Pocket Excavation: There should be uniformity in excavation, location, etc.
3. General Site Preparation: Uniformity of grade, tillage, and topsoil depth should be checked.

4. Location/Spacing of Plants: Tagging or staking of trees, shrubs, and ground covers may be required.
5. Plant Protection: Check the storage conditions for the plants. If wrapping, staking, and pruning are required, check to see if the workmanship is proper.

Final Inspection After Planting

The last phase of an inspection program is governed by the specifications. The more detailed the requirements, the more detailed the final inspection will be. An inspection checklist, based on the specifications, should be developed for this inspection — and strictly followed.

Determining Maintenance Impact

The lasting success or failure of a planting composition will be determined by the level of effort and care taken to perpetuate the designers' original objectives. The amount of enclosure of the walls, the attractiveness of accents, and the shapes of the original forms are important if the images of the space are to remain. Why spend many hours for research and design if you plan to simply walk away from a project after the final inspection?

In order to address this important aspect of the design program, the planting designer must develop a maintenance plan, a statement or plan of action to determine the amount and type of care to be taken to ensure the continuation of the composition theme. Such a plan should include:

1. Description of the projected levels of service needed to maintain the composition: This should include all forms of minimum maintenance for the plants (i.e., watering, weeding, mowing, clipping, etc.).
2. Estimated annual and seasonal costs to reach the minimum maintenance levels: This should include equipment, energy, and supplies.
3. The dates of the maintenance services for each season, plus a program for special services required for the project.

Numerous reference materials are available for determining what must be done to ensure the growth and development of the plants chosen for a composition. The designer may even wish to add a maintenance specialist to the planning team to assist in the development of a total service program.

Resource E
Installation Graphics (Fig. 5-1 to 5-15)

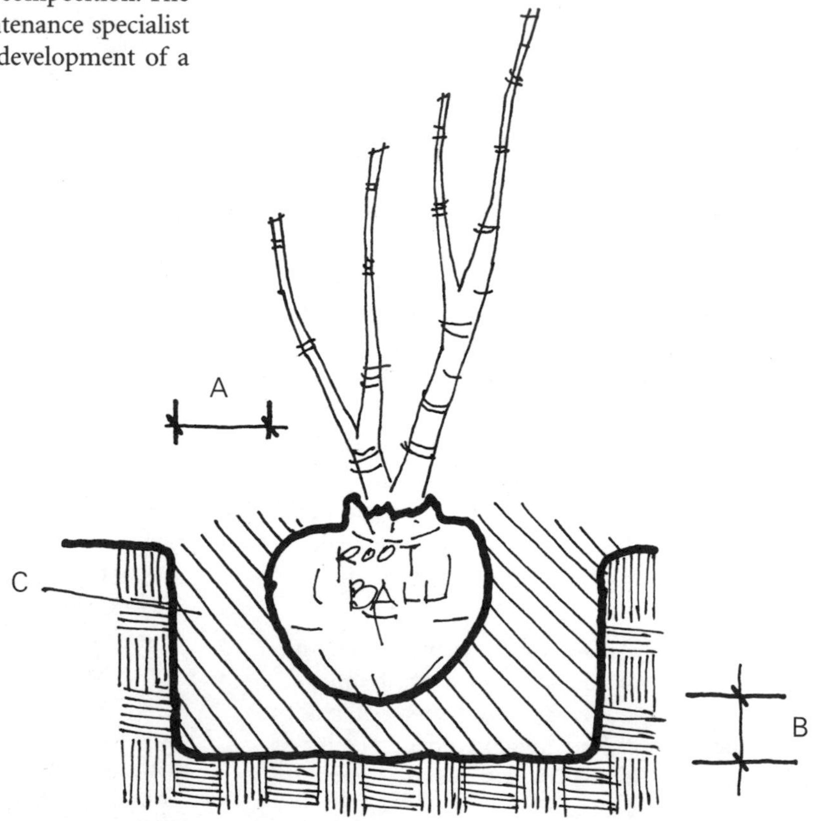

Figure 5-1
Detail—Multi-trunk tree.

A. 6" to 12"
B. 6" minimum
C. Prepared soil

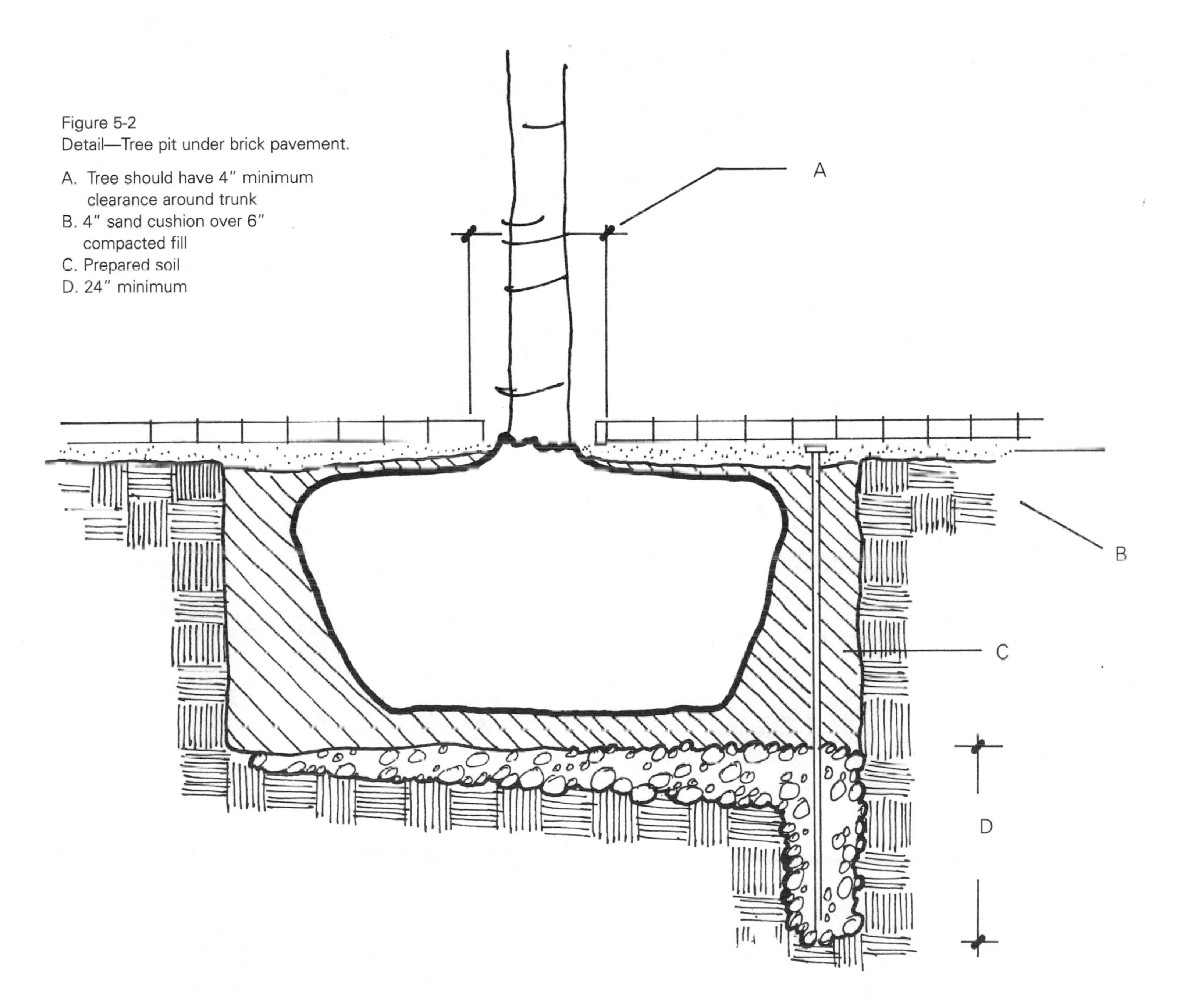

Figure 5-2
Detail—Tree pit under brick pavement.

A. Tree should have 4" minimum clearance around trunk
B. 4" sand cushion over 6" compacted fill
C. Prepared soil
D. 24" minimum

Figure 5-3
Detail—Large tree with 2" X 4" bracing

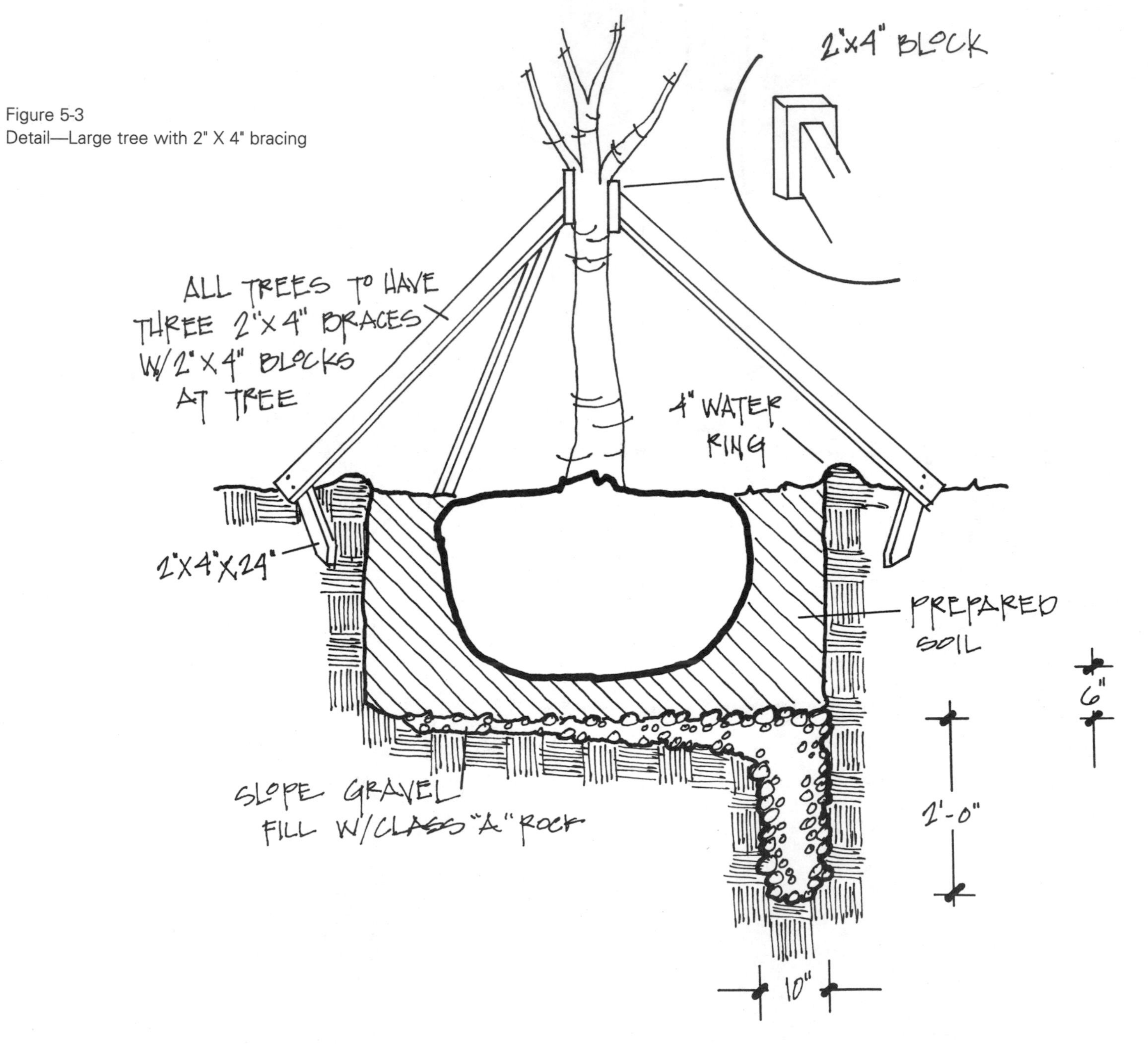

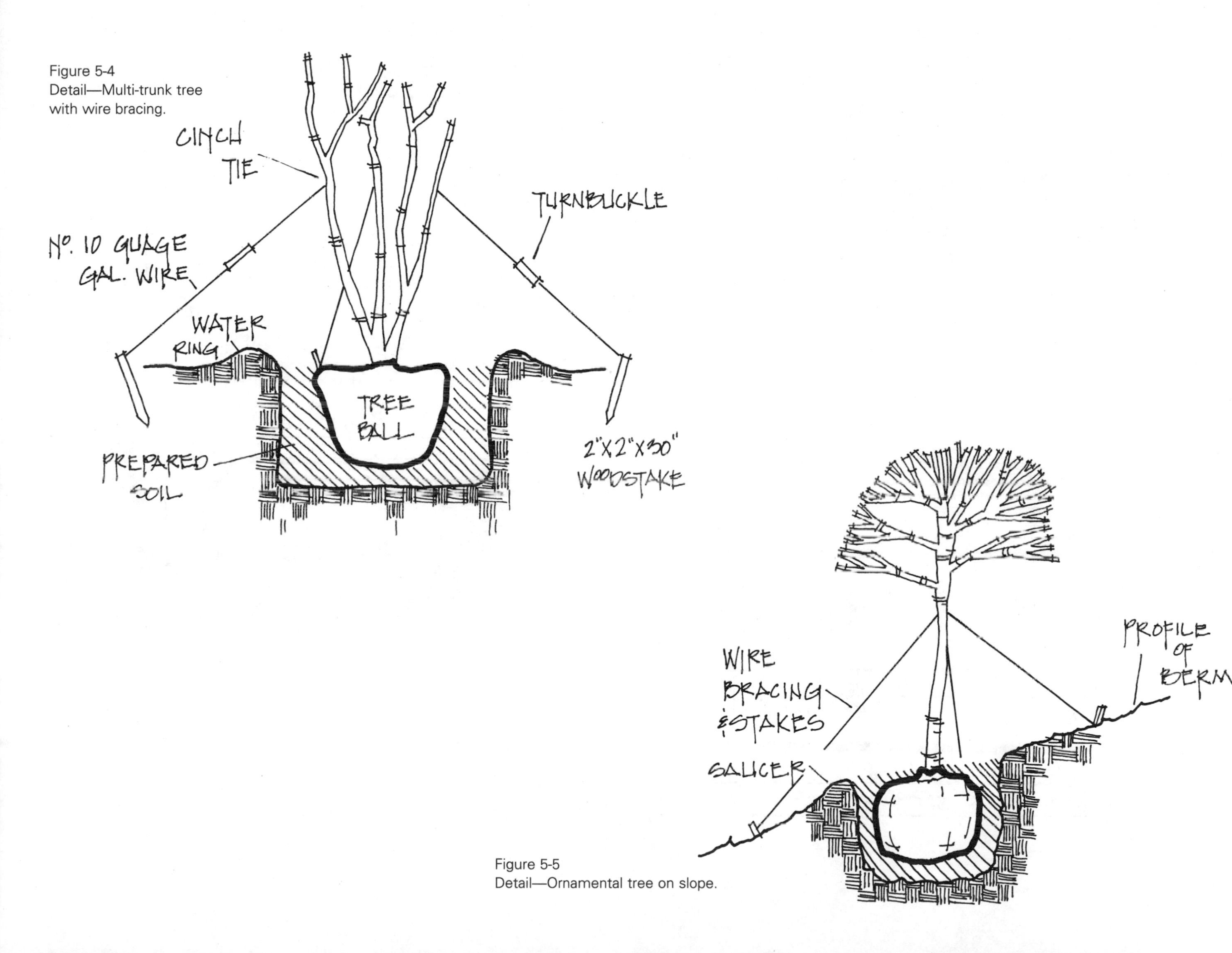

Figure 5-4
Detail—Multi-trunk tree with wire bracing.

Figure 5-5
Detail—Ornamental tree on slope.

Figure 5-6
Detail—Gravel mulch.

A. 2" to 4" mulch layer.

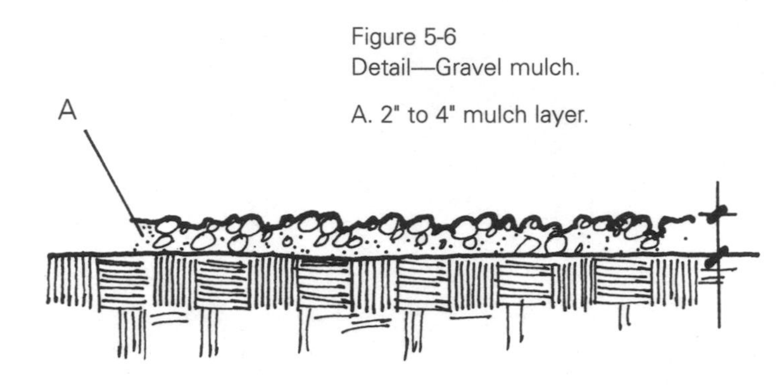

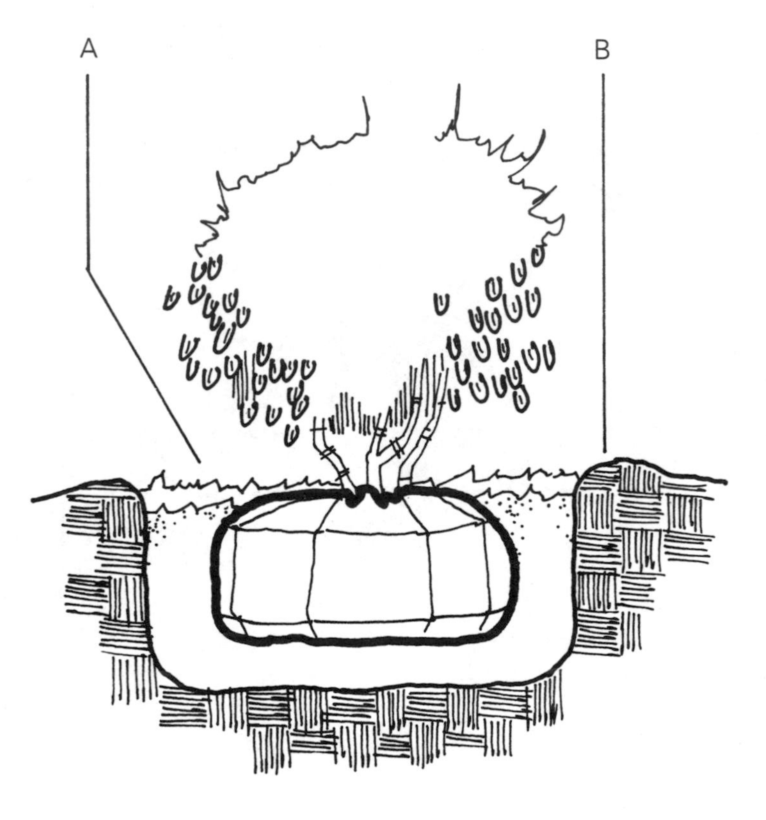

Figure 5-7
Detail — Annual planting in plastic pot.

A. Decorative bark
B. 10" to 18" maximum
C. 12" to 14" maximum
D. Crushed gravel
E. Concrete base

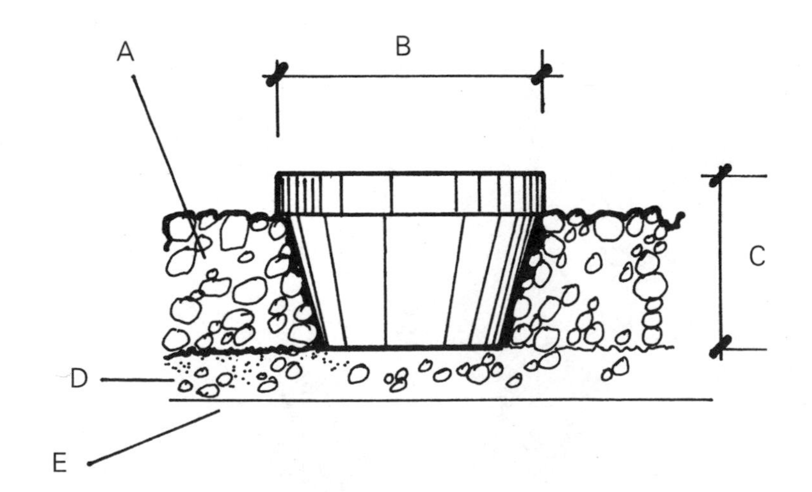

Figure 5-8
Detail—Shrub pit

A. 1" to 2" mulch
B. Saucer around shrub pit

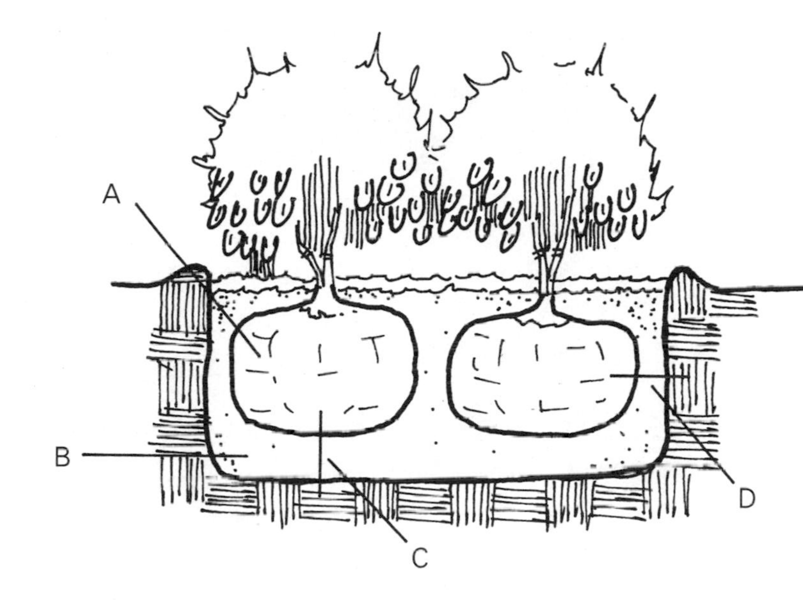

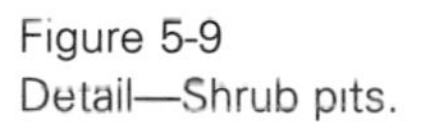

Figure 5-9
Detail—Shrub pits.

A. Remove burlap from around plant ball
B. Prepared soil
C. 4" minimum
D. 4" minimum

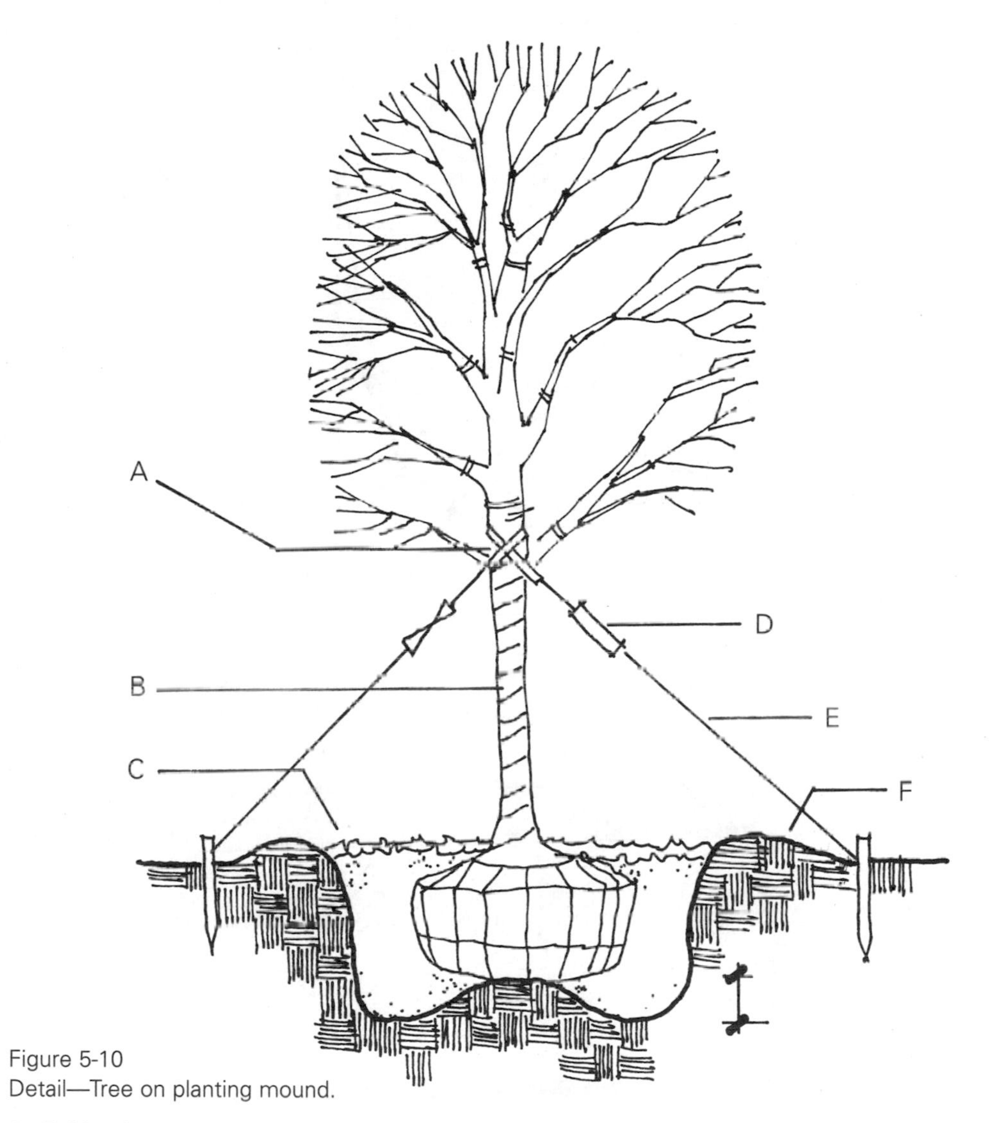

Figure 5-10
Detail—Tree on planting mound.

A. Rubber hoses
B. Tree wrap
C. 2" mulch cover
D. Turnbuckle
E. Guy wire
F. Saucer mound around pit

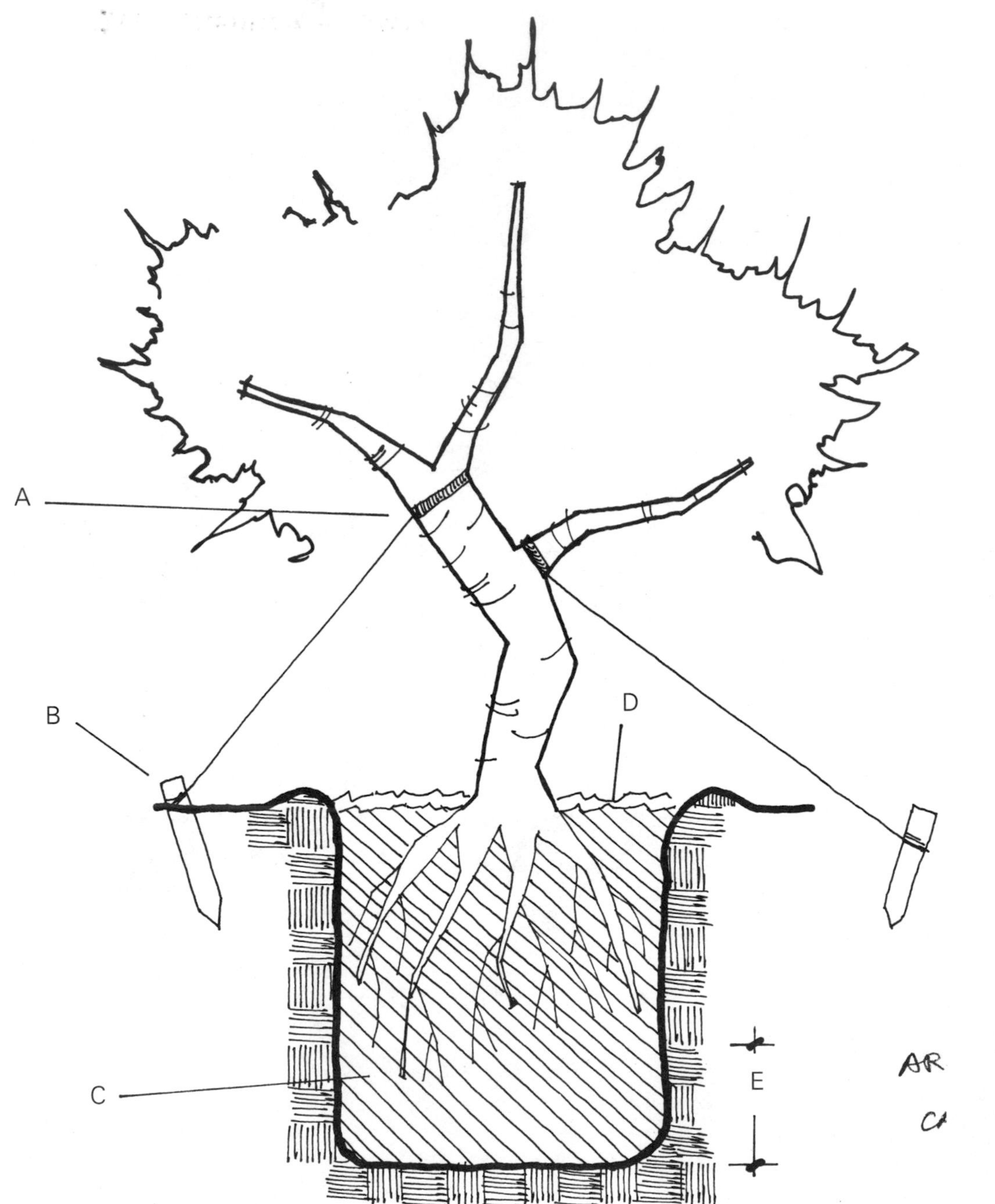

Figure 5-11
Detail—Specimen tree (bare root)

A. Rubber hose
B. 2" X 4" stake
C. Prepared soil
D. 2" mulch
E. 6" to 12" minimum

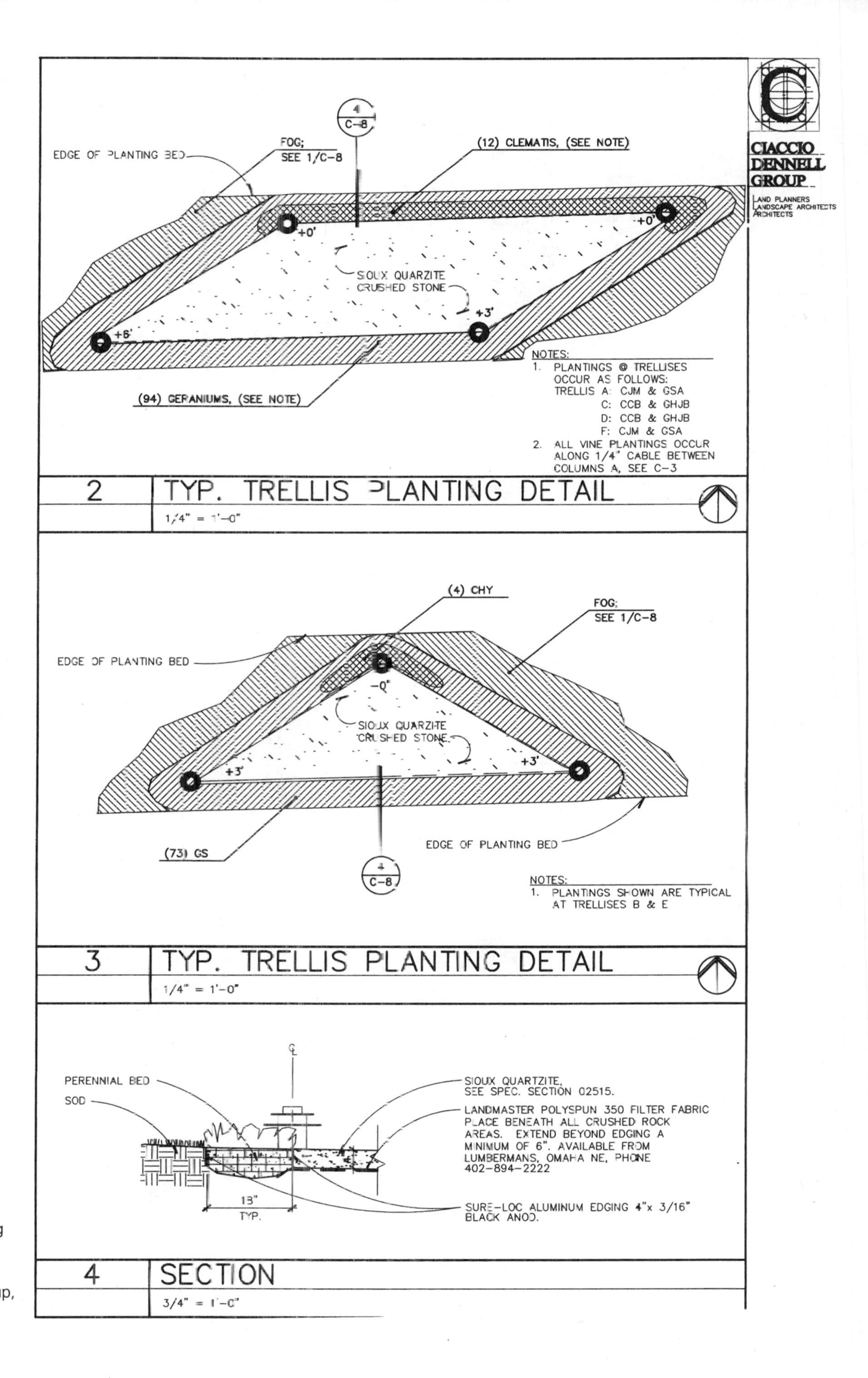

Figure 5-12
Typical trellis-planting details. Courtesy of David J. Ciaccio, Ciaccio Dennell Group, Omaha, Nebraska.

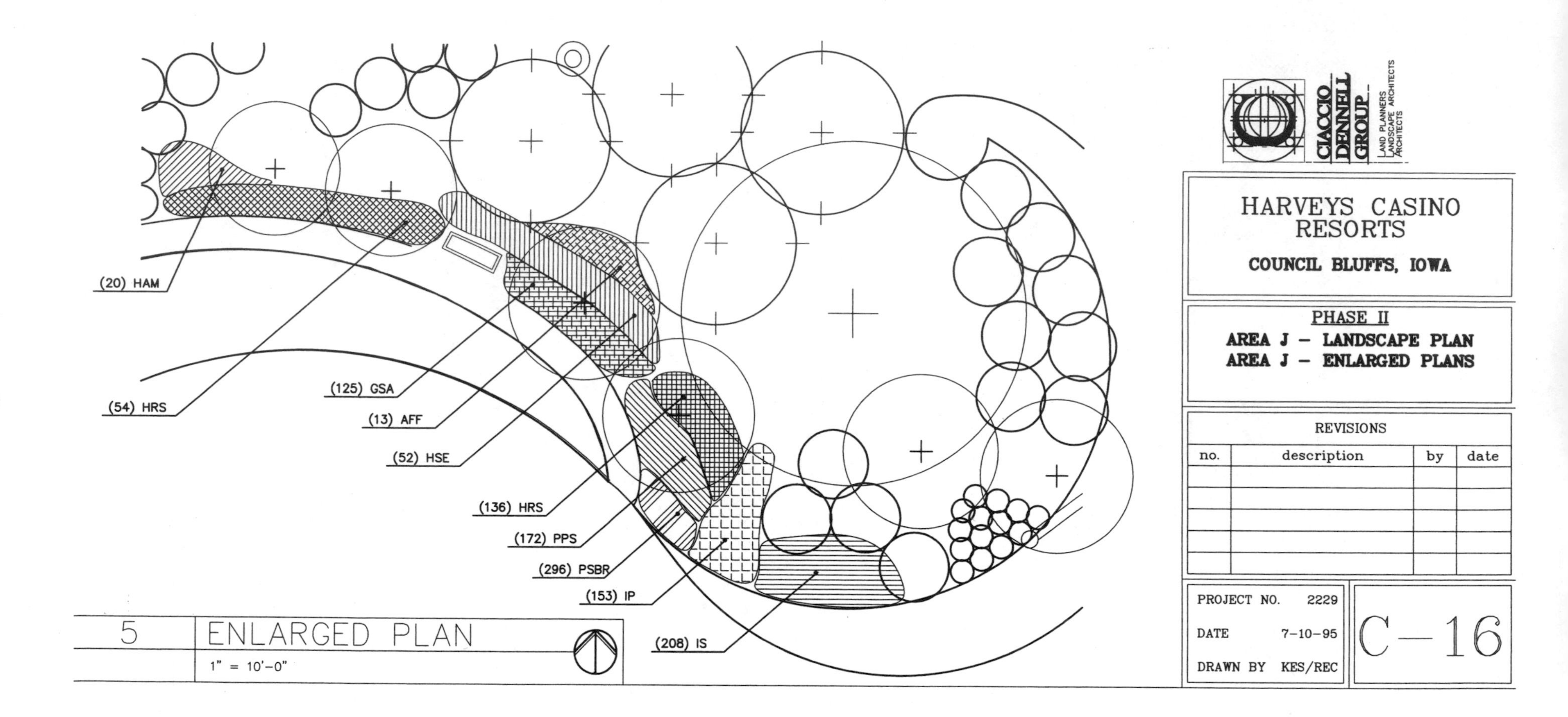

Figure 5-13
An enlarged planting plan of annual/perennial beds. Courtesy of David J. Ciaccio, Ciaccio Dennell Group, Omaha, Nebraska.

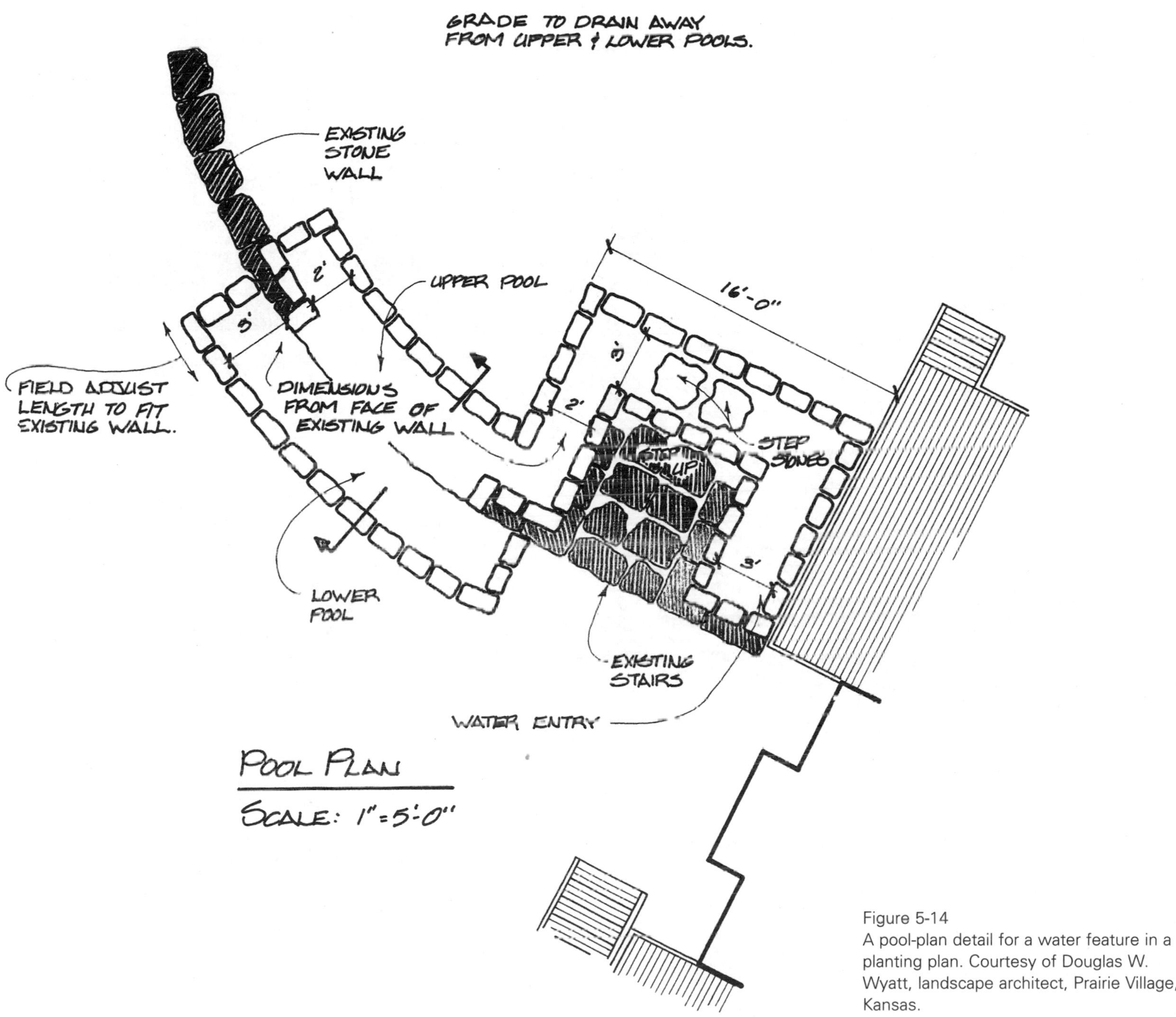

Figure 5-14
A pool-plan detail for a water feature in a planting plan. Courtesy of Douglas W. Wyatt, landscape architect, Prairie Village, Kansas.

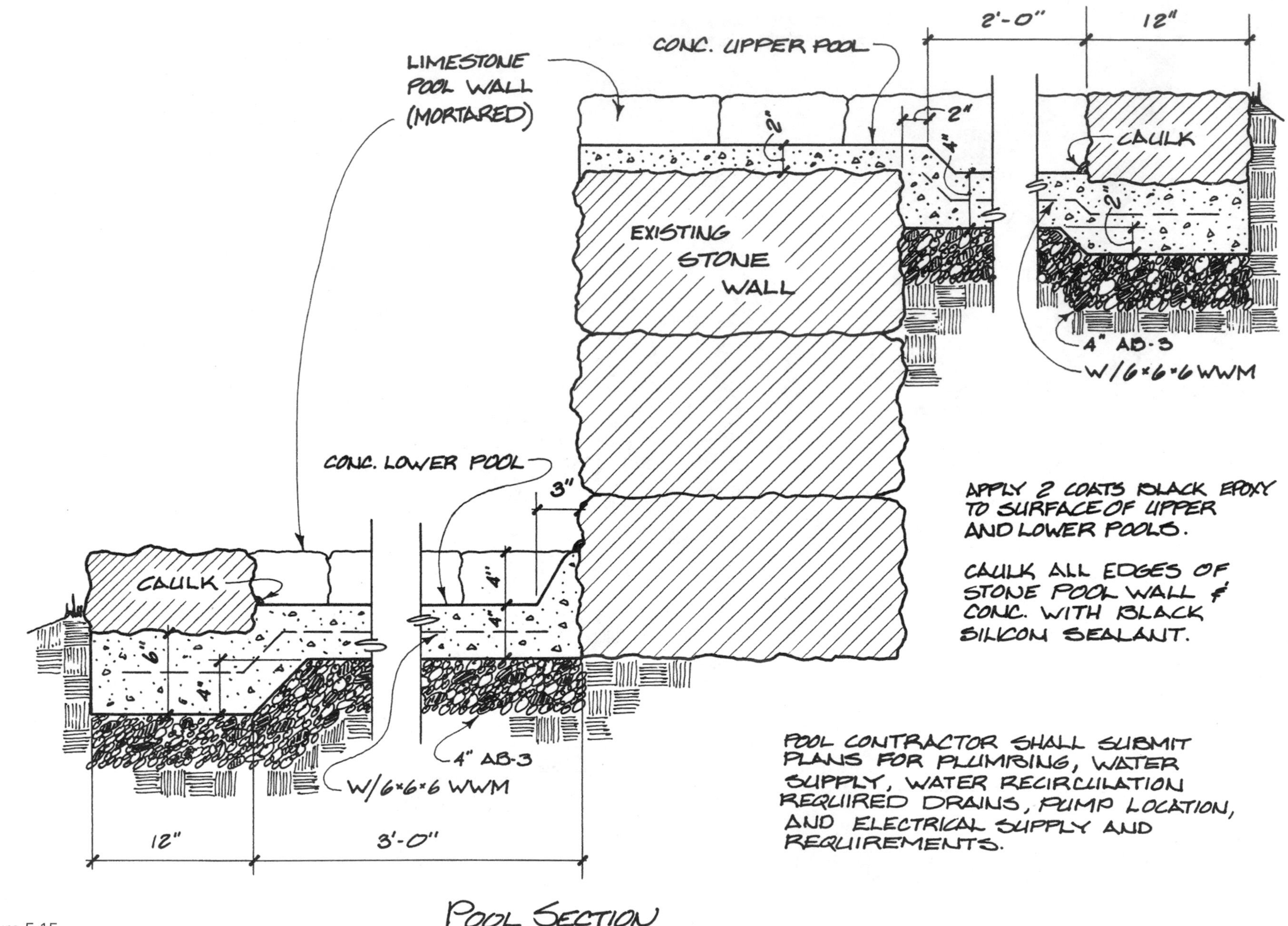

Figure 5-15
A section detail for the water area. Courtesy of Douglas W. Wyatt, landscape architect, Prairie Village, Kansas.

References and Bibliography

Davis, David A., and Theodore D. Walker. 2000. *Plan Graphics*. New York: John Wiley and Sons.

Dice, Lee R. 1952. *Natural Communities*. Ann Arbor: University of Michigan Press.

Eckbo, Garrett. 1969. *The Landscape We See*. New York: McGraw-Hill.

Leszczynski, Nancy A. 1999. *Planting in the Landscape*. New York: John Wiley and Sons.

Motloch, John L. 2001. *Introduction to Landscape Design*. New York: John Wiley and Sons.

Robinette, Gary O. 1972. *Plants, People, and Environmental Quality*. U.S. Department of the Interior, National Park Service.

Shelford, Victor E. 1963. *The Ecology of North America*. Urbana: University of Illinois Press.

Spurr, Stephen H., and Burton V. Barnes. 1964. *Forest Ecology*. New York: John Wiley and Sons.

Sullivan, Chip. 1997. *Drawing the Landscape*. New York: Van Nostrand Reinhold.

Walker, Theodore D. 1991. *Planting Design*. New York: John Wiley and Sons.

Watt, Kenneth E. F. 1968. *Ecology and Resource Management*. New York: McGraw-Hill.

Index

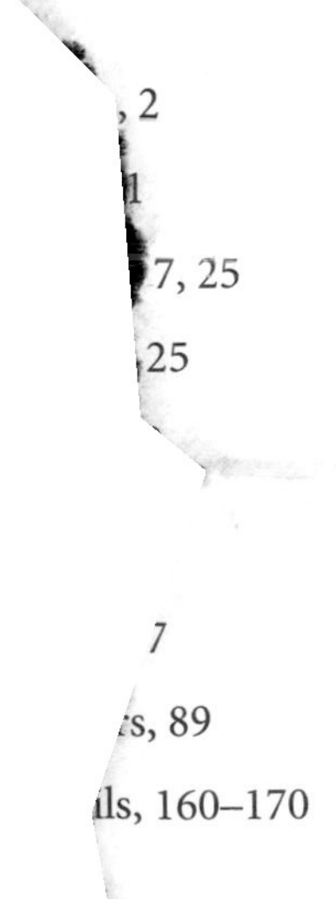